Feminism: history
305-4209

Hyenas *in Petticoats*

Hyenas *in Petticoats*

A LOOK AT TWENTY YEARS OF FEMINISM

Angela Neustatter

HARRAP

London

*To Olly and my sons Zek and Cato who are
far from being fully reconstructed new men,
but who have been loving and supportive
through this project.*

First published in Great Britain 1989
by Harrap Books Limited

ISBN 0 245 54618–9

Printed and bound in Great Britain by
Mackays of Chatham Limited

CONTENTS

ACKNOWLEDGEMENTS

My thanks first to the women who spoke to me and wrote to me for this book. Their words have made the book what it is.

Thanks then to researcher Sara Miles who has worked with speed and enthusiasm and has managed to smile in the face of my erratic *modus operandi*. And much appreciation to the other people who have helped with research: Rachel Krish, Bridget Wheelan and to those near and dear friends who have listened to my thoughts, read chapters, come up with comments and criticisms.

Thanks also to the Equal Opportunities Commission for opening their library and giving me lots of help, and to the Women Artists' Slide Library for the help they gave.

A special thanks, too, to Jeni and Derek Norman who opened their warm and sepulchral home to me when I needed to escape to tranquillity and write.

INTRODUCTION

THE Women's Liberation Movement has just celebrated its twentieth anniversary – two decades of activity, activism, consciousness raising and campaigning. During this time the women involved have been reviled as strident, butch, ugly, man-hating harridans, hell-bent on the destruction of our traditional way of life. But they have also been celebrated as inspirational, powerful, a source of spiritual salvation for other women and the architects of a vision which will make life happier for men as well as women.

It has been an extraordinary movement in that it has put women very firmly on to society's agenda. It is now impossible to ignore what has gone on in the past twenty years, not to hear the voices from the battlefront, pointing out women's inequality in so many ways — from the fact that they were, and still are, paid less than men and have always been discriminated against in the workplace, to the fact that they are victims of rape, domestic violence and sexual harassment because our society has only slowly begun to question the idea that men are entitled to have power over women. Has anyone failed to hear of the women who set up camp at Greenham, galvanizing an incredible amount of public hostility because they were prepared to leave their families and live in a conspicuously unfeminine way for the sake of their politics? Or of the strongly voiced arguments for child care provision which would enable women to work? Haven't we all seen the growth of feminist thought and ideas and seen them being published by the mainstream publishing houses as well as the feminist presses, influencing subject-matter in a wide range of women's magazines, as well as getting space in the national press. Women now create art, theatre, film, on a scale unimaginable before the movement. Many families have been influenced by the ideas voiced aloud, that women should not do many hours of invisible, unpaid domestic labour, that fathers should share in the care of their children. And much more.

But what led these energetic, committed women to set out to change the agenda for women, to work towards a world in which they would be visible and important? And what has been the impact of the movement on the lives of women who read the important early works and were stunned by what they read? Or those who felt it was a movement which had little to do with them, or had little place for them? How far has it been possible for any woman to spend twenty hours of her life in a society where a status quo which kept women as second-class citizens was being loudly challenged, without being touched by it? And what are the feelings of women who have disliked some or all of a movement professedly working on their behalf?

These are some of the questions which intrigued me when I was asked to write a book looking at twenty years of the new feminist movement. What I have aimed to do in these pages is to offer some answers by presenting a picture of how women have been active and reactive in what has gone on. The basis of the book is the voices of ordinary women, some gathered through personal interviews, others from letters written to me in response to my own request for thoughts and experiences, in advertisements placed in *Woman* magazine, *Time Out*, *The Guardian* and a variety of local papers, ranging from Liverpool to Bristol.

Without these voices, which come from old and young women, of different classes, creeds, colours, attitudes and politics, the book would have been merely a chronology of events. It is the memories and emotions which women have voiced about feminism, how it has shaped and coloured their lives, how at times it has been painful and destructive, at times exhilarating and life-enhancing, how some see it as a force for enormous good, others see the harm it has wreaked — which bring the book to life.

I have added my own voice at times because it is my history too. My involvement with the Women's Liberation Movement has been small compared to that of the early activists, although I feel profoundly glad that the women's movement happened when it did in my life, affecting my adult existence. I have demonstrated on behalf of some of the causes, put my name and voice to some campaigns, and I have used my journalism to write about what feminists have been doing. But I have also felt ambivalent about some of the more radical attitudes and activities and I have disliked intensely the putting down of women who were deemed not to be 'right on' enough, and the abuse of heterosexual women by the political lesbian lobby, however much I can understand, intellectually, the arguments. And while finding utterly repellent those men who are dedicated chauvinists, who treat women at best disdainfully, at worst violently, I cannot subscribe to a view which seemed to be around in the movement for a while, that each and every man is a case of Original Sin.

The first two chapters are a chronological account of how the movement laid its roots and how it evolved and fragmented, and the last chapter takes a look at where it is now and what women who have been involved in it have to say. These accounts are based on press reports, the writings and speeches of the time and the reflections of women speaking to me recently. In between these chapters, I have focused on specific issues which, though important, have not been as widely written about as, say, the Greenham campaign, the miners' wives, the politics of health or the issues around violence (which are touched on in the first chapters). My themes, then, are sexuality and the split which occurred in the movement over the belief of radical lesbians that heterosexual women 'collude with the enemy'; the politics of appearance and the discussion about whether feminists should adorn themselves; the way women's work has developed in visual arts and the theatre; how feminism has made its mark on journalism; the issue of children — to have them or not — and a look at how far equality has really got. There is also a chapter called Voices, which consists of excerpts from the letters women wrote to me which I believe speak vividly for themselves.

In each case my aim has been to show how feminism has interfaced with life, how a feminist perspective has developed around the issues, and to show some of the conflicts which have been a very real part of the movement.

I chose the title for this book because it was the term applied to

Mary Wollstonecraft, one of the earliest and most courageous battlers on behalf of women's rights. When her extraordinary piece of writing *Vindication of the Rights of Women* was published in 1792, Horace Walpole labelled her 'a hyena in petticoats', and it seemed to me that his sentiments — the sense of loathing for a woman who dared to deny her femininity by opposing the rule of men over women — were effectively repeated two hundred years later.

This is not a polemical book nor is it intended as a definitive history of the women's movement — there are people far better qualified to write that than I am. My aim was to convey a sense of the important issues which arose through the movement and the changing atmosphere and thinking throughout the past two decades. And my hope is that the book will appeal not only to women who have been passionately involved but also to women who have not felt themselves, in the words of one interviewee, 'fully paid up sisters', women who may not believe in all of the causes but who have stood up for their rights in an individual way, women who have watched and listened with interest or with irritation. In other words, this book is intended for the range of women who gave their time and thoughts to me for these pages.

1

LAYING THE ROOTS

1968—1970

IN February 1968 *The Sun* marked the anniversary of women's winning the vote with an editorial stating: 'Fifty years after the emancipation of women *The Sun* is under no illusions as to the real position, the real power, the real influence of women today . . . Making news, making impact. Today. Every day.' Anybody reading this twenty years on is likely to react with a sardonic sneer, at the assumption of that statement. For it is generally agreed that 1968 was the year in which the new women's movement came, tentatively but positively, to life. Before this, women had been protesting and talking in a disparate way about the issues of birth control, abortion, equal pay and equal opportunities, but it was not until that year that women came together to formulate their thoughts on the fundamental discrimination and oppression they perceived and to consider ways to fight the psychic as well as the practical effects of their position.

The line *The Sun* was taking had a good deal to do with its professed position as a progressive, liberal paper. For at this time the title belonged to an offspring of the old union supported, Left-wing *Daily Herald*, not the anti-feminist, misogynist tabloid which has proudly displayed women as a sexual commodity, since Rupert Murdoch became the proprietor. It took a consistently positive line on women in its editorials, for example, stating on the issue of equal pay: 'Not only are women underpaid, they are undervalued', and commentating that they were being wasted by employers who would not offer equal opportunities. Even so, *The Sun* could not resist a bit of reassurance to the

threatened male when the new feminists were showing a per-
ceptible head of militancy. The report of a survey published at
the end of 1969 showed that women could compete on equal
terms with men but said comfortingly that 'all this boss talk is
sheer bluster'. It went on: 'Intelligent girls always knew when to
conceal their intelligence'.

There was at this time a widespread feeling that women had
already achieved equality, and — however extraordinary it might
seem in retrospect — plenty of people who felt it had all gone too
far. Journalist William Spicer voiced an anxiety echoed by many
when he wrote: 'I wonder if the growing pressure on women to
go out to work is not going a little too far. As a man it is
frightening and a little depressing to learn that three out of every
four wives no longer believe that looking after a home and
children (to say nothing of a husband) is a sufficiently rewarding
full-time occupation.'

Nor were men the only ones who felt this anxiety. The press, a
valuable gauge of the moods and *mores* of an age, carried many
articles by women protesting at their discontented sisters and
urging women to hang on to femininity, to the *Me Tarzan, You
Jane* status quo. Janet Morgan, first women secretary of Oxford
Union Society, voiced her feelings in an interview in the *Daily
Mail* that year: 'I sometimes think the sex war for equality may
have gone a bit too far. I think absolute equality is impossible.
Aggressive women make me shudder. Militant feminists who
take a determined stand on women's rights seem to forget that
women still have an advantage simply because they *are* women.'

Despite these protests, a growing number of women were
beginning to feel that being a woman actually put them at a
substantial *disadvantage* in a patriarchal society, and it was this
which led to the emergence of the Women's Liberation Movement, a movement that was to grow into the irreverent, ebullient,
exasperating force that impacted on the lives of women and
men, whether they liked it or not, over the following decades.

Anita Bennett, an American who had come to Britain and
been involved in the demonstrations for a woman's right to
choose at the time of David Steel's 1967 Abortion Act, was one
who recognized the need for a specifically women's voice on
issues which affected them. She had long been active in varying

political activities and she began to see that women needed to start talking about themselves, and their own needs, the oppression in society that applied to them as a group and where they must, if necessary, be in opposition to men. She recalls: 'The abortion issue brought women together because it was so obviously about them. Clearly it was not right that men should decide what happens to our bodies. From this very particular view of male control and how it affects us we began to talk about other ways in which that control is exercised, ways that are not always so visible. There had been talk of equal pay and other specific rights before this time, but this was different. We began to understand the psychological grip men had on women as well.'

The crux, then, of the feelings which were gradually being unearthed, was that an inequality existed which was enshrined not just in law in the form of unequal pay and discrimination in job and education opportunities, but which also underpinned the whole culture in which women were living, providing an underlying valuation of women as inferior to men and an acceptance that women were programmed by gender to perform different tasks from men, to play a specific and separated role in society. This came as a shock even to those women who understood the struggles of earlier feminists, and had reached an understanding of how profoundly the feminine role ascribed to and taken on by women, had locked them into a strait-jacket of oppression.

Ann Oakley, whose feminist analysis of domestic labour *The Sociology of Housework* (published 1974) crystallized for many women the resentments they felt, said of the motivations for the new movement: 'From its beginning this movement has seen the position of women in a different light from earlier feminists. It has taken up some of the early more radical themes — the bondage of marriage, the economic and emotional poverty of housework . . . It has sought for a theoretical understanding of why women are oppressed. In the second place it has seen this oppression as existing within attitudes and ideologies as much as in actual behaviour.'

What was going on represented a breaking through what Betty Friedan termed the 'Feminine Mystique'. This was the cult of the feminine which had been energetically promoted in Britain and America after the Second World War when politicians and press, propagandists and manufacturers came together to 'persuade' women that a mixture of biological destiny, their innate domestic skills and their gentle nurturing qualities (in contrast to the male qualities of aggression and drive, intellectual rigour and the toughness necessary for survival in the outside world) meant they should inhabit the domestic sphere and leave the world of important work, careers, power and universality to men.

Friedan had interviewed many women in America at the end of the 1950s and early 1960s, and it was her discovery of their profound distress which inspired her to write *The Feminine Mystique*, published in 1963. These women, with husbands and children, nice homes and all mod. cons., were expected to fulfil the American Dream of a cosy nuclear family where Mum is supremely contented looking after home and children, providing care and sex for her husband. The media devoted enormous time and newsprint to pointing out how fortunate she was to be boss in her own home, mistress of her own time, in charge of the vital organization of domestic matters. And if there were problems, she was told, in true Freudian spirit, that they lay with her and that she must work at being the passive counterpart to the dynamic aggressive male. The woman who failed this goal was culpable and could only undermine the well-being of society.

Yet women spoke out to Betty Friedan and their resounding howl of despair was: 'I want something more than my husband, my children, my home. I want something which makes me feel I exist.' And in her book — which caused a storm of fury and protest across the United States and which had her and her family ostracized by their community — Friedan blamed women's frustration on a culture which taught them that since their 'success' depended on being desirable to men, and on getting married, they must not appear too intelligent, too ambitious, but rather should concentrate on being decorative, adorable dependents. This, she argued, provoked deep guilt in women who secretly considered a lifetime spent living in this way intolerable. She wrote angrily: 'The problem that has no name — which is simply the fact that American women are kept from growing to their full human capacities — is taking a far greater toll on the physical and mental health of our country than any known disease.'

But while Friedan and her family were reviled locally, *The*

Feminine Mystique hit a female nerve. It became a bestseller and was for many women a seminal read. As one woman put it: 'I read this book and it seemed to state, there on paper, so much that I felt but didn't admit. I could not have gone back from that stage, I just had to start doing something about my life. It was drastic. It meant in due course splitting up with my husband, living as a single mother, struggling to support us. But for the first time since I was a child I felt as though I was allowed to be who I wanted, and I felt strong being that person.'

The Feminine Mystique was also published in Britain. Eva Figes, whose own book *Patriarchal Attitudes*, one of the key British works of early feminist polemic, was published in 1970, recalls: 'I read Betty Friedan and knew it was important, that it would have real impact. I hadn't really considered the situation of women that way but my own position as a wife made me realize the absolute truth of much that she said. And it was exciting because this was the first sign that something was happening and it didn't seem long at all before there was a sense that women were voicing discontents.'

What these women were feeling and what *The Sun* had to say clearly represented very different perspectives. One reason for this is that a great many women did go out to work after the Second World War and this was seen from the outside as a sign of equality. The fact that most were working part-time in low-paid service industries with conditions which offered little or no employment protection, and none of the prospects which men in 'proper' jobs had, and were expected also to continue running the home, was not taken into account. The vote, which was awarded only to women over thirty in 1918, had been extended to all and it was widely assumed that because women could vote they had equal power with men.

But at least as significant was the equality mythology which developed with the arrival of the Pill. Women, freed from the risk of unwanted pregnancy, were certainly equal with men in being able to choose sex when and as they might want. However, that did not alter the fundamental power structure within a society which had separated men and women from working together, or co-operating in any fundamental matters, and designated women to the role of pleasing, seducing, and caring for men. Indeed, many of us found that, far from breaking down barriers between the sexes, the Pill merely provided a new slant on male power-mongering. Women who dared to say that they did not want to have sex with a man, were accused of being frigid, and such was the climate of the time that male disapproval led to profound feelings of inadequacy, leading a great many women to indulge in 'permissive' sex as much from a wish to please and mollify men as from actual desire. As Jenny Sands reminisces: 'If you said you didn't want to sleep with a man they would say things like "I suppose you are cold" or "you're frightened" and at that time catching a man, knowing men fancied you, was all important, so many of us gave in. But I remember feeling upset on many occasions because the fact that I could "choose" to have sex didn't bring me any closer to real companionship with men which was what I really wanted.'

In fact while the Fifties had kept women down by putting them on pedestals, worshipping them rather as the Victorians had, as the angel in the house, as objects to be loved and cherished as a man's private prize, the Sixties worked hard to turn women into a commodity. The new fashions packaged them most effectively as playthings in skimpy clothes and mini-skirts, faces made doll like and vacuous with thick panstick make-up, black eye liner, layers of false eyelashes, and with it all went the trivializing terminology — chicks, dolly birds. The new genre of macho pop stars gave a spurious glamour to the no strings one-night stand, a prime example of the way male power can reduce women to the fawning desperation of groupies. And yet to a society which equated sexual freedom, on whatever terms, with emancipation, the belief that women were truly mistresses of their own destiny, took root.

Unrelated in lifestyle, but presenting another deceptive picture of female equality was the 'hippy' woman who travelled the Eastern trail with her man, wore similar clothes, appeared to live on equal terms and united with him in a disdain for the world of establishment values. But inside the communes and shared homes the status quo was seen to be remarkably traditional. Women would care for the children, cook the meals, wash the clothes and generally tend their men, who often enough, less traditionally, would not even be going out to work. And it was conspicuous that 'serious rap' was almost always among men, while the women performed their tasks in the background and assumed the earth mother identity, investing the business of childbearing and mothering with a spiritual as well as practical significance, creating from it an absolute *raison d'être*.

A more honest equality appeared to exist in the political student movement of 1968 which occurred in Britain, in Europe and in America. Here young men and women could be heard voicing the same protest and passion over Vietnam, and Cuba, the peace movement, the Civil Rights struggle, the demonstrations in support of workers in France, the Soviet invasion of Prague — demonstrations in which the sexes were indistinguishable in their tattered jeans and elongated sweaters adorned with agit-prop badges and emblems, the model of genderless unity. But under the surface it was very different. Stokely Carmichael in his endlessly quoted homily made plain how little the revolutionary male perceived his sister as equal: 'The only position of women [in the Civil Rights movement] is prone.' Amanda Sebestyn, who went on to become a member of the *Spare Rib* collective, comments: 'I remember tackling one of the men I demonstrated alongside and asking "Why are you people always going on about women and sex?" Socialist men were deeply into trashing monogamy, and there was a strong sense that they were more interested in us as the perks for their ideological work than for what we did for the cause.'

And Anita Bennett comments: 'Very charismatic men like Tom Haydn were organizing Left-wing communes in which the men would be surrounded by a posse of adoring women. Before long the women began to talk among themselves and see that all this ideology had nothing to do with them and their happiness. We began to see men less sympathetically, to talk of them as phallocrats.'

Years later, Betty Friedan recalls the double bind women found themselves in — on the one hand despised for not having the right 'qualifications' to be proper revolutionaries, yet relegated fairly and squarely to the most traditional place. She describes how men would 'come home from a demo, wipe tear gas from the eyes, lie down on the sofa and wait for dinner to be prepared. It was a shock to find that although the men felt we shared their politics they left their revolutionary politics at the door.'

The press too took a markedly traditional view of women's role

in the 1968 uprisings. Apart from photographing good-looking
girls at demos, or taking the 'how could a nice girl like you . . .'
approach, it largely ignored the female involvement. In 1988
when *The Sunday Times* magazine carried a 'remember 1968'
feature based on press reports from the time, devoted to the
revolutionary movement, women's names were conspicuously
absent. Margaret Warters, producing a history of the women's
movement in the same year, for Radio Four, recalled: 'Women
barely rate a mention in all the memories of fighting on the
streets during the Sixties. But women were there taking the same
risks, in the US, in the South working with the blacks in the Civil
Rights movement, in London in the anti-war movement.'

In Britain and America, the Women's Liberation Movement
grew out of the student protest activities where women, exposed
to political analysis, and the process of looking at power and its
meanings within society, began to ask questions about their
personal situations, about their subordinated status which they
had previously accepted as immutable.

But the act of asking the questions led to the realization that
solutions to the dilemmas they were uncovering could not be
solved in conjunction with their revolutionary partners on the
barricades, because few of those partners had any real interest in
the cause of women's rights. One woman recalls a male friend's
reaction when she told him that she was going to the protest
against Miss America in Atlantic City rather than to a big demo
in Chicago — he was appalled. And a revealing insight into the
value attached to the woman issue was the label 'chicks' lib' it was
given by revolutionary men. Joyce Gelb in her essay 'Feminism in
Britain. Politics without Power?' (*The New Women's Movement*. Ed.
Drude Dahlerup. Sage Publications, 1986) says: 'These women
turned their often radical politics to the concerns of women: they
organized at the local level. Out of this base came the early
emphasis on consciousness raising and organizations such as
rape crisis centres and shelters for battered women.'

Sheila Rowbotham, whose energy and incisive writings have
been a vital contribution to the British women's movement, said
(*Dreams and Dilemmas: Collected Writings*. Virago, 1983): 'In the
diary I kept during 1967 there are persistent references to
incidents I'd seen and books I'd read from a women's liberation
point of view. I can remember odd conversations with women

who were friends of mine, and particular very intense moments when I was hurt and made angry by the attitudes of men on the Left. But it was still at an intellectual level. We didn't think of meeting consciously as a group, far less of forming a movement. We were floundering around.'

But this was, of course, part of the process which led to a more concrete formulating of ideas. Conversational floundering around was an activity which allowed women to voice diffuse thoughts and emotions, it gave them the chance to explore feelings which had perhaps never been acknowledged before and which many felt were theirs alone. As Ann Oakley puts it: 'Before the Women's Liberation Movement could be born, there had to be the recognition among women of a shared female condition — a condition that constrained all women, regardless of their individual circumstances . . . The genesis of the movement lay not in the identification of a particular goal for which political organization among women was needed, but the personal experience of women whose dissatisfaction was the image thrown back at them by the mirror.'

Although the British movement was strongly influenced by the American Women's Liberation Movement, the Socialist and Marxist ideologies which underpinned the beliefs of many women in Britain, were not popular in the USA. Anita Bennett says: 'I was a Socialist and there was a good deal of hostility towards Socialism in the States at that time and the women's movement was certainly not free of it. If you declared yourself a Socialist you were accused of putting Socialism before feminism.'

In America, practical advances in equality were made far earlier than in the UK. In 1963 the Equal Pay Act was passed making discrimination in pay illegal and the 1964 Civil Rights Act legislated against discrimination in hiring, firing, benefits, promotions and job conditions — although this was done at a time when rights for blacks were higher on the agenda than equality for women. In 1966 the National Organization for Women, with Betty Friedan as a founder member, was formed by a group of delegates at the National Commission on the Status of Women, to lobby the Government to take seriously women's demands for changes in education, employment and reproductive rights. Robin Morgan recollects the exhilaration of the Jeanette Rankin Brigade March on Washington in 1967, which was joined by thousands of women: 'There a group of women split off to discuss the possibilities of building an autonomous women's movement.'

In Britain, groups began to form around the country, and before long the term 'consciousness raising' was given life, as a positive recognition of the new awareness women felt they were achieving. Anna Coote and Beatrix Campbell (*Sweet Freedom*, published 1982) have a vivid memory of what it was like: 'Small groups of women began to get together. They began to talk to each other in a way they had not done before. They discussed their day-to-day experiences and their feelings about themselves, their jobs, their husbands, their lovers, their children . . . What was new was that they were now drawing political conclusions from their personal experiences.' Jean McCrindle, involved with women's groups in America, sent 'raps' about men from the groups she attended. Some of the women who founded the New York Radical Feminists group wrote: 'Women are the only oppressed people whose biological, emotional and social life is totally bound to that of the oppressors', a statement which struck an immediate chord with many women. And in that statement was an intimation of the move to come, among some feminists, towards separatism and certainly to the choice — even by women who continued to have heterosexual relationships — to meet exclusively. Although men had been admitted to some of the very earliest group meetings when no policy had been formulated against their attending, since the essence of what the women wanted to discuss was directly related to male behaviour and the way in which this impacted on women's lives, it soon became clear the truth would only really come out in women-only groups.

For women such as Madelaine Lloyd the fear of speaking out in front of men resulted from a fear of hurting them: 'There was lots I wanted to say about the imbalance which seemed to exist in my life with Michael and I wanted to be allowed to be angry, to say things which sounded quite brutal. But I knew if I did that in front of Mike he would feel terribly upset, terribly attacked and betrayed, and I didn't want to do that to him. I didn't think it his fault that my career had been cut to fit in with the kids, or that I felt undervalued because he didn't discuss his work decisions with me, but with a male friend, or even that I had kept quiet about my sexual needs for fear of making him feel a failure. He is a good and caring man and really wants to get things right, but he is also a product of the culture he grew up in.'

Lucy Majors explains: 'Many of us had kept our real feelings quiet for years because too often if we spoke out we got derided or misunderstood by men. What we were experiencing as women talking together was too important to risk that way. We knew the only way to be able to be absolutely honest, to take risks in sharing feelings, was to do it among women only. There were certainly women who came out saying they hated men, but for most of us that wasn't the feeling or the point. It was simply that we wanted to feel safe and that wasn't possible with men there, even men who wanted to learn and understand.'

Another point was that many women wanted to be able to talk about things which seemed important to them, and did not want to have to tailor their conversation to appeal to a man. An understandable sentiment at a time when women were regularly parodied for being capable only of gossip and small-time tittle tattle, a point made publicly by Judge Faulkes in a divorce hearing when he said: 'If you want to make your wife happy, chat her up when you come home in the evening. If she bores you stiff prattling about everyday rubbish, try to look interested.'

But not all women were enthusiastic about these early groups. Journalist Linda Melvern, who was working on a newspaper as a reporter in Doncaster, at the end of the 1960s, remembers deciding to go along to a local feminist group and: 'Feminism was heavily into consciousness raising and for a start I couldn't understand the language, but what I was aware of was a lot of grovelling in the psyche for "revelations" and "feelings" which seemed to me grossly self indulgent and not to lead anywhere. It didn't seem to me to be the point. I was interested in the mining community. At the time widows' pensions were being cut and I felt strongly that women should be concerning themselves with this kind of issue. Then the final straw was when the local women's group made a radio programme on feminism and used the money they were paid to give themselves a party. It made me furious because the whole thing seemed to be about talk but not about helping women who really needed it, the kind of women I was meeting as a reporter, who desperately needed practical and financial help. Discussing male oppression would have been a luxury for them.'

But talk was the point of the burgeoning groups and plenty of women have justified this. Barbara Lewis, who was a single mother after a recent, traumatic marriage break-up, said: 'I was so full of pain, anger, emotions which were quite paralysing and all I could think about was finding another man as a way of proving I was all right, still an attractive woman, still a winner. I know, and I even knew then deep down that that would have been no kind of solution, but it took being able to cry, shout, rage, gain support through talk in my women's group, to make me feel strong enough to let my husband go, in my head, and to build a life for me, on my own.' Elizabeth, a twenty-year-old from one of London's seediest housing estates where harassment and male aggression are part of everyday life, also expresses the value of talk for her: 'I didn't know how to deal with the aggression around. I felt constantly frightened and intimidated and as though, somehow, it were my fault, that I was to blame if a man was unpleasant to me. Talking with other women I began to see that this really wasn't so, and I began to discuss ways to deal with it. That was valuable because it gave me strength and it also helped me to like men who didn't behave that way, rather than regarding them all as potentially frightening and horrible.'

At this early stage the groups only touched on the issues and campaigns which were later to take a much more central role, while the importance of therapeutic talk and consciousness raising continued to be stressed. From the early days the friendship gained through these groups is the thing which many, many women remember with delight. A fundamental camaraderie emerged, and women found that they could enjoy supporting and being supported by each other. For many this was exciting, startling, shocking even. It was a new phenomenon, for although women had recorded deep and vital friendships formed during the war years, when men were absent and the need to share the daily fear and anguish created a sisterhood, the years after the war did a great deal to separate women one from another. During these years the emphasis was on 'rewarding' soldiers who had been at war and providing for them a return to normality. Built into this ambition was the belief that homes and wives were the key to their readjustment to civilian life. The onus then was on women to be contented players in this reassuring game of happy families. The absolute aspiration for women, the symbol of success and fulfilment, was to be a wife, mother and homemaker and any sense of self sufficiency, contentment at living alone which might have developed during the war years, was now seen as a pathological or deviant state. To achieve society's approval a woman needed a husband. To remain unmarried and to be a spinster was a sign of conspicuous failure. But men were in short supply in the post-war years and so women were effectively pitched against each other in the competition to 'win' the husband they had so energetically been assured they wanted and needed. In such a climate it is hardly surprising that female friendships were, for the most part, superficial, wary and disposable. It was accepted that a 'best friend' would always take second place to a man, that once a women was engaged or married the best friend would get scant time and attention and only that on terms which did not disturb the man involved — a situation vividly portrayed in Terence Davies' film *Distant Voices, Still Lives*. And a stalwart of literature and films of the post-war years is the tale of the 'best friend' who steals a husband or lover. Novelist Fay Weldon, looking back on her first marriage, remembers the sense of unease which circumscribed women's friendships in the early Sixties: 'I lived a conventional life with a husband and baby, in the suburbs, and it always struck me as curious that although there were lots of us in the same situation we never talked to each other, never intimately, only on the price of sugar level. Then if a husband came in, the woman who didn't 'belong' would immediately go away because somehow women weren't supposed to talk to each other for fear of marital disloyalty. Men felt very threatened by women talking. So as well as competitiveness between women — and that was very real, as was the flashing of the wedding ring by women who had them at those who hadn't, there was fear that one's man might be upset by too close a friendship and then, horror of horrors, you might lose him. So women were very isolated in this situation and I remember feeling it was all very odd and weird.'

She contrasts this feeling with what she felt, at the end of that decade, when she went to a women's group: 'Suddenly there was a sense of sisterhood, a feeling of women actually liking each other. I only went to the group twice but it was enough to make me realize the sense of communality with other women which could exist and from this I went on to write about issues to do with women. It was a wonderful, exhilarating sense of saying things which were unsaid. I felt I was speaking not *for* other women but about things which concerned them.'

Marsha Rowe, co-founder with Rosie Boycott of *Spare Rib* magazine, recalls the intensity of experiencing her first meeting with a group of fifty women: 'So much of our lives had been concealed from each other, it was as if we had been strangers. Other impressions were the way the room seemed to swirl with emotion so long suppressed and that I was frightened. After everyone left, Louise, a friend, and I couldn't sleep and sat up for hours feeling terribly shaken and near hysteria, clinging to each other every now and then for reassurance.'

Although women already involved with politics were largely responsible for the fact that the informal airing of feelings and dissatisfactions among them acquired some kind of formal shape and eventually became a proper movement, by no means all women who feel feminism has been significant in their lives, came to it this way. Books such as Germaine Greer's *The Female Eunuch*, Eva Figes' *Patriarchal Attitudes*, Kate Millett's *Sexual Politics*, Robin Morgan's *Sisterhood is Powerful* — passionate, enraged outpourings — have been absolutely crucial in drawing many women towards feminism. In some cases they legitimized feelings women already had and gave them shape and authority; in other cases they helped women make sense of experiences; for others they presented a whole new way of looking at the world.

Barbara Rogers, now editor of *Everywoman* magazine, remembers reading Betty Friedan's *The Feminine Mystique* at school. 'It was just a book in the library which I picked up, and it was staggering, particularly talking about housework and acknowledging the tedium of it, the way it wastes women's lives and they are supposed to feel virtuous doing it. I kept saying to my mother "there's this book which says housework is stupefyingly boring, it goes nowhere and you just have to do it again". This didn't lead anywhere at the time but later when I did get involved in feminist issues I could see how it had affected the way I looked at various things "women do".'

For Linda Melvern reading Simone de Beauvoir's *Memoirs of a Dutiful Daughter* was most important because: 'Very early on de Beauvoir realized that her destiny was in her own hands, not in the hands of the man she might one day marry. It was so fundamental. I may not have liked joining groups and all that, but I was tuned in to the concepts of feminism and I could see that to support the broad principles was important.'

Australian writer Dale Spender, who has devoted her extra-ordinary energy to writing exclusively on feminist issues, found reading the writings by the new feminists 'a kind of salvation'. She explains: 'I was brought up in suburban Australia where women grew up and got married and there really wasn't any question about it. I had trained to be a teacher and I can remember in my early twenties enjoying the work hugely and thinking I wanted to concentrate on it. But everyone kept telling me I would never be happy until I had my own kitchen. In the end I believed them and I married a local man in 1967. I can tell you, getting a kitchen certainly didn't make me happy, nor did marriage. Once we had got over the idea that we were allowed to have sex and we were not united in finding clandestine ways of doing that, there was nothing we had in common. I was interested in books, my job, ideas and he just didn't want to know. His idea of a good afternoon was sitting with his feet up watching football and drinking beer. He didn't seem to under-stand when I suggested that if I did that with him sometimes, he should do things I enjoyed with me sometimes. And I remember feeling that, somehow, I had to be available to my husband all the time and most of my energy got subsumed in washing, ironing, cooking when I got home from work. One day I was ironing and he was watching television and he said "I really don't like to see you ironing". He wasn't offering to do it, he just felt uncomfortable seeing me doing it in front of him. At that moment I thought "bugger you, mate, do your own ironing".

'We split up and apart from the sheer joy of being able to eat, smoke and type in bed, I had lots of time to read. I came across *Sisterhood is Powerful* and it was as though I'd seen the light. This collection of writings was saying things which seemed so import-ant, so right. I went on to read Greer, Millett, Juliet Mitchell, Eva Figes and plenty of others and I just knew that what they said was right, that I had to be with them, one of them.'

For Eva Figes being a single parent was the catalyst to working out a feminist perspective on the world. Alone, once she separated from her husband, with two young children, she realized 'what a conspiracy male domination was. Men were going on about the importance of the family and it was this which allowed them to justify the way women were treated at that time. Yet that was shown to be completely hollow when a woman found herself alone with children, as I did after the divorce. In terms of supportive legislation there was nothing. I found that getting maintenance was a farce. I lost my house and there was nothing I could do.'

Fay Weldon's marriage and domestic experience was cata-paulted from a state of 'not discontent' by what she describes as 'two significant occurrences' which caused her suddenly to view the world from a different angle. She explains: 'Two women I knew took their lives. One was Hannah Gavron, a sociologist, who had written a powerful and important book about the captive housewife; another was Assia Wevill, a talented and intelligent woman, who lived with Ted Hughes after Sylvia Plath died. She killed herself and her child in a way which conveyed her desperation, her inability to work out how to live her life in a way which would work for her. And as I thought about this I began to see how wrong it was that society automatically blamed her rather than looking at the individual circumstances of her predicament and understanding that blame was inappropriate. But in those days women were seen as labile creatures, the victim of their emotions; and it was quite natural for women to be condemned as mad or sad, if they couldn't cope — and certainly if they chose so drastic a way out.

'It was then I realized how important it was to be on the side of women, to be working out exactly what it was that made things go wrong for them.'

Small incidents, sudden recognitions of an injustice, some-thing said and suddenly absorbed, education or a relationship, have all been catalysts for women, the moments they recall — perhaps years later — as the time when they began to think in feminist terms. Not that all put it like this. Among the letters sent in response to my requests were many replies from women saying 'I am not quite sure if I am a feminist', 'I don't belong to any group', 'I wouldn't like to call myself political' and 'I am definitely not one of those ardent women libbers', yet the things they say are all about the voyages of internal discovery which fired the gatherings together of women in the early days.

Majorie described how: 'I fought my first "feminist" battle — although I did not recognize it as such — when I was about to get married in 1953. I knew that I did not want children so I went to the FPA and asked to be fitted with a diaphragm. Shock! Horror! I wasn't married and I was a virgin. I pointed out that to be fitted with one after I was married was like bolting the stable door when the horse had gone. After a lot of argy bargy they relented, but only because I was a professional woman and because my prospective husband also had a degree.'

As the 1960s drew to a close the energy and excitement generated within the groups now alive and active all over the country, was heady. There was a sense of something important and revolutionary happening. For women who saw this new feminism as important and right it was a time of hope.

But by no means all women who heard what was going on were enthusiastic. Plenty felt threatened by the idea that the goals they had committed the bulk of their time and energy to, were now being devalued and undermined. As Jane Brown put it: 'I felt content with the domestic life I had, without work, and without exploring my relationship to my husband. But I felt suddenly that I was failing, getting things wrong, that women out there had dictated that I should start unravelling the contentment I felt.' And columnist Lynda Lee Potter defended, vigorously and subjectively, the traditional way of things when she wrote: 'I've got two children, a big, old house, a smashing husband who doesn't believe in equality or equal pay or complete emancipation or cleaning his own shoes. Why should he when he's got me to do it for him?'

That a great many women did not have things so good, and did a great deal more than cleaning shoes because it was assumed to be women's work, was the point the new women's groups were making. They wanted to provide support for the ever growing number coming forward and stripping away the veneer of contentment they had built up over years. Women must be given an opportunity to speak out against the status quo, to vent their anger and to strive for change, was the message of the groups and that was the direction in which they were determinedly moving.

Margery Proops may have been saddened by what she saw but she recognized the reality of the situation when, in November

1969 she wrote in her *Daily Mirror* column: 'There is hardly anything less attractive than a militant woman . . . and I feel real sorrow and regret at finding myself forseeing the time when female militancy will no longer be restricted to the few.' Within the year militant demonstrations would take place, feminists would gather together to be publicly strident and the movement would gather momentum.

2

BRITAIN'S MOST DANGEROUS REVOLUTIONARIES

1970s—1980s

O N 20 November 1970 the Miss World beauty contest took place with pomp, packaging and ceremony as it had done since 1951. The competing girls desported themselves on stage, in front of guest Bob Hope who was full of bohomie and patriotic references to Vietnam. The tune being played was 'Ain't She Sweet' and a good time, it seemed, was being had by all. Until, that is, a posse of ill-kempt women, who contrasted bizarrely with the gloss and glamour of the occasion, burst on to the stage mooing like cows, blasting whistles, whirling football rattles and bearing placards with the titles 'Mis-Conception' (a bid for free contraception), 'Mis-Treated' (a demand for free housework), 'Mis-Placed' (demanding free abortion) and 'Mis-Judged' (advocating an end to beauty contests).

'The Beauty and the Bovver Girl' was how the *Daily Mail* described it, and Heydon Cameron reporting said: 'The Miss World contest was interrupted last night by fifty women. Mr Hope was in the middle of his act as the judges were selecting the seven finalists. Suddenly girls jumped from their seats in the auditorium . . . They hurled smoke bombs, stink bombs and pamphlets. Comedian Bob Hope fled from the stage. It was the signal for the demonstration to begin.'

The *Daily Express* did not disguise its partisan feelings: 'The trouble was caused by *women* — women with the slogan "We're not beautiful or ugly, we're angry"!' While the contestants, identified contrastingly by the journalist as 'girls', were labelled 'cabbages' and 'poor cows' and deemed 'an affront to the dignity of women' by the interlopers. But it was Bob Hope who got the last word in: 'Anyone who would want to try and break up an affair as wonderful as this, they got to be on some kind of dope.'

But in fact it was not dope which stimulated the women into action, but a determination to focus attention on what they described as 'the physical confines of the way women are seen and the way they fit into society. . . . It was a blow against passivity, not only the enforced passivity of the girls on the stage, but the passivity that we all felt in ourselves.' A group of the demonstrators produced a pamphlet called *Why Miss World?*, which aimed to make the connection between a piece of entertainment generally regarded as harmless good fun, in which women displayed themselves in the hope of winning the ultimate accolade of being labelled the world's most beautiful 'girl', and the way females, from birth, are pitched into the beauty stakes, and taught very early that the approval which really counts is that of men.

The writer, attempting to explain the attitudes and actions behind the demo, described her own angry, subjective feelings: 'I felt the event symbolized my daily exploitation. I saw the contestants being judged by men, and I know what it feels like to be judged and scrutinized every day when I am just walking down the street. I saw women being forced to compete with each other . . .'

She wrote: 'Suddenly the signal which we had been waiting for so anxiously, came at the perfect moment. It was our robot-like response which surprised us most of all. When the moment came it was easier to act than to consider . . . We threw smoke bombs, flour, stink bombs, leaflets . . . Bob Hope freaked out, ran off the stage. We got thrown out by Mecca bouncers: Sally was arrested for assault (stubbing her cigarette out on a policeman). Jenny was done for an offensive weapon (a children's smoke bomb). Some went on to the Café de Paris where the Miss Worlds were having dinner; two more arrests — Jo and Kate for throwing flour and rotten tomatoes at the Mecca pimps. Maia was arrested for abusive language (telling a policeman to fuck off).'

This was, as Coote and Campbell (*Sweet Freedom*) have noted, the first conspicuous act of civil disobedience and the arrests which followed may have been strictly correct according to the law of the land, but it seems likely they came, too, as a horrified reflex reaction to the sight of women so mutated from the desirable norm. There seems a clear parallel with the arrests and imprisonment of women Suffragettes at the turn of the century.

The following year, Anne Sharpley, one of the few women journalists at that time prepared to take a sympathetic line on feminism in her writing, covered the trial of the arrested women when they appeared at Bow Street court. She explained that three of the women conducted their own defence and described how they challenged the police's right to give evidence against them because they were men, and how they questioned and challenged throughout the trial, asking: 'Do you enjoy manhandling women?'. 'Are you married and what do you think about the Women's Liberation Movement?' And Sharpley observed: 'Mr Geraint Rees at one point said, "I am not going to let this develop into a forum for the Women's Liberation Movement — whatever that may be".'

In her article for the *Evening Standard* she painted a vivid picture of the women: 'They seem to overflow the dock, all long hair, arms and laughter. Their hairy coats slung on the back of the dock, they pass sweets, peel oranges', and she pinpointed moments of wit such as when the pregnant J. Robinson declared: 'I threw flour over the heads of the people and one fat, ripe old tomato was obstructed in the course of its flight by the helmet of PC McGhee who dutifully stood in the way.'

Summing up, Sharpley put forward her own thoughts on the Women's Liberation Movement. 'Is it important? Yes, if only because there are few of us who wouldn't admit there is a lag in the acceptance of women and if Mrs Joyce Butler's anti-discrimination bill doesn't go through *something* has got to get us, men and women, out of our complacency. Is it 1905 again? [the year Emmeline Pankhurst and mill girl Annie Kenny opted to go to prison instead of paying a fine]. Well *is* it?'

Women's Liberation may have been drawing to its cause an increasing number of women over the past few years, but to the general public it was pretty much a non-event. The Miss World Contest changed all that. It was an outrageous and colourful enough protest to catch the imagination of members of the general public, and while most were certainly not won over to the protesting women's viewpoint, they did at least pause to listen and to look at the odd headline and began to understand some of the reported points being made. Patricia Ashdown Sharp, summing up the decade in the *Daily Mail*, made the point: 'If any single event proved that 1970 was the year Women's Lib. got itself moving it was that incident during the Miss World contest when a battling horde of feminists forced poor Bob Hope to close his eyes and think of Vietnam.'

The demonstration was also a watershed for the press which realized that from now on there would be some mileage in covering women's events. The term 'Women's Lib' was coined and widely used in the popular media. In the view of Lisa Tuttle, author of *Encyclopedia of Feminism* (Longman, 1986), the term was not so much a friendly diminutive as a put-down. She describes it as: 'a demeaning abbreviation for Women's Liberation . . . the shortening of 'liberation' to 'lib.' is trivializing and reflects male unwillingness to take women seriously.'

The other major news story of 1970 which galvanized many column inches of animated press coverage, was the day when American women held parades and demonstrations protesting against male domination, and demanding equal pay and opportunities. It was not, however, their grievances which were reported, but the fact that it had been suggested women should refuse their men sex for that day. However, plenty of women were making plain that they did not want to align themselves with a tactic which would be so thoroughly alienating to their men, or with women who made the kind of remark attributed to one demonstrator: 'I used to lie in bed with my husband and wish I had the courage to bash his head with a frying-pan.' John Sampson in *The Sun* informed his readers: 'Pleas from many ladies of the Women's Liberation Movement that women refrain from all love-making for the next 24 hours were being openly defied. And some women were saying that, instead of staying away from their jobs as urged, they will merely take a long lunch-hour or lecture the boss on being fair to women. One St. Louis Missouri woman even called on members of her sex to ignore the strike altogether.' Another report told how women showed their disapproval by turning up for work in their most feminine clothes and presenting their bosses with chocolate and flowers.

Meanwhile, the *Daily Express*, purporting to report the event as news, told how: 'Thousands of the mothers of America today "dumped" their babies in city hall grounds. Elsewhere women marched, protested and shouted. And the babies howled. But their mothers were on strike — the Women's Strike for Equality was on the march. In New York most were young, wearing men-catching mini skirts or trousers and crying slogans like the airline hostesses': "We want our babies *and* our wings". Others — like the female warriors at the "Male War Centre", the Pentagon — filled dustbins with bras, panties and corsets.'

Just in case all this was making the British male anxious, knowing as we do that what America does today we are likely to be doing tomorrow, Joyce Hopkirk was at pains in the pages of *The Sun* of 25 August to defuse any such thoughts: 'Is there any chance that the dreaded sex strike — threatening to halt love-making in America tomorrow — could spread to Britain? Horrified husbands, fearing that the fiery Women's Liberation Movement of America — who are organizing the strike — might find sisterly support over here, need not worry. Our militant feminists, it seems, feel just as strongly about the need for equal pay and opportunities, but they think those love strike tactics might well rebound. It was all very well for Lysistrata to persuade all Greek women to withdraw their favours until their men stopped fighting, but it is unlikely that women nowadays would show that kind of solidarity.'

Earlier in the year an event took place which showed just how powerfully solidarity among women was growing. In February the first National Women's Liberation Conference was held at Ruskin College, Oxford, and for those who attended it was an exhilarating event, a landmark for women who either had not realized the extent of consciousness raising in the past few years, or who had wondered how a universal unity and focus could be achieved. Sheila Rowbotham recalls: 'We thought perhaps a hundred women would come. In fact more than five hundred people turned up, four hundred women, sixty children and forty men, and we had to go into the Oxford Union buildings because Ruskin was too small. I'd never seen so many women looking so confident in my life before.' While Anna Coote and Beatrix Campbell remembered: 'Like so many events at that stage of the movement it happened almost by accident taking everyone by surprise. They expected three hundred, but nearer six hundred came . . . there were bound to be disagreements at such a diverse gathering. But there was a great sense of exhilaration. The women knew they were in at the start of something big.'

The press coverage of this event was minimal compared to that given to the Miss World activities, but Mary Holland (sent by a male news editor who told her 'it's easily the most amusing thing this weekend') wrote a lengthy report for *The Observer*. The conference began, she said, with 'an impassioned attack on the press which, these women feel, is part of a conspiracy, part male, part capitalist, for the oppression of women. These women are young, violent, radical and very attractive with their long hair and maxi coats.' The speech, which was greeted with roars of applause, advocated violence if necessary to 'smash the myth of feminine passivity'.

During the afternoon Audrey Wise, tagged 'a militant trade unionist from Coventry', made a speech calling for a broadly based Socialist movement and, boldly in this context, she declared that 'feminism is not enough'. She said: 'I don't want to be an equal economic unit any more than I want to be a decoration or a drudge. I want Women's Liberation to be a movement for people as people whether they are men or women.'

The coming together of women sharing, broadly, an ideology and bursting with conviction, commitment, enthusiasm, determination, was the thing many women recall as being a highpoint of those early days. And from this meeting was formulated four demands to be promoted and campaigned for under the flag of the Women's Liberation Movement. A description of these was published in *Women's Newspaper* (issue 1, 6 March 1971):

'EQUAL PAY — We have to understand *why* we don't have equal pay. It's always been said that a woman's place is in the home. We don't want to do equal work and housework as well. We don't want to do equal work when it's shiftwork. Equal pay means not just the same money for the same work, but also recognizing how many women work not because they want to, but because they *have* to, either for money or for friends. Equal pay is the first step not just to more money, but to control over how, why and for whom we work.

'EQUAL EDUCATION AND OPPORTUNITY — We don't want to demand an education equally as bad as that of men — we want equal resources, not equal repression. We want to fight for real education, to make our own jobs and opportunities.

'24-HOUR NURSERIES — We need somewhere for the kids, but we have to choose as to whether the kids will be kept out of the way or given their own space, and whether, freed from children, we just manage to survive through working or make the time to discover who stops us from living.

'FREE CONTRACEPTION AND ABORTION ON DEMAND — We have to be free to choose when and how many kids to have, if any. We have to fight for control over our own bodies, for even the magic Pill (or in the case of mistakes) abortions on demand only gives us the freedom to get into a real mess without any visible consequences. We still can't talk of sex as anything but a joke or a battleground.'

In 1971 Sally Beauman devoted several thousand words in *Nova* magazine to an article looking at the impact of Women's Liberation so far. She said: 'It was inevitable, I suppose, that Women's Liberation should become the media beanfeast that it has. Inevitable that *Time* and *Newsweek* should run cover stories on it within six months of each other; inevitable that one by one the other magazines would capitulate . . . until it was there in *Cosmopolitan* magazine — target of the Women's Liberationists from the beginning. Right there snug between the ads for vaginal deodorants, and ultralucent lipsticks — an excerpt from *Sexual Politics* by Kate Millett.'

Among the most publicly audible women at this time were those who saw the business of feminism as being inextricably bound up with Socialism. They saw that the roots of much of women's oppression lay in a capitalist system which exploits both men and women and many saw it as logical to fight alongside men in the struggle to change this. But, the argument went, women suffer additional discrimination and oppression because of the way sexuality, marriage, child rearing are structured and these issues also need addressing specifically. It was from this feeling that some women either separated part of their activities from those of men, or separated completely in order to concentrate wholly on issues concerning women. An increasing number began to talk of the need to work without men, to espouse separatism as a way of life, and to argue the need for women to cease all possible involvement with men. It was in this atmosphere that *Shrew* published an editorial justifying the woman-only rule at their workshops, which presents the essential argument of separatists: 'It seems to us that Sisterhood really only exists when the individual goes out and relates to and acts with other women in the light of this consciousness. We identify with other women in terms of our common oppression and servitude and we have a solidarity between us born from this.

'Sisterhood is an attempt at redefining our relations with each other. Instead of seeing women in terms of stereotypes and therefore denying them their true nature, we learn to see women and act towards them as full personalities. Learning ourselves to see and treat women as the equals of men. . . . Men divide women from each other. As lover, husband and father to her children, a man is central to a woman's life while her own sex is peripheral, incidental. We need to be liberated not only from men and their domination of our environment but also to be liberated in relation to other women.'

Meanwhile, Dinah Brooke whose passionate lyrical writing has won her a reputation as a fine novelist, brought a personal perspective to the theme of *Shrew's* leader when she delivered a paper at Hornsey College of Art exploring her identity and the expectations around her as she grew up. 'In this present society and in most of the societies we know about, most men despise all women and most women despise most women as well, and that includes themselves. A woman's identity is formed in fact in ways which are almost a prescription for schizophrenia. The conditioning processes of society, advertisements, magazine stories and articles, films, novels, TV and the expectations of people around her insist that she needn't bother to be a person but should find her true fulfilment being a wife and mother.'

But within Socialist feminist thought there was a recognition that, alongside women's oppression, are other important oppressions — that of different nationalities and race, on the basis of age, religion and class, and that these, in the words of Lisa Tuttle, 'cut across gender lines, ensuring that women in different groups, while sharing a universal oppression with all other women, will also share equally important interests with men of their same race, class, ability etc. Rather than arguing that oppression on the basis of sex or class is the fundamental oppression, Socialist feminists argue that every issue is a women's issue, so that it is neither possible nor desirable to separate the *Woman Question* from other political questions.'

It was during the early 1970s that several books which touched women's hearts and minds in an extraordinary way were published. These included Eva Figes' *Patriarchal Attitudes*, Shulamith Firestone's *The Dialectic of Sex*, Kate Millett's *Sexual Politics*, Juliet Mitchell's *Woman's Estate* and Germaine Greer's *The Female Eunuch*. This latter attracted not just a great deal of attention as to the thesis being expounded, as would be appropriate to a Professor at Warwick University, but stimulated a continuing fascination with the personal attributes, lifestyle and thoughts on any subject of the author. Donald Zec, the late *Daily Mirror* columnist, wrote a piece which paid little attention to the content of the book save to sum it up glibly and adversarially: 'Miss Greer's accusations seem to be these: woman has become a stereotyped sex object, made fraudulent by make–up and men's insistence of phoney beauty; that marriage imprisons both parties and love should be a communion between equals, not a male dominated affair with the little woman biting on her lip at the role of submission.' Zec dwelled with delighted approval on the author's physique and personality, using a run of adjectives which emphasized her womanliness: 'She has the profile of a Garbo and the rump of a show jumper and if there is a wittier, wiser, gayer, franker Prof. going the rounds the world ought to hear from her.'

But for plenty of women who had no particular interest in Germaine Greer's rump or gaeity, *The Female Eunuch* was a prodigious exploration of ideas and experiences, the drawing together of of thoughts and feelings which had been fermenting in their own minds. Annette speaks thus: 'My formal introduction to feminism came at about seventeen, having discovered and read from cover to cover (twice!) *The Female Eunuch*. I think it was the first time I'd actually read anything which reflected *so* clearly many of the things I'd been feeling for a long time. I recall thinking how positive it was to see an acknowledgement of many of the doubts and sense of injustice I'd had around being female. Practical involvement in feminism came about a year later. I signed up for a course in Women's Studies. During the course of the next year I worked at the Women's Centre several evenings a week, went to many meetings, talks and joined my first consciousness raising group.'

Sue recalls the impact of what she read and the discussions it led to: 'I was vaguely aware of feminism during my early twenties — I started reading and talking to other women and was so excited that I wasn't the only person to see the limits of traditional women's roles in life. I was rather shocked that so many people ignored or were hostile to what made perfect sense to me . . . I didn't try to resist feminist ideas at all — so much fitted with my own ideas, reassured me, stimulated me, that it fitted like a glove.'

A year after the first Women's Liberation conference at Oxford, the first International Women's Day March took place, drawing together 2,500 women, and as some kind of a tribute to this event the United Nations declared 1972 the International Year of the Woman. Workshops were being set up around the country to campaign on specific matters and in these days there was a lot of emphasis on practical matters — for example, Sheila Rowbotham was much involved in a campaign to pressurize the Government into providing State child care which would then liberate women to work on equal terms with men, and would give them economic independence, and, at a grassroots level, she was involved in a local child care scheme run by a co-operative of women. The discussions centred on ways women could combine giving children the time and attention considered desirable with satisfactory careers — schemes for job sharing, shorter working weeks, flexible time, came up on the agenda. In due course the notion that sharing child care with the father of the child (when he was around and involved) was an important step, not just because it liberated women but because it was valuable for child and father, was widely voiced. And it was at this time that groups began to campaign to have child benefit (then family allowance) paid directly to women.

With the focus on the domestic areas of women's lives, it is hardly surprising that housework — that all-embracing, life-consuming care of the home which, throughout the 1950s, women had grown to understand was a measure of their success as a woman — began to be examined in the light of a feminist perspective. Ann Oakley had demonstrated an interest in exploring women's attitudes to what had simply become accepted as 'women's work' when she decided to make this the subject of her Ph.D in 1969. She went on to write two books: *The Sociology of Housework*, which examines the social significance of housework in our society, and *Housewife* on the historical development of the housewife.

It was the realization of what a dreadful and deadening fate housework could be, which writer Zoe Fairbairns described as her lead-in to feminism. Watching her mother toiling daily at unchanging, dreary tasks which appeared to make her so angry, Zoe came to the conclusion that there was a choice in life: either you were married, put up with the housework or you didn't get married, thus avoiding it, but the 'punishment' was that you were on the shelf and to be pitied. 'There were very few role models to suggest otherwise', she observed. She later wrote an article on the subject in which she said: 'Into the anger and anxiety of my late teens came feminism, not as the historical curiosity I had believed it to be, but as something contemporary and urgent and speaking to me. It spoke about the "Politics of Housework". The phrase alone was stunning. It argued that the division of labour in the home went beyond private family squabbles about whose turn it is to wash up. It argued that without women's unpaid, unacknowledged work, world economic systems would collapse, as would domestic ones.'

It was the fact that housework is unpaid which led to the formation of Wages for Housework in 1972, a campaign founded by the formidably energetic Selma James and run by the Power of Women Collective, which took as its controversial, combative central theme the line that women who service the nation's homes and male workers are performing a task of national value and that, therefore, they should be paid by the State in recognition of this. The thinking here was that economic independence is a primary requisite of liberation for women, rather than that women must leave home and work in order to be liberated — indeed, a point Selma James made emphatically is that some women would prefer to stay at home, particularly if

they have children, provided it did not reduce them to powerlessness and poverty. Paying for housework, within a money-
motivated society, her argument went, would also raise its status
and thus the self-esteem of women doing it. Speaking in 1972,
she said: 'I was in contact with single mothers who were fighting
the cohabitation rule. I knew that those women were right. I also
saw that Women's Liberation somehow saw the single mother
and her fight as being outside the liberation struggle. It was very
clear to me that women needed money.'

But it was here that Selma James found herself in conflict with
a sector of the women's movement which took the line that
paying women to do housework would only cement the idea that
this was 'women's work' and would make still tougher the job of
breaking down the division of labour in society, between men
and women. They felt, too, that the lack of value given to a form
of labour to which many women devoted long hours of their time
would go on.

Lisa Tuttle lays out the Socialist argument in her *Encyclopedia
of Feminism*:'It (housework) is one of the underpinnings of the
capitalist system: women as an unpaid labour force function to
maintain the paid labour force, and thus keep wages down and
profits up, since otherwise society would have to provide these
services. . . . One way of abolishing housework is to take it out of
the private sphere by making it communal.'

Zoe Fairbairns recalls her reaction to the campaign: 'My first
response to the slogan "wages for housework" was to see it as an
extraordinarily good joke, and I mean that as a compliment to
the women who thought it up. It was subversive and embarrassing and enraging and could not go unanswered.'

The memory of being involved in the Wages for Housework
debate comes quickly to mind for Angela Phillips who reflects
back on the 1970–74 period as intense, hectically busy and
tremendously exciting. She says: 'There was a big division over
this issue. It was the biggest political division, partly because
Selma James was a very charismatic political speaker who
gathered a group of women around her and wanted people to
take on her analysis, but plenty wouldn't and there was lots of
resistance. What she was saying was completely contrary to most
people's analysis. I remember once when I said I didn't agree she
just said "one day you will."   The period shortly before this

campaign was set up, had marked the emergence of another powerful, propagandising, outspoken woman who often found herself in discord with members of the women's movement — Erin Pizzey who founded the first battered women's refuge, Chiswick Women's Aid, in 1971. The refuge in due course received some public funding and caught the imagination of a public which could easily see the right in condemning domestic violence once it was thrust under their noses — individuals (and conspicuously the police) continued to be less willing to intervene when they saw or heard of it happening. But once it was out in the open and acknowledged then, yes, it was to be taken seriously and of course the poor women deserved some place to escape to. Erin Pizzey's refuge opened up the issue of violence against women and soon other women set up refuges for victims of domestic violence across the country. When rape crisis centres followed not long after, the links between pornography and violence to women began to be explored. It was ironic, then, that the woman who acted as an all-important catalyst found herself, within a few years, frequently at loggerheads with other members of the women's movement, and particularly those involved in the Women's Aid Federation to which almost all those running refuges were affiliated. Part of the blame was put on Pizzey's autocratic style, while some women objected to the fact that she did not necessarily counsel the women at the refuge against going back to their men or that men as the instruments of patriarchy are fundamentally hostile to women's best interests, as other refuges run by radical feminists did. Jane, who went to such a refuge after being severely beaten by her lover, recalls: 'The women there could not understand that I was deeply ambivalent about Des. On the one hand I was scared and angry at what he had done to me, but on the other there were good things in our relationship and I wanted some sort of help on how perhaps I could live with him. Ultimately that proved impossible, but the fact that the women counselling me had no time for the idea of sharing life with a man was not helpful.'

But it was Pizzey's stated belief that some women collude in their men's violence, are 'violence prone', and that domestic violence may be a psychological problem rather than a problem of male power, which caused many feminists to dissociate themselves from her. Sandra Horley, a Canadian who was later to become director of the Chiswick refuge and who has written *Love and Pain* (Bedford Square Press), a book dealing with male violence, and who says her conversion to feminism came through seeing the apalling suffering of women both emotionally and physically at the hands of men, explains why Pizzey's analysis was so unacceptable: 'By saying women are in some way giving men permission to brutalize them, you are letting men off the hook and throwing the blame on to the woman. We all have choices in life and men choose to batter women. It is the course of action they decide to take. Women are as much upset and distressed by men as vice versa but they very rarely become violent — that is their choice, it's not that their feelings are less powerful. Until, as a society, we say men are wholly to blame for domestic violence and that it will not be tolerated, they will not stop. But there is a curious unspoken approval of men hitting women, keeping "the old lady" in line. How often have you heard men saying "she asked for it" or "it's what she needs once in a while". That is intolerable and we have to support women absolutely in this, otherwise they will go on keeping their pain a secret as they have and continue to do, for so long.'

Pizzey was not bowed by the hostility directed towards her and in a conversation with Suzanne Lowry, author of *The Guilt Cage* (Elm Tree Books, 1980), she interprets the reason she was banned from all meetings and refused the approval of the women's movement, as an example of how doctrinaire the movement had become. She said: 'Anyone who came near the movement had to have a dictionary in one hand — everything was polemic and dialectic and so on . . . There was a party line that had to be toed, and it actually excluded about ninety per cent of women in the country who in fact believed in half the tenets that the women's movement was fighting for.' (It is not perhaps surprising that a movement which drew to it so many passionate, opinionated, persuasive women as well as those who were less flamboyant and outspoken, women who felt perhaps for the first time in their lives that they could achieve a sense of potency, that an ideological vision was realizable, if only all others would share their particular attitudes and methods, should be the site of conflicts, disagreements, splits large and small.

Sheila Rowbotham recalls how, by 1974, there were problems emerging within her women's group: 'Political strains upon the structure of the London workshop were quite severe. Behind the arguments about structure were big differences between women who were separatists and those of us who were not . . . We began to shift away from the London workshop towards national women and Socialism conferences and towards making local links with women in Hackney and Islington . . . These meetings continued for nearly two years and we did bring together women from health groups, consciousness-raising groups, the Abortion Campaign, the Working Women's Charter, Women in Manual Trades. In the Arsenal group we appeared to be successful and productive . . . but we never managed to overcome many tensions which had been there from the start. The personal never did become quite the political even in our small group. . . . Awkward silences appeared as people felt unwilling to take the initiative in case it was dominating . . .'

Another woman recalls: 'Antagonism with feminism came when we realized, yes, we could be strong and because we never were strong, having got strength we didn't know how not to turn it on each other. Discovering anger is very powerful. Working-class women have more oppression and even more anger.' By now working-class women were beginning to look at how their class was a particular oppression for them and to turn angrily to criticize middle-class women for their role in this. One working-class women's group published *Working-Class Women's Voice* in the 1980s, which directed the kind of undisguised antipathy which had been targeted at men since the earliest stirrings of feminism, towards middle-class women. In response to my request for an interview I received a letter stating:

'We, personally, have told middle-class women what they and their women's movement have done to exlude us. *We* didn't benefit from that; they or The Movement didn't change. We don't benefit from being the subject-matter of middle-class books. We're just seen as "interesting". We know that many women, working-class, are doing projects with middle-class women out of isolation. They find themselves being grateful that middle-class women are paying them attention. They may feel proud to be the subject-matter of middle-class reading . . . but

middle-class books don't change classism. Working-Class
Women's Voice is for working-class women to come together as
one, rather than being isolated with their experiences of different forms of oppression. It is a place where they don't have to
look for praise and appreciation from the middle-class.'

   The divide between women of different classes and different
colours has been an enduring issue for feminism which
continues as the 1980s draw to a close. While working-class and
middle-class, black and white women have joined forces in many
of the struggles against patriarchy and female oppression, they
also recognize the inequalities of birth which in many cases imply
fewer choices than middle-class women, poverty and lack of
status.
   Black women, for example, are becoming strongly aware that
racism — which white feminists do not experience — creates
barriers. This has been particularly true in radical circles where
white women have at times felt that discrimination on gender
lines must be the primary battle and that this should not be
diluted by preoccupation with racism. Rita expresses it this way:

'I have been aware, all my life, that being black was going to be a
handicap. From when I was very little people used to make racist
remarks and for me the strongest feeling of oppression lies there.
I know well that being a women also oppresses me, lessens my
chances of getting decent work, means some man can have
control over my sexuality if I want to get married and have kids,
that it makes me vulnerable in a way men are not. But I feel that
I can do something about all this. Perhaps I can develop skills
which are good enough to get me a decent job in spite of being a
woman. I can choose not to marry, but I can never choose not to
be black and that is the thing by which I am always judged first. I
have not found the women's movement very sympathetic to this.'

   Nor do all black women want white women attempting to
empathize with the racism they experience. Writer Joan Riley
put it emphatically: 'I have listened to white women talking
about the suffering of blacks, about how they try to feel the
feelings, how dreadful it must be to endure double oppression
and so on, and it makes me very angry. I don't want to be labelled

any kind of a victim, let alone a double victim. Yes, I'm black, and yes I've experienced racism, I've written about it, but I'm not a victim. I've learnt to fight back, I've learnt that I can be strong, that I can be the person I want to be. I am involved in many of the issues of the women's movement and that is fine, but I feel patronized when white women who are not the same and will never be the same, act like they want to suffer on my behalf.'

As the women's movement gathered strength and confidence through the 1970s it became clear that far from being a gimmick, it was a dynamic force which was growing. And so it was possible to see a change in the way women's activitives were reported. The reaction to the women's movement in its infant days may have been hostile but in a jokey, slightly dismissive way — the general attitude seemed to be that 'the girls' were getting a bit out of hand, and reprimands were in order, but that after all none of it really meant a great deal. In the early 1970s, however, it became plain that women were deadly serious about their demands and that far from fading away, their campaign was gathering momentum for 'Women's Lib' week by week. Clearly the most fearsome thing was that they did not seem to mind if men were upset, antagonized even. Indeed some seemed actually to be telling men they didn't give a f . . . if they jumped off the edge of the globe. Observing all this at a North London women's meeting, Lesley Ebbetts wrote in *The Daily Sketch*: 'The women photographed here are, as far as men are concerned, Britain's most dangerous revolutionaries. Direct action they plan, leaving men to do all the housework, refusing to cook their meals or do their laundry. Actively and savagely competing with them to get their jobs. Denying them sex when they want it . . .'

Within the year it was time for a bit of palliative journalism to try to re-assert the status quo. James Laing in the guise of reporting an American survey on women's attitudes to men, delivered veiled sneers throughout, ending up with his ace hand: 'Significantly, back where Women's Lib. all started — in America — an opinion poll taken only three weeks ago showed that more than 60 per cent of women just like being women. They enjoy being wives and mothers and wearing bras and minis. And just to boost the male ego, more than 67 per cent of women think that men are kind, gentle and thoughtful.' While Kate Wharton, eschewing female solidarity, wrote in *The Daily Telegraph*: 'I may be wrong but the over-riding impression that Women's Lib suggests is of deep sexual unhappiness among its members.'

People with far higher profiles than these journalists were also making known their views on the destructive effects of feminism. Brigitte Bardot who, some might argue, seems to have been made markedly unhappy taking what men dished out on their terms, said on television in 1973: 'Women get more unhappy the more they try to liberate themselves and act like men. A woman is a tender and sweet person and she'll lose that if she tries to be like a man.'

Prince Charles who believed, even fifteen years ago, in having his say on matters of the moment, declared: 'Women's liberationists annoy me because they tend to argue all the time and start calling you a male chauvinist pig and frankly it becomes rather uncivilized. Basically I think it is because they want to be men.'

There are women who remember their work in the National Abortion Campaign, launched in 1975 to defend and in due course improve the 1967 Abortion Act, as the time that they connected a woman's right to have control over her body with other aspects of reproduction and with health generally. The natural birth movement, which had been around for some time, was concerned with helping women give birth with as little medical intervention as possible, but it took feminists to make the link between male domination of medicine and the power that afforded men, who would not experience childbirth, but who were able to ordain the kind of birth experience women would have.

This led women to explore the way the professions surrounding health have elevated men and subordinated women, so that, for example, most doctors are male and almost all nurses are women, and they began to see how this has led to a patriarchal control over health which dictates, from a male perspective, how women's health will be regarded and treated. Talk around this subject unleashed many angry, anguished feelings about how little right women felt they had to ask a doctor for information, to challenge his diagnosis or treatment.

Within the political discussions around health, women began, too, to question the dismissal of 'female complaints' such as thrush, cystitis, PMT. They began to ask why women should be penalized by being seen as infirm because they happen to suffer ailments, by definition of gender, which men do not. From the outrage and anger which bubbled up, came an assertiveness which was the spur to women's health workshops and clinics and, in due course, to a range of carefully researched books.

Within the women's movement were women doctors, health workers and others who held workshops and talked about alternatives; the Well Women clinics were set up, run by women for women, and Janice Bumsted, former director of the Marie Stopes Clinic, remembers: 'It seemed very important that women should feel they understood their own bodies, knew their bodies and felt good about them. A lot of women who had seen dismissive and bullying male doctors for years were effectively ready to hand themselves over to be done unto. I saw my job as involving a lot of talking about knowing your own body, insisting that women had a right to the kind of treatment they felt was right.'

Judy Graham became involved in women's health through working politically on the Lower East Side in Manhatten with blacks and Puerto Ricans. She says: 'I found a lot of women being abused by their husbands, getting pregnant, having abortions and then ending up being given hysterectomies to stop them getting pregnant. And in the middle of this it seemed the women had no real understanding of what was happening, why it was happening and they certainly had no power over it. We set up an advisory service to help them and from there I moved to work at a women's hostel where five of us got together and set up a health clinic. That engaged me, it seemed a way I could use feminism in a very practical sense. It was something of concern to me, as a woman, and I could see how vital it was for other women. We held courses to try to teach women to understand their bodies, to know how to get information about what was wrong when they had a problem, and to understand the different treatments which might be offered. As in Britain doctors simply didn't give women information, it was all paternalistic stuff where women were told what would be done to them, but without explanation.

'My own memories of being a patient and feeling incapable, a lesser being, were so strong and as I did this work I saw so clearly how all the beliefs in society about women being inferior to men underlie what is on the surface perhaps a kindly and caring approach.

'What was nice on the courses was that nobody was an expert but those of us who set them up studied so that we had some information to bring. They actually got put on television and written up and it was clear they provided a model for other women to use when setting up their own courses.'

The British version of the assertive health guide for women, first produced in America, *Our Bodies Ourselves* (published 1976), was adapted for Britain by Angela Phillips and Jill Rakusen and became a bestseller. To Carolyn Faulder the growth of women's health has been one of the most important developments within the range of feminism. She recalls: 'I went to the US at the beginning of the 1970s because a woman was on trial for practising medicine without a licence — she had inserted yogurt up a woman's vagina [to alleviate her cystitis]. Luckily she was acquitted, but significant from my point of view was that she introduced me to all sorts of women involved in examining how women could get some autonomy over their bodies. I came back to Britain very excited and convinced *Nova*, for which I was writing at the time, to let me do an article on the subject. We got a great many letters and the article got reprinted around the world.'

Some measure of the continuing importance of the politics of health can be seen in the fact that these authors were asked, in 1988, to update the book. *Spare Rib* started a health page, edited by Sue O'Sullivan who went on to edit an anthology of health writings from the magazine. She says: 'Health is an intensely political issue. Feminist concern with health aims both to free women from notions of biological determinism and to turn upside-down accepted definitions of women's bodies, minds, emotions. We attempt to seize knowledge and understanding of these in order to have more control over our lives.'

One of the most crucial issues in the politics of health is the question of rape. A woman who has been raped may lose any sense of control she already had over her life. It is male power over women, misogyny and violence at its most destructive and yet for centuries it has been tacitly condoned as the act of a man who 'gets carried away' (implicit in this is the suggestion that the woman has led him on), who is rather too much of a red-blooded man for his own good or who, conversely, is pathetic and inadequate and more to be pitied than despised. In these definitions of who and what the rapist is, lay little if any concern with the desecration of the woman's life or her right not to be assaulted. In court, as has been well documented, women have always had to defend their 'good character', though they were not supposedly on trial, while judges all too often ticked off the plaintiff for the clothes she had been wearing, the place she was in, her demeanour on the occasion of the rape. It is scarcely surprising that women have not willingly reported rape to the police who historically have been disbelieving and unsympathetic to raped women, nor put themselves forward for the legal ordeal.

In a society where a large part of the culture deifies male strength and prowess over women, where sexual violence is part of daily entertainment and where the man who does not publicly command the submission and adoration of women is likely to be derided as a wimp or a failure, it is hardly surprising that rape is a common occurrence. A clearer indication of just how wide-spread it is has emerged since the women's movement made it a political issue, allowing women who have been raped to speak of the experience in the safe and supportive environment of women-only groups and centres, and helping them to unravel the knotted mass of pain, guilt, fear and fury which they had so often supressed. Although Germaine Greer, interviewed in 1982, took a theoretically more belligerent view saying that she was angry about rape, violently angry, 'but I am not going to hang myself just because some wretched little man sticks his dick into me'.

It was in 1976 that the London Rape Crisis Centre, the first of its kind, was opened by a group of women who had been thinking and talking around rape from a woman's perspective. Most urgently they saw the need for a place where women knew they could talk about their rape experience at any time of day or night. Inspired by this model, which clearly answered a profound need, other groups set up their own rape crisis centres around the country. In 1984 the London centre produced a book, published by The Women's Press, looking at what rape is, how it is 'dealt with' in our society, how women may feel, what they can do for themselves, the kind of help available to them.

The focus of the book is wholly about the needs and rights of the women who have been raped, and there is no quarter given to the pathology or emotional problems of the men who rape. In the introduction the authors describe how from childhood women are taught to fear rape, and how not to invite and incite it by their actions. They produce a catalogue of familiar daily examples of sexual harassment which range from workmen whistling at women, to men getting too close, touching, leering, and they say: 'With every comment on our bodies, with every leer, men are letting us know, quite clearly, that they have access to our bodies and that we have no control over that access. They are saying in effect, "if I choose, I can rape you — so make sure you don't antagonize me" . . . And if you *are* raped you can be sure that you (and everyone you tell) will be able to find numerous rules that you have broken, or numerous things you might have done to avoid it or stop it happening. Many women never realize that rape does not "happen", it is caused — by men.'

American academic Susan Brownmiller's thorough documentation of the prevalence of rape throughout history, *Against Our Will*, was published in 1975, providing a thorough feminist analysis of an offence which she describes as 'a conscious form of intimidation by which *all men* keep *all women* in a state of fear'.

In 1977 women went out on the streets to make known their anger at the fact that a woman, because of her sex, is at risk if she goes out at night. Reclaim the Night was the name of the demonstration held annually around the country which began in Leeds on 23 November 1977 with women out on the streets in that city, Manchester, Newcastle, London. It was in the latter city that a group of women 'visited' *The Guardian* newspaper, perhaps hoping that this publication of avowed liberal persuasion would be sympathetic. Not so. The then news editor and sundry male workers around the place at first laughed, then became cross when the women continued to demand to be listened to. Eventually the women were pushed out and once they were gone, the men, by this time quite edgy and markedly unpleasant in their dealings, broke into all-boys-together laughter and dismissed the women as 'frustrated', 'man hating' and not the kind of 'girl' the chaps in question would want to 'get a leg over'.

It was the typical kind of response shown to women who dared to display militancy and antipathy on the subject of male behaviour.

From these demonstrations grew the group Women Against Violence Against Women. By 1980 the Ripper murders had reached their toll of thirteen victims and fear around the country was high, particularly in Leeds where he operated. So it was that the first demo which drew five hundred women, was held there. Jane Gaskell, reporting for the *Daily Mail*, wrote: 'The women who have joined the new feminist groups do not belong to any mobile Rent a Women's Libber hit squad. Many are typical North of England or Scottish lasses now letting go with anti-male resentment.' Cinemas in various cities around the country showing Brian de Palma's gruesome film about the murder of women, *Dressed to Kill*, were sabotaged.

Meanwhile, some feminist barristers were refusing to defend rapists on the grounds that by doing so they would effectively have to put the woman who had been assaulted on trial. And even though nobody could argue that the legal profession generally takes a pro-woman line, attitudes to rape as a serious crime have changed. Sentences have become tougher. Public attitudes to the offenders have also hardened and greater sympathy is now directed at the victims of rape. Some efforts have been made at police level to provide specially trained policewomen to question and help women alleging they have been raped. Elizabeth Wilson in her book *What is to be Done About Violence Against Women?* (Penguin), published in 1983, said: 'During the past decade, women have also worked for changes in the law, for changes in the way the law is administered and for changes in the attitudes of court and police. In the mid 1970s several notorious rulings in controversial rape cases in the British courts provided a focus for feminist anger and did also arouse concern among reformers and within the legal profession.'

The importance of knowing just how many women are raped annually (and throughout the 1980s the figures rose steadily) is clear, for as the women's movement began to demonstrate how widespread and horrifying a crime rape is, some magazines and newspapers began to report it more seriously and more fully. This in turn brought greater public attention to the issue — although none of this necessarily guaranteed better treatment for the raped woman.

In 1984 The Woman's Safety Survey conducted by the campaigning group Women Against Rape, the first large scale survey
trying to chart the incidence and effects of rape and sexual
assault, written and analysed by women, was published. It
showed that one in six women had been raped and nearly one in
three sexually assaulted, and even that was widely held to be
below the actual figure.

Rape was one issue on which feminists were united, and which
led to a wider discussion, continuing throughout the 1980s,
about pornography where violence and sex are frequently
interlinked, and where the sexual debasement of women via
sexual power is a recurrent theme. A member of Women Against
Violence Against Women, writing in *Spare Rib*, asked: 'What is
going on in their heads when (men) derive pleasure from seeing
women bound, gagged, hung up on a meat hook and raped?'
The response of Helen Buckingham, a prostitute, was simple:
'Pornography is an expression of man's desire to have the effect
on women that he knows he does not, in reality, have.'

Ruth Austen, a twenty-one-year-old community worker from
Liverpool, whose commitment to feminism is of the feisty, equal
rights brand, and who is not keen on 'anything which resembles
man-hating', sent me a poem expressing some of the sense of
alienation and distress for women she sees embodied in pornography:

> 'Without faces no body could be seen,
> Man was able to abuse because,
> Faces were ripped or veiled in silk,
> I felt the lives of those women cry,
> Hidden and ground down on stone,
> Thick enough to conceal pain.
> We cannot just sit here and watch,
> Women die and men devour,
> Without facial recognition.'

But Elizabeth Wilson, a sociologist with a psychiatric social
work training, believes the motivations in the male enjoyment of
pornography are complex. She says: 'I do not myself believe that
pornography "speaks" male power in some simple way. It seems
rather to reveal the disintegration of male sexuality under the

pressures of a commoditizing, fetishizing culture. Far from being the celebration of male power, pornography sometimes seems designed to reassure men and allay fears of impotence; where it is violent and sadistic it displays fear and loathing not only of women but also of male passivity.'

This perspective is not of interest to the majority of feminists who consider the problems and deficiencies which lead men to want pornography as irrelevant. They are concerned with what pornography is and why it is harmful to women, not whether it is therapeutic for men. Andrea Dworkin, whose seminal writings on sexual matters including pornography and the inherent violence in the sex act, have earned her a formidable reputation, has expressed with passionate anger the way she sees pornography as dehumanizing women, and leading to sexual exploitation, forced sex, physical injury and 'social and sexual terrorism'. The result of the imagery of women in pornography is discrimination against them in all areas of life, she argues: 'Male power is the *raison dêtre* of pornography, the degradation of the female is the means of achieving this power. Pornography is the ideology that is the source of all the rest.'

Even if feminists were united on this, its motivating purpose as erotic material poses questions which have been the subject of vexed debate within the movement. Radical barrister Helena Kennedy says: 'At the meetings I went to I found people talking about how to stop the publication of material which is obviously diminishing to women and hostile, but they also talked about the nature of pornography and in this context came up a lot of questions about whether as women we are depriving ourselves if we deny that we can experience any kind of erotica. The problem is that pornography and erotica can be so closely linked.'

That pornography is offensive to and about women, and that it would be better if it did not exist, was — and probably still is — the view of a great many women. But the question of censorship provoked a volatile debate which had women who would probably happily have joined forces in creating a funeral pyre from the spoils of the porn merchants, arguing against each other. The disagreements then were not to do with women defending pornography but were based on a fear of bringing in censorship which could then be extended in ways that might be harmful to women. Those arguing from this standpoint pointed out that the pro-censorship anti-pornography lobby were, on the whole, reactionary and hostile to much that the women's movement stood for and censorship, it was pointed out, had been employed to control 'aberrant' sexuality such as homosexuality in the past (and although they were not to know it then would seek to do so again with the Tory Government's Clause 28 introduced in1988). It had been used to constrain and restrain female sexual behaviour, imposing standards of morality designed to tie women to a single man, and have her condemned if she transgressed and used her sexuality in ways a patriarchal society did not condone.

Barbara Rogers who, as editor of *Everywoman*, has carried a number of articles on the harmful effects of pornography, believes this so-called liberal attitude is damaging to women. She recalls writing an article for *Tribune* some years ago in which she said women should stop worrying about lining up with Mary Whitehouse. She explains: 'That argument was being used a lot to keep women from complaining about pornography, it was a clever device to make women feel that they were being repressive and reactionary. But I think it is vital that we do stand up and say we find pornography damaging, that it offends us and these are authentic feelings. I cannot see why it's being illiberal to not want men getting pleasure from women's powerlessness and degrada-tion.' Throughout the Seventies, committed activists in the women's movement attempted to bring some kind of feminist public consciousness to bear on these and other matters, women who had not involved themselves with organized activities, were reaching towards feminism in individual ways.

Commenting on her interest in feminism, Kathryn states that it was 'mostly a matter of the heart — something I felt rather than "intellectualized" about. Now I'm doing a Women's Studies course and getting academically involved with the subject too. What I've got from the reading is not just facts and information but an intense feeling of pride in the courage and achievement of women. I have never resisted feminism. On the contrary I have embraced it. It gives me something to hold on to in a world shaped by patriarchal values, from "the brotherhood of man" to "man-sized tissues".'

Patsy has a slightly different perspective: 'I read Betty Friedan, Germaine Greer, *Spare Rib* and joined in discussions at the local mother and toddler group. But when I saw close friends separating from their husbands I felt hostile to the women's movement, that the attitudes were destroying family life. I changed my views during the early Eighties when my children became teenagers. After years of playing the part of "perfect wife and mother" I felt that I was left with nothing for myself.'

Fay Weldon sees the insistent voice of feminism which surrounded her but which she had not consciously articulated herself, as the spur to the genre of writing based on empathy with women which she forged. She says: 'There was a kind of pressure around which I was under, too. My life until then, until I was about thirty, epitomized what had been going on and of course my eruption into writing was going along on the crest of a wave. I both helped to make the wave and was carried along by it. But at the time I didn't analyse it as feminist stuff. I know I was considered something of a heroine of the movement, but I've never felt that was quite right because I wasn't actually proselytising or crusading and I was never saying things were simple. They weren't simple for me and to some extent I was working my own life out on paper. My books are seen as very aggressive towards men but I don't think I've ever maintained it was men's fault. It's as much women's fault for putting up with it.'

Helena Kennedy, who organized one of the first mixed-sex—and mixed-race chambers, describes herself as a late developer. 'I came from a working-class family and my politics were essentially class politics. I had the feeling that women were downtrodden, but then so are working-class men and I've always felt that middle-class women have a better deal than a lot of men. I could never see that their oppression was comparable to that of someone working on a shop floor.

'The power in my family was my mother and then there was an aunt and my grandmother who were all strong women with great heart. They helped people through poverty, death, war. When I went off to study for the bar I became slightly conscious of the way women were discriminated against, but also I was flattered by the "spoiling", being one of very few women among a lot of men. It was when I began practising that I came into contact with quite a number of women who were questioning the way the law treats women and that was when my political learning took place.

'They were very concerned with getting changes in the law to improve the way women are dealt with, and I began to see very clearly how women are so often punished for not being the guardians of morality, for behaving in an "unwomanly" way. If they are aberrant and act with violence or aggression, as men do, they are labelled mad or sad. And you see in court that judges cannot bear it if a woman is assertive and does not use feminine wiles or a feminine defence.

'I started going to far more women's meetings in the early Seventies and I went to some of the annual conferences. I found it was very difficult for me as a woman who was articulate, not a bit cowed. I had to learn how other women find speaking in public painful and it was only through seeing this that I saw the advantage of being in a place where women's voices were heard without being interrupted.'

Shirley first became aware of feminism when her daughter, her eldest child, went to university and joined a consciousness —raising group there. 'Until then I had enjoyed being a wife and mother and at work I had always had equal pay. I was very interested in my daughter's view which I gradually came to share, although never her condemnation of men. Through *Spare Rib* I joined a small self-help group for a particular ailment and we had a group therapist from the Women's Therapy Centre.'

Heather states: 'I'd been very unhappy with my life and in fact already held many of the views the women's movement brought to the fore, but I was generally regarded as too outspoken and even odd — especially by my husband! What the women's movement did was to actually bring out into the open what had been fermenting in many women's minds for a long time.'

Journalist Mary Kenny, who in the late Eighties acknowledged that she is seen by many women as a renegade who has betrayed her earlier convictions, nevertheless remembers vividly the reasons that for a while she espoused many of the most controversial feminist causes. 'My awakening came from where I lived in Dublin. I felt, in a primitive way, that women at home needed a more independent life and I remember thinking that I never wanted to have to ask a man for money. My mother was left widowed, she had a well-to-do brother, but he would say to her "of course you can have money but for serious things, not for frivolities like hats". I saw that kind of thing all around.

'I went to London in the Sixties and it was when, after that I returned to Ireland, that the next move to feminism occurred. I thought how dare these men say women can't have contraception. Then whenever I wrote something on an issue concerning women's bodies or their rights I got a deluge of letters and it was obvious there was something important going on. I did join groups — we used to meet in the restaurant of a woman married to a Pole who is very much a Marxist and seemed awfully glamorous.'

As the 1970s gave way to the 1980s women started to band together to oppose nuclear arms and the Women's Peace Movement became a conspicuous, voiciferous force which attracted a good deal of attention and kept disarmament in the news longer than would probably have happened otherwise. But it also antagonized many traditional peace campaigners of both sexes by claiming that women occupy the highest moral ground because bombs are manufactured primarily by men, and therefore all men are implicated in the guilt; and because women are the bearers and (usually) the carers of society's young, making sacrifices to fulfil this role and are more concerned therefore about their children not growing up with nuclear arms. There were also those who maintained that women are an inherently more peace-loving, pacifist sex than men.

In 1981 the Greenham Women's Peace Camp was established outside the Greenham missile base and over five years a caucus of women kept a constant vigil, campaigning relentlessly by their presence and, at times, with force and civil obedience as when they broke through the perimeter fences or refused to move after eviction orders had been served. Other women visited to offer solidarity; Greenham attracted international publicity and local opprobrium both from those worried that the women would affect property values and more significantly, from those who found abhorrent the idea of women sacrificing cleanliness, domesticity and confirmity to a cause which involved opposing the might and wisdom of our leaders and their policies for defending the nation. But in 1982 the Peace Camp drew together 30,000 women who held hands around the bases as a symbol of mass solidarity.

Barbara Harford and Sarah Hopkins, editors of *Greenham Common — Women at the Wire* (The Women's Press, 1984), describe their time at Greenham, the hardship, the deprivation, the discomfort it meant for long-term campers but also the elation at the sense that they really could impact on a world which seemed hell-bent on nuclear proliferation: 'Beyond Greenham these connections are becoming tangible. This was demonstrated most vividly on 24 May 1983 and later in November when 102 peace camps were set up in the UK. A loose network of women has grown within the UK and is extending beyond national boundaries to Europe, Australasia, America, Japan and Canada.

Women went to Greenham filled with heady conviction, a sense of having the power to change events, and excitement at such sisterly solidarity. They had no idea what the level of deprivation, discomfort and outside hostility would be if they were to make a permanent commitment to the camp, as many women did. Novelist Caroline Blackwood wrote a book about Greenham, *On the Perimeter*, which recorded her feelings, observations and belief in the importance of this 'anti-apathetic' five-year demonstration. They'd been made to sound almost mythical in their horror. They'd been described as 'belligerent harpies', 'bunch of smelly lesbians' and 'witches of Greenham' . . . They were also accused of being in the pay of the Soviet Union. And in her writings Blackwood encapsulated some of the extraordinary rage which informed the abuse of the women: 'Greenham makes people very angry, particularly men. So many people lost their temper even at the mention of the word. Yet Greenham is one of the most significant things, if not the most significant, going on in England at present.'

That it was both a momentous political gesture and a vital part of the development of feminist consciousness for many women, would be hard to dispute, yet Greenham, ironically, was another site of bitter conflict for the women's movement. According to some women who spent time there, Greenham was 'taken over' by a powerful lesbian contingency which managed to intimidate heterosexual women and which used the camp to dwell on political ideas which were nothing to do with peace.

Ann Pettit, one of the earliest Greenham campers, gave an interview in 1986 for a tabloid paper, in which she spoke of how 'it became a haven for nutcases and women trying to escape from hideous realities. This was not what we had come for. The camp became increasingly separatist and husbands couldn't come to visit with children.'

The separatist element of the camp also infuriated women who would certainly call themselves feminists and who are sympathetic to the peace movement. Rabbi Julia Neuberger puts it this way: 'I think the fact that Greenham excluded men and attempted to give women the moral high ground in the peace issue was appalling and very alienating. It is outrageous to suggest that men are not equally concerned about the world and their children's future.' Polly Toynbee wrote in *The Guardian*: 'To me, from the start, there was something repugnant and demeaning in the idea that women, through some biological necessity, cared more about the world being blown to bits than men did.'

For all that, Greenham's importance as an emblem of women's determination, and as a venture which drew many women of very different types to spend time there, should not be underestimated.

Nor should the separate Women's Peace Movement which continued to exist, albeit without the limelight, through the 1980s. A vivid picture of the women as they stayed to the bitter end was portrayed in a review of the film *Carry Greenham Home*: 'That women's only eloquence is their readiness to commit themselves to the nomadic squalor, the rain and mud, the tangles of plastic and bundles of old clothes which keep out the cold, the cropped camp hair, the boiled cabbage.'

But where the Seventies had been the heady days of optimism, of group activity, and a sense of communality at the shared feelings about a woman's lot, the Eighties were the days when women were looking far more critically at what feminism was about. Janet Radcliffe Richards' (book *The Sceptical Feminist* (Routledge and Kegan Paul) questioning and turning on its head much feminist gospel, was published in 1980. These were also the days when women were making quiet headway at work in domestic relationships, in the arts and in the public eye, but the passion and single-minded conviction of the women's movement had faded and women were questioning where things would go from there.

3

SEXUALITY AND SCHISM

SEX AND POLITICS

'WE were led to believe that the Pill was our liberation. It was a licence to be promiscuous and I was and I regret it. But we did it because it was our joyous sexual freedom. All that seemed to matter was getting lots of sex, because it was somehow good for you.'

In questioning whether the sexual *mores* of the late Sixties and early Seventies were about women pleasing themselves so much as fulfilling a fashionable construct of the 'with it' woman, Jane Sellars, now thirty-eight, has touched on a theme echoed by many women looking back to the time when the Pill arrived and gained its credibility as the modern woman's aid to sexual autonomy. The reasoning went, if you were free from fear of pregnancy then you were liberated, and many of us bought that line, disregarding the insistent little background voice questioning whether it really *was* the epitome of freedom to be laid by a chap because he was decent enough to fancy you and finding ourselves, as Joanne describes, 'going to bed with men out of politeness'. And then the insistent voice, still supported loudly by a large chunk of society, male and female, kept on, *alto voce*, saying even if America's *Vanity Fair* magazine had sanctioned unmarried sex with its article 'Nice Girls Do', the fact was you were quite likely to get called a slag, a tart, or just plain cheap if it was known that you were too easily available. 'The office bicycle' was the particularly nasty label given to a woman on a newspaper where I worked, who slept around markedly less than most of the men there. Promiscuity was voguey for the chaps, but a double standard still applied for the other half who, after all, had had the role of guardian of men's morals as well as their own, thrust upon them for centuries.

These were the thoughts which emerged as the focus of the Women's Liberation Movement, moved on from such practical and vital matters as equal pay and child care, and feminists began to re-examine the legend of women's self-determining sexuality in the 'swinging era' and question whether it was one more example of a culture designed to benefit men being marketed to women as avant garde pleasure.

With hindsight, then, women have questioned the history of the Permissive Era, a history which is wrapped in nostalgia and sentimentality like no other. The bits of news footage, the celluloid interviews, the books and articles written, do not on the whole touch on the casualties of this era — the women who couldn't get laid because they weren't attractive enough or trendy enough, or up-front enough, for despite all the love and peace talk around, surface appearances were at a premium. In such an atmosphere women who could not offer a pert bum, a dollish face, a pair of FAAAAANTASTIC legs sprouting from a mini skirt, soon became aware that they were failures. Success in those days was measured on a sexual yardstick.

Val Clark, a polytechnic lecturer who remembers 'frightening the boys' from a very early age because of her height and abrasive manner, nevertheless succumbed to the *zeitgeist* of the Sixties. She says: 'I am certain one of the difficulties for women at this time, a reason they found it difficult to feel they were "good" enough physically, was that up until then we had been taught to flatten our tummies with rolls-ons, wear a foundation garment which would hide the crease in our bottoms, bras to make sure our breasts looked the way the ads. said they should. Then suddenly you were expected to take off this stuff and produce a body which looked entirely different and, we believed, worse.'

Margaret recalls: 'I felt very unconfident during the Sixties because I wasn't good at being a raver. I didn't look good or feel comfortable in the Biba diminutive dresses which seemed to be *de rigeur*. When men talked to me, and were clearly chatting me up, I got panic-stricken thinking, "I don't want to go to bed with this man. I don't want to go to bed with any man without knowing him properly", and I spent the whole time thinking I must let him know I wasn't game because sex was surely all he was after. I am sure it was lousy for men too, because probably lots of them would have liked to develop something more than the one-night stand, but the general atmosphere of the time prohibited that.'

But for some women there was an empowering element in being able to play the male game. My own memory is of deciding, while living in Amsterdam, that I would like to know whether I could be promiscuous on the same basis as men — without any commitment. Having grown up dreaming of white wedding dresses and believing sex was for very special relationships only, this was a decision of some moment. For six months I entertained a string of lovers, enjoying what they had to offer in varying degrees, but critically because I knew I wanted nothing more from them. With the early morning light, they got their marching orders. It was an interesting time, not ultimately satisfactory because the means defied any enduring end and ultimately I felt that sex was more fun with commitment, but the point was, I had experienced a kind of equality in being able to take sex quite separately from involvement and apart from helping me to understand how men could do it, it gave me a sense of having got into a locked door. I'd entered their domain and coped. It gave me an uncanny confidence.

Jessie, now forty and at home with two young children, recalls: 'I thought it was a wonderful time because it broke through all that dogma about having to be a nice girl in order to get married. Suddenly marriage was not on the menu and it allowed one to enjoy men as they came, rather than having to forever assess them as potential husbands. I felt I got to know and like men on a friendly level during this time.'

That women's recollections of this era vary, embracing both those who remember it as exhilarating and exciting as well as those who felt it a time of stress and striving, is not the point. As feminism brought in a new consciousness, women began to examine the accepted 'line' on liberated sexuality, from a different perspective. Inverting the 'hip' ideas they had absorbed, many began to look at how those ideas were not designed with women's welfare in mind.

Anita Bennett expressed a common enough view that: 'We needed to bring critical analysis to precisely times like the Sixties which are simply talked of as the never-had-it-so-good era. We needed to understand that having failed as a Sixties' sex object didn't mean you were failing as a female. That has been all important to some women. They've carried those damaged feelings with them through the years.'

But while critical analysis has been valuable, it is also important to see how far women had come in at least 'being allowed' to enjoy sex, how different things were from the earlier decades. For the first half of this century Freud's influential view was that women should be the giving partners to their men, with the primary function of sex as reproduction. Although a well-adjusted mature woman could experience a vaginal orgasm this was something of a bonus. But this selfless, restrained approach to sex, which went hand in hand with the belief that women who were enthusiastic about sex could be ranked alongside prostitutes, had begun to be questioned after the Second World War. Some marriage manuals (thus named because sex outside marriage was not to be encouraged) included advice on 'how to make it good', while a number of surveys reported that sex was unsatisfactory for a large proportion of women. During the Fifties, Alfred Kinsey published his report *Sexual Behaviour in the Human Female* in which he advocated that women should not only be aware that orgasm was a good thing for them, but that they should count orgasms as a way of measuring satisfaction. This idea was taken up in books and magazines. But Kinsey's suggestions for women to achieve clitoral orgasm without men's participation, by masturbating, was not taken up, at least not in those immediate post-war years.

In the mid-Sixties, William Masters and Virginia Johnson added their findings and views with the publication of *Human Sexual Response*, which was based on a 'scientific survey' of 700 volunteers viewed during the different stages of sexual arousal and coitus, while others were observed masturbating. This work not only identified woman's ability to have orgasms as greater than a man's but also pointed to the intense clitoral orgasms women could achieve through masturbation. However, this was not seen as a triumph of possible autonomy for women. The view was taken that if women did not have good sex lives with men, masturbation was a way of resolving a problem — *their* problem. Nevertheless the view that sex should be pleasurable for women was a tenet of Masters' and Johnson's work and they suggested that men should work at stimulating the clitoris with the penis during intercourse, as a way to help women achieve the best orgasms possible in the circumstances.

Sexual pleasure for women, then, was very much on the agenda. Magazines began to carry screeds on the subject, agony aunts assured wives that they were entitled to ask their men to 'please' them, the avant-garde *Nova* magazine introduced orgasm counts and quizzes for readers. At the time the women's movement was coming into being, sex was being advocated for everything from a happy relationship to a glowing skin. Sex shops selling aids for women stopped being kept under plain cover, Ann Somers' shops flourished; the sex parties at which women gathered to buy ecstacy creams and vibrators, potions for men's 'privates' and underwear with the funniest bits cut out, became a feature of quite a number of women's lives. Nancy Friday published *My Secret Garden* (see page 73), a tomb-like book of interviews with women about their sexual predilections, fantasies and yearnings. And in 1971 Shere Hite started work on her trilogy of books examining female sexuality, and although men were sandwiched in the middle with volume two to themselves, the final book, *Women and Love: A Cultural Revolution*, was concerned solely with the perspective women had on sex and relationships having lived through a decade of feminism.

At the same time an 'ordinary housewife', who had none of the degrees and academic back-up of Hite, entered the sexual arena, making plain how important a part of marriage she thought sex to be. Marabel Morgan, an American born-again happy wife, with neatly cut hair, conventional make-up and clothes which seemed to inform the world at large that she was not a sexual being, told in her bestselling books *Total Woman* and *Total Joy* how she regenerated her marriage to lawyer husband Charlie by gearing life almost entirely to being sexually alluring, trying old tricks and new ones to make him feel desirous of her. Between her pages was found a comprehensive range of suggestions for ways other women could follow the Morgan example, ranging from laying the dinner table with damask linen and candelabras the minute the kids left for school, in preparation for *his* homecoming, or phoning him at the office in the middle of the day and telling him, in the huskiest of voices, what naughty garment she was wearing, to dressing up as a spy in a trench coat with nothing underneath, or a French maid in the most classic 'sexy' uniform. The success of her books was that she gave women the feeling they could inspire lust while benefiting themselves with happy and fulfilling sex lives.

There was no hint of feminist analysis in Morgan's advice, as in the other ubiquitous articles, TV shows and films, which all implied that women should dedicate a substantial amount of their time and most of their emotional energy to pleasing men, although an interesting point made by Barbara Ehrenreich, Elizabeth Hess and Gloria Jacobs in their book *Remaking Love* is that unconsciously Morgan *et al* were finding an area of initiative and control in an otherwise dependant life. But these women were far closer to the doctrine of psychoanalyst Helene Deutsch who commented in her book *Female Sexuality, the Psychology of Women* (New York, 1945): 'The sexual act assumes an immense, dramatic and profoundly cathartic significance for the woman — but only under the condition that it is experienced in a feminine, dynamic way and is not transformed into an act of . . . secular equality', than to the emergent feminists looking for a change in the sexual power structure.

But when feminism focused on sexuality, it was that power structure which suddenly became an important issue. Coote and Campbell explain: 'The effect of discussing the problem in consciousness-raising groups was to start to politicize it. As sex, love and monogamy were scrutinized, they were seen not simply as autonomous functions of "human nature" but as aspects of a power struggle. Women began to interpret conventional practice as the glue which held together the patriarchal order.' And Kate Millett writes in her influential work *Sexual Politics*, published in 1970: 'A disinterested examination of our system of sexual relationship must point out that the situation between the sexes now and throughout history is a case of that phenomenon Max Weber defined as *herrschaft*, a relationship of dominance and subordinance. What goes largely unexamined, often even unacknowledged (yet is institutionalized nonetheless) in our social order is the birthright priority whereby males rule females.'

These discussions led to the belief among some women, mostly calling themselves revolutionary feminists, that the primary cause of woman's oppression lies in man's sexual dominance of her. They argued that heterosexuality is not a natural impulse but a cultural construct in a society which makes heterosexuality 'compulsory' by condemning the alternatives. These discussions resulted in the quest for separatism, which caused a deeply damaging schism in the movement. To quote Beatrix Campbell again: 'The Women's Liberation Movement . . . was no longer a safe and sisterly place. Almost more than class or nationality, sexual desire and orientation seemed to divide and disturb.'

But before the eruption, as women realized how irrevocably they were bound to men for sex, they began to question how they could be truly independent when their only source of sexual satisfaction lay with men. This resulted in the search for autonomous sexuality — which meant going back to Freud and refuting his stricture that women enjoying clitoral orgasms were immature. An important contribution to this debunking was Anne Koedt's essay 'The Myth of the Vaginal Orgasm', which argued cogently that women are far more likely to achieve orgasm, certainly successfully, by stimulation of the clitoris than with penetration of the vagina. Nor should they be 'oppressed' by a male-orchestrated dictum which holds that the best and most appropriate orgasms occur this way and that if this does not happen for women, they have a problem. One woman, Linda, found massive agreement when she 'confessed' at a group discussion: 'I don't think I've ever really had an orgasm — not the kind you hear described in books where the earth moves, stars explode, your insides dissolve and all that. I tried saying something once but my boyfriend got very upset and critical of me so I shut up and assumed that I just wasn't the orgasming type. I became very good at faking it, though.'

Eleanor Stephens went to Berkeley, California in 1973 and found that sexuality groups were teaching women to look at their genitals, to touch themselves, to make themselves feel good, and in due course to reach orgasm. Looking back on her course, at which almost everybody achieved orgasm through masturbation and 50 per cent said, in a four-month follow-up study, that they had achieved this within their relationships, she commented: 'Amongst all the issues raised by the women's movement, the feminist approach to female sexuality is one which has, for many women, completely transformed our feelings about ourselves and our lives. Just as women are questioning many of the institutions, ideas and social relations defined for us by men, so we are no longer prepared to accept traditional sexual attitudes and practices.' Writing about it later for *Spare Rib* she said: 'Most women joined these groups as a last resort, having spent hundreds of dollars and hours in conventional psychotherapy, hypnosis, encounter groups, anything that offered hope. And most commonly they would go from one relationship to another looking for the right lover who would teach them the secret of sexual satisfaction.'

A 1971 issue of *Shrew* magazine contained an article: 'Sexuality: discussions in a small group' which described what happened: 'We chose sexuality for the following reason: it is of central importance to Women's Liberation and at the root of women's oppression. At first we thought of the large themes — and the obvious — the nature of woman's sexuality — how it was different from man's — orgasm, childhood, the pressures which shaped our sexuality. We discussed these and they in turn led to talk about fantasies, fashion, bodies, lesbianism, masturbation, pornography and jealousy. The more we talked about sexuality the more plain it was that we were talking about our whole lives.'

Although in these group discussions women questioned the attitudes to sexuality which most had grown up with, and expressed support for anyone who did not want heterosexual sex, the majority still approached the issue as heterosexuals who did not want to give up sex with men but who wanted to be able to achieve sexual pleasure without them if they wished.

Tina, who feels that men in her working-class life would be much threatened by the idea of women masturbating and reaching orgasm (although Deidre Sanders in her book *The Woman Book of Love and Sex*, published by Michael Joseph in 1985, found that a large proportion did), says: 'I was quite happy with my husband, he's a lovely man, but he wasn't really satisfying me and I felt sort of itchy a lot of the time. Then I read an article in a magazine saying it was okay to "please yourself", as they put it, and I was a bit shocked really, then I found myself reading it again and again, and each time the words "there's nothing wrong if you, as a woman, want to find your own sexual pleasure" hit me. I began to see that was right. So I tried playing with myself and it felt very uneasy, kind of wrong, at first. I suppose I'd always believed men should do these things to you.

But I kept on and I got more "advanced" and one day I had an orgasm, an amazing orgasm, and it felt wonderful.'

Barbara felt: 'It might have been easier to be unfaithful because that would have seemed "normal" to him, it would have been something he could have reacted to in a macho way and been forgiving and all that. I think if he knew I was doing very nicely without him he would have been totally confused and quite upset. It's different if you both masturbate together but it's the business of the man being irrelevant which hurts. After all, for centuries men have been told of the importance of their sexual prowess, and in a way I feel sorry for them. I don't see getting my own sexual pleasure as a way of punishing men.'

Other women in relationships with men found themselves feeling guilty at getting pleasure on their own. Jean comments: 'I felt as though I was humiliating Jeff in a way, because actually I had more satisfaction by myself than with him. But I didn't want to be without him because our sex together was about love and affection. Yet I knew that if he found out he would be mortified.'

In this climate lesbian women who had kept their sexual life well guarded felt freer to 'come out' and certainly it was seen as a vital function of the liberation movement that they should be supported in doing so. In her book *A Corridor of Mirrors* (The Women's Press, 1987) teacher Rosemary Manning records the strength she drew from feminism's positive atmosphere. It was this, she says, which 'allowed' her to speak out publicly about her lesbianism after many years of living covertly.

Kathryn sees her experience as illustration of the pain a presumed and promoted 'norm' of sexuality can inflict on women (and no less on men who are homosexual). She says: 'I had started out as a lesbian but then I thought I should try men, having been brought up on the idea that marriage was the ideal, which led to several years of misery and discontent and wondering what was wrong with me. Finally, I rejected men and was then celibate for some time. With the development of gay rights in the Seventies I felt able to come out as a lesbian.'

Stella, twenty-two, daughter of a hairdresser who lives on a council estate, feels, too, that presumed heterosexuality caused her considerable suffering and she thanks the women's movement for helping her throw off that 'oppression'. She says: 'My sexual relations until recently had been a response to social pressure from the age of sixteen. Losing my virginity in cold, sordid circumstances to be equal with my girlfriends and involved in the mating game, was horrible. Feeling this, my decision to become involved with women was cold and rational but I am not a separatist. I have many male friends. But feminism has allowed me to escape the manacles of repressive sexuality and simply to enjoy sex.'

Suzanne, a middle-aged mother of two children who talks of twenty-five years of marriage to a 'particularly dominant' man and who left to try to 'find myself' away from his control, felt able in the climate of the Seventies to experiment with lesbianism. She says: 'I turned to a lesbian relationship out of sheer curiosity. The fine thread between being very good female friends and actually making sex happen is a big jump. I guess I just prefer men.'

The liberation approach where women, freed from feeling they were irrevocably limited to heterosexuality, began to 'experiment' with lesbian affairs, often seeing them as an extension of close female friendship rather than as an absolute change of sexual inclination, won particular opprobrium from the emergent revolutionary feminists. These feminists were beginning to formulate an analysis of the sexual power structure of society which argued that men control women through sexuality and that this is the primary issue. From this followed the thinking that lesbianism (and as far as possible separatism) was the only honest sexual identity a 'woman identified woman', a truly committed feminist, could logically have. A woman who consorted with both sexes, therefore, was not only supporting the traditional power structure but 'polluting' the political importance of lesbianism.

These ideas burst upon a movement which, by the mid Seventies, because of the trust which had built up over the years, allowed women to be critical of one another. But the revolutionary lesbian issue was not about criticism in an environment underpinned with sisterly solidarity; it was a political stance which effectively labelled women who did not concur with the notion that 'to fuck a man is to collude with the enemy' as traitors to the cause.

One of the first conspicuous statements about this issue came from America in 1974 and was used as a long-running feature in the London Women's Liberation workshop newsletter. It not only saw the need for women to withdraw from all sexual relations with men and, if they were to be sexual at all, to be so with other women, but it contained the bombshell concept that heterosexual women were as 'dangerous' as men — and possibly more so. 'The Clit Statement', as the feature was called, made plain that sisterly solidarity was out of the window with its snarling views: 'straight women think, talk, cross their legs, dress, come on like male transvestite femme drag queens.' And then: 'The danger of straight women is their disguise. They look like women . . . they are men in disguise.'

At first British feminists thought that since this paper came from America it could be dismissed as the US's particular brand of extremism. However, it soon turned out that they were mistaken, for there were women in Britain coming to very similar conclusions. These women believed that the most important, powerful way men and a male system oppresses women is through heterosexuality, through individual control of women, through the family, through the extraction of women's labour for men's benefit, and that feminism should have a radical way of attacking this.

Sheila Jeffreys, a lecturer, was formulating these thoughts while living with a man, though having always led a fairly separate social life. In 1977 she ended the relationship for 'political reasons', taking the line that with her views it was a contradiction to be living with a man. In the same year she delivered her paper 'The Need for Revolutionary Feminism Against the Liberal Takeover of the Women's Liberation Movement' at the National Women's Liberation Conference. She recalls: 'I went to the workshop expecting about five people to be there. In fact there were a couple of hundred. It was obviously what was needed at the time.'

The ideas were the subject of much heated discussion in groups around the country, and caused a furore at the Birmingham Women's Liberation Conference in 1978. But it was not until 1979, when Sheila Jeffreys and a group of women she had come together with in Leeds to form the Leeds Revolutionary Feminists, published their paper 'The Case Against Compulsory Heterosexuality', that the gloves were really off.

The group stated that all feminists could and should be

political lesbians, explaining: 'Our definition of a political lesbian is a woman-identified woman who does not fuck men . . . Men are the enemy.' And in the debate which followed this paper, published in *Wires* magazine, women are defined as collaborators with the enemy and their 'important work' for the movement was seen to be being undermined 'by the activity they engage in with men. Being a feminist is like being in the resistance in Nazi-occupied Europe where in the daytime you blow up a bridge and in the evening you rush to repair it.'

Explaining the thinking which led to this emotive paper, Sheila said: 'If you want the liberation of women it does not make sense to remain in a relationship where you are giving your most precious energies — sex and love — to a man. If you truly love and care about women, then you want to ally yourself with the oppressed, not to be relating to the ruling class, and that is what happens with heterosexuality. I believe the only real changes for women have come through them separating from men, working and pushing forward. In the last wave of feminism it was spinsters who were doing that, women who were not putting their energies into men and I do think the heterosexual relation-ship is undermining to women and if the rewards were not so great I don't believe it would be the chosen way, but if you reject it you have to face the fact that you will be punished in the present culture. And I know the arguments about drawing men in to support us, but they haven't been interested in our liberation for thousands of years and I don't believe they are interested now in giving up their power — why should they be? Besides, what I want is revolution, which means being free of male control, not sticking-plaster for the wounds.'

The authoritarian line of the Leeds feminists, its attack on women who had seen themselves up until then as comrades in arms with the revolutionary feminists, even if there were certain differences of opinion, caused an explosion of fury which led to a split in the movement which even ten years later has not properly healed.

Marsha Rowe, in Leeds at the end of the Seventies, recalls: 'It was quite horrific. There was so much anger and pain. Sheila was a cause of real trouble and damage', while another woman remembers: 'Things had turned to war. The hatred and rage we saw among women was terrifying. Here was our precious sisterhood, something we had nurtured as all important for ten years, being blown apart.'

If the public notion that feminism was about man-hating needed any nourishment, this was it. Feminists began to be caricatured and the tag of lesbian won new currency as a form of abuse. Satire and lampooning of the women's movement became fair game.

For all that, the revolutionary feminists' ideas *were* taken up by women, admittedly not a large number in proportion to Britain's female population, but enough to be substantial within the inner circle of the movement. Several of the women I interviewed say they have 'chosen' lesbianism as a political gesture. Certainly Rosemary McAuchty, an Australian who came to Britain to do her Ph.D, did so. She was , she says, promiscuous for many years, and was also involved in feminism, (although aligned to the Socialist faction which placed greater emphasis on drawing in men's support). Rosemary choose lesbianism as a direct result of meeting Sheila Jeffreys and being won over by her theory. She explains: 'Sheila made me see that it was a moral choice, that in a society where men hold the power and that position is reinforced by their having control over women, it is not morally right if you care about women, to go on supporting heterosexuality. I thought about it a lot and I stopped having sex with men, in fact, because I was very much involved with feminism. I stopped seeing much of men at all. And I found that as you stop assuming your relationships will be with men, you begin to see women differently. It is possible to find them attractive and of course they are as attractive as men. I know people believe you must have to psyche yourself up to "fancy" a woman, but that just isn't the case. If the world and politics changed I could get off with a man, they don't make me sick, but if you see relationships as about sharing and friendship it is logical you are going to have more to share with a woman who understands where you come from.'

Small though they were in number, the convert lesbians, with what seemed a holier-than-thou brand of feminism, exerted a powerful influence. Helena Kennedy, who regularly attended meetings, talks, and conferences, was one of many women I spoke with and heard from who recall the sense of being 'wrong' because of their heterosexual relationships, who found them-

selves confused at suddenly being disparaged by other women.
She says: 'I felt there was a strong desire to punish heterosexual
women. Although I was very active in feminist politics in many
ways I felt that paled to nothing because I was living with a man.
And what made me particularly angry was that all the ideas many
of us had considered so important about involving men in child
care, in domesticity, working towards a greater sensitivity in
them, were simply being chucked out in this blanket men-as-
enemy political drive.'

For Joanne, there was 'an uncomfortable rift that was often
there in the group I went to between heterosexual women and
gay women. I particularly recall an occasion where two of us
heteros were totally outnumbered by gay women. It was impossible to share our experiences because the gay women were just
not interested in what I and the other woman had to say —
because we weren't gay.'

The irony was that many gay women also found themselves
outlawed, for the political lesbians in no way wished to be
identified with women who claimed they had been lesbians for
life and were discriminated against because of it, and who
therefore aligned themselves with gay men feeling the same. To
quote Rosemary: 'We don't link up with gay men because they
are not generally interested in tackling the oppression of women.
Indeed, often they have many of the advantages afforded to men
in our culture. And also gayness in men can often stem from
hating women, so clearly we don't support women aligning
themselves with them. We think the liberation of women more
important than the liberating of gays generally and that the
cause is not best served if they lump themselves together.'

But most women disagreed with this standpoint, both those
who saw themselves as having been outside the mainstream of
the movement, no more than touched by what was going on, and
those who were actively involved. They felt — and still feel,
judging by the responses I received in 1988 — that feminism and
lesbianism should not be indivisible and that withdrawing sexually from men will not solve the most pressing problems for
women. What was voiced, over and over (although there were
dissenters too), was the feeling that as a direct result of women's
efforts, lesbianism has become, and should be, quite acceptable
now, and several women felt they might at some time have a

lesbian relationship.

Lynne Segal asks in her book *Is the Future Female?* (Virago, 1987): 'Are there no sturdier weapons than the penis? One way and another we are forced to leave behind the complex historical formation of men's social power — and how this social power confers a symbolic power to the penis as the defining characteristic of the male — to return to a naked sexual capacity which can be, and therefore is, used to control women.'

But amongst those who opposed the dogma being spread by the revolutionaries were women who felt they had earned their stripes in feminism and were not amused at what they saw as a moral hi-jack of the movement. A book of seventeen articles on the subject of sexuality published in *Feminist Review* were put together into a book *My Secret Garden* (published by Virago, 1979), while magazine articles, talks, workshops battled with the issues raised and the deep schism which had occurred.

Beatrix Campbell stated: 'As a lesbian I was opposing separatism, reduction of our political problematic to "men are the enemy" because it stood in direct opposition to sisterhood, which became transposed in some variants of feminism into a cult of woman. It took many forms, from resurrection of the matriarchy, through Earth-Motherhood to bovver girl with a bottle of Newcastle Brown. What was common to all these was a sentimentalization of femaleness and an essentialism based on a cult of women-are-wonderful or rather women-without-men-are-wonderful.'

Wendy Clark, author of *Sexuality: A Reader* (Virago, 1987) commented: 'Heterosexual feminists are faced time and again with the fact that given all the feminism that exists, the damning critiques of men and male behaviour, they are still attracted sexually to men. Lesbian feminists, like myself, still do not see men as the enemy, and continue to define ourselves primarily through an erotic and sexual attraction to women. My criticism of men does not equal lesbianism. My desires and my sexual practice are not predicated on a dislike of men.'

Because revolutionary feminism works from the basis that women are able to function better without men it has no interest in change or reform in men. However, many women believe that the sexual power structure can better be changed with male support, that sensitizing men to women's feelings and needs will ultimately win more than turning from them. Anna explains her feelings:

'I want to live with a man, I like sex with men, I like the idea of having a child with a man around, so I am disposed to try to put energy into trying to change men. As I see it, each and every man is not a terrible guy out to oppress women. Some men behave appallingly, and as a movement it is important that we make plain how unacceptable this is. But I see men, know men, who really do live in an equal partnership with their women, who are very involved with their kids, who actually see the benefits of feminism, and they, to me, are a far more optimistic sign than a load of women living in women-only houses.'

Miranda expresses similar feelings: 'If you treat half the species as the enemy then they will behave like the enemy and that is bad for everyone. I look around at quite a lot of the teenage generation and it seems to me the boys are quite different in their behaviour from the boys I knew when young. I think that is progress and political lesbianism and separatism can only push that way back.'

The revolutionary lesbians caused huge waves, but they also brought the subject of sexual relationships sharply into focus, forcing women to look more deeply, more questioningly at the basis of their choices and lifestyles. But most, rather than turning to lesbianism as a solution, looked — and continue to look — to ways of making an enduring heterosexual relationship work on terms which are acceptable to them.

4

HOLDING THE BABY

FEMINISM AND MOTHERHOOD

THE week I started on this chapter, the Duchess of York gave birth to her first child and the world seemed to go mad. The tabloids ran ecstatic banner headlines, page after page of newsprint spun words to convey the joy Fergie was unquestioningly assumed to feel, and Margaret Thatcher announced: 'The nation will celebrate with you'. The new baby as the embodiment of hope and happiness, was the news of the day. The deification of woman as mother reached its apogee.

The birth of babies to well-loved and famous people acts as a kind of emblem in our society, so that the celebratory brouhaha is wheeled out to reinforce a status quo where women are congratulated not simply for their unique ability to produce progeny, but in the implicit understanding that, having produced a child, they are prepared to take on the task of caring for her or him. It is an artful, time honoured device to make women feel special and admirable when they go forth and multiply, so they will uncomplainingly spend the next decade or so providing primary child care. It is taken for granted that they will assume and accept motherhood, although it comes with no pay, no employment protection, no specified hours, and no statutory breaks, indeed, with condemnation if they don't match up to the standards society demands and a huge dollop of guilt if they don't feel unerringly gratified that biological destiny has honoured them with this job.

But the mother on her own, left in sole care of her children, day in day out, is a relatively new phenomenon. Historically, women who could afford it, paid to have their children cared for much of the time, and for those who couldn't, the extended family and close communities provided practical support. But after the Second World War all that changed. The population needed a boost: it was no good women, who had perhaps enjoyed full-time work during the war, putting their energies into that now that things were back to normal. Home-making and bringing up children were the goals promoted for women to aspire to and women's magazines were quick to extol their virtues: and to speak of the creativity and the sense of a woman being boss of her own domain and educator in the domestic sphere. Contemporary child development experts added their ponderous voices, emphasizing the importance of the mother's presence for young children. At the same time the State nurseries (which had been widely available to enable women to work during the war) began to be whittled away. What women felt about being packed back into the Doll's House after years of war work, or what younger women felt about their destiny, was not much discussed in those times. As Caterina Barnes, the activist mother of Beatrix Campbell, now in her sixties, notes: 'In those days women didn't talk to each other about whether they felt happy with their lives, whether what they were doing was what they wanted to do. So none of us knew whether the others were wondering underneath what on earth they were up to in this situation.'

It took Betty Friedan with her sympathetic manner to draw from women their ambivalent feelings, and to expose the culture which had been evolved around these women, in her seminal book *The Feminine Mystique*. She found that central to the anguish of these women was their feeling of being trapped, underused and undervalued, in their role as mothers at a time when the message constantly pumped at them was that women love to be mothers and that motherhood is what makes women fulfilled.

For many women, reading *The Feminine Mystique* was a vital step towards feminism, and Germaine Greer, Eva Figes, Kate Millett and other of the early feminist polemicists produced works which, amongst other things, challenged the myth of motherhood as all fulfilling, and suggested that this was based on patriarchal need rather than an honest assessment of women's fundamental contentedness. Militant feminists began to express their anger at the way mothers are pushed into a position of powerlessness and inferiority, at the enormous sacrifices to career prospects, the cutting back of freedom they must put up with because they take on the job of producing and rearing the next generation. But many ordinary women objected to these views because of their conviction that having children and assuming the traditional mothering role was what they wanted. As Lucia Valeska, a founder of women's studies at the University of New Mexico, has pointed out, becoming a mother is not a choice made from a position of neutrality, but has been reinforced historically as a means of survival. She says: 'Since motherhood was the primary and often the only route to social and economic well-being for women, having children was a material asset and to be childless was historically negative. Indeed, the term was often directly equated with barrenness. Few women were autonomous: survival depended on marrying and bearing children. No man wanted a barren woman. So under these circumstances no "sane" woman chose not to have children. To be childless still carries a negative stigma.'

Many women felt that to voice their feelings about the oppression of childbearing was a betrayal of children they already had. But gradually women who had been shocked by the constriction which took place when they had their first child started to express their feelings — their isolation, the sense of having lost their personality, the sheer exhaustion, and the anger they felt towards men who offered token help but no real commitment to sharing the work. Madelaine, who had desperately wanted a child in her late twenties, describes how she felt when she had one. She, like numerous other women, only came to feminism when she became a mother. She says: 'It was a revelation when I had a baby. The weight of hundreds of thousands of years of history seemed to come true. It came down to being me who couldn't go out and shut the front door and my husband who could. I became vulnerable, dependent, and suddenly I realized what it was all about. I tried to talk to my husband but I became aware of how women are on a different wavelength, of how most men just don't understand these things. I'd be dying for him to come home and then five minutes after he was in, I would be at his throat because I had been with a screaming baby all day. I felt without power, the balance of status and approval didn't come with the package. I went through a bitter phase and we had lots of rows. I was very grumpy, very thin and quite ill, I think. I used to stamp around the park for hours thinking, "I'm going to escape" and thinking "how . . . where" . . .'

In expressing their angry feelings about motherhood, women were rebelling against the myth of fulfilled motherhood, refusing any longer to play society's game of obedient Madonnas. For many women it was a relief to speak out, ambivalent feelings of love towards their children alongside rage at their own situation as mothers.

Ann Oakley sees a crucial conflict for women educated for a world outside the home and then confined to life inside it. She expresses her reaction to motherhood poignantly in the introduction to her book *From Here to Maternity* (Penguin, 1981): 'My first child was born in 1967 when I was twenty-two and had accomplished a university degree. I thought it was my vocation to be a mother. When my son was sixteen months old my first daughter was born. Both children seemed to me absolutely lovely and I delighted in them, but the time that followed was an unhappy haze of nappy washing and pill taking, as I found I could not make my dream of domestic contentment come true. I felt depressed and oppressed. I felt constantly tired. I felt isolated. I felt resentful of my husband's freedom. I felt my life was at an end.'

But feminists who spoke out thus were liable to be harshly criticized. They were condemned as mutants who could not experience mother love, who had turned against their children, who were outside the norm. Men and women everywhere came forward to state that they saw motherhood as the most important and valuable task, something women could rightly feel proud of dedicating their lives to. But this was to misunderstand the issue. Women were *not* saying they had no wish to be mothers, or turning against their children, but they were questioning why women should make sacrifices no one would ask of a man with children. As one woman put it: 'My child is so precious to me and ultimately because I love him so much I am prepared to put up with the high price this society with its emphasis on "individualism" demand — in other words shutting everyone away to cope alone no matter how tough their circumstances, taking no interest in kids as the next, all important generation. — But it makes me angry as hell.'

Another woman feels anger at the condemnation of women — even in the 1980s — who want something other than to be at home with a child: 'There is a strong suggestion that if, as a mother, you want to work, you are selfish, prepared to damage your child for your own satisfaction, yet ask a man to give up a career he finds satisfying, which gives him his own money in his pocket and which allows him some contact with a world outside domesticity, and most would leave home. Indeed, plenty do but they are not condemned loudly for that.'

Novelist Fay Weldon, who has combined writing at home with bringing up children and therefore does not feel the anger of sacrifice, nevertheless remarks: 'Women with children are tied, and profoundly tied, while men do seem to go on doing what they want. Men's whims are women's necessities.'

During the Seventies, attention was focused on the restrictions motherhood put on women rather than on the belief that men should be an integral part of parenting. Because of this, many women's groups put substantial energy into attempting to set up community-organized child care in their own districts. Michelene Wandor recalls: 'In the early days facilities which would allow women some time for themselves, the chance to work if they wished, while knowing their kids were well looked after, seemed an answer, and so we worked hard to try to organize this. We also campaigned hard for the State to understand the importance and do something about it, but realistically we knew that small initiatives would be a quicker alternative.

'I had young children, having always wanted to be a mother, but when the kids came and I realized how thoroughly they took up my time, which meant I couldn't continue with my own work, I understood the importance of back-up. There was a vociferous group of us in the early days believing this to be an answer.'

Sheila Rowbotham, the writer, helped to set up a community nursery in Hackney, while Angela Phillips, a mother with two young children and a campaigner on child care and the rights of mothers and children, was still involved in setting up *ad hoc* child care in the late 1980s.

At least it was possible to make progress with these practical issues. But it was far harder for women to free themselves from a constant sense of guilt towards their children. Immersed in a culture which embraced the views of Freud, Melanie Klein, John

Bowlby and others who had cited the mother as the person who can make or break a child's happiness, the parent who by giving or withholding appropriate love and attention will create or prevent trauma, women felt their every action was critical. Virginia Held, mother, and professor of philosophy, observed: 'Over and over, one encounters the argument that if a women chooses to become a mother, she should accept a set of responsibilities and obligations that are quite different from the responsibilities and obligations of being a father. Many people expect a father to contribute some of his income for the expenses his child makes necessary. A mother is expected to give up whatever other work may interfere with her availability to care for her child and to take full care of the child — cheerfully and contentedly, to whatever extent, and as long as the child needs it. And if it is thought that the child will develop difficulties due to early separations from a parent, it is the mother who is thought responsible for preventing them.'

Joanne recalls: 'My husband and I both wanted children and George was delighted when I was pregnant and when both children were born. And yet I realized from day one with my elder child that the whole, huge weight of responsibility for making life all right for her, lay with me. George was a "good" father in that he spent quite a lot of time with the babies and wanted to be involved in child rearing, but in no way was he being made to feel that the psychological welfare of the kids required him to make everything else secondary.'

Given such forceful discussion of the dark side of motherhood it was not surprising that some women began to question whether they wanted to have children at all. This was given weight by the abortion campaign leading to the 1967 Abortion Act (which set out to allow women to have legal abortion, albeit on restricted grounds) which had made campaigning for reproductive rights — which meant the freedom *not* to have children — an important issue.

But going against centuries of female culture was not easy. Letty Cottin Pogrebin, a journalist, writing in *Ms* magazine, expressed it thus: 'Scores of feminists of every age, race, marital status and sexual persuasion are talking seriously, thoughtfully and candidly about motherhood. We refuse to believe that women are hollow shells unless and until we have brought forth issue. Truly, feminists are talking about choice . . . yet this notion of choice is a new one for our generation. In the minds of so many women motherhood is prescribed, non-motherhood is deviate. Childless women are to be pitied. Motherhood is synonymous with womanhood. For women who grew up believing in the inevitability of motherhood, the notion of choice is in itself disturbing and heretical.'

But exercising this was also a way in which women could assert control over their lives. The number of women who chose not to have children, but its impact was. The idea that women could choose, coolly and calculatedly, to turn away from biological destiny, was shocking indeed.

Lisa recalls the reception she got when, after three years of marriage, she announced to her family and friends that she had been sterilized: 'My mother didn't like it and couldn't understand at all but she tried at least. Other members of the family treated me with a kind of repugnance, as though there must be something wrong with me. Friends varied from those who felt it was fair enough if that was what I wanted to those who wondered aloud how anyone could really value a career and freedom above the "creativity" of having children.'

Adrienne Rich, the poet, described how, after having three children, she decided to be sterilized. Waking up from the anaesthetic she was confronted by a nurse who asked: 'Been spayed have you?'

The hostility adopted towards women who choose not to have children is demonstrated by Ellen Peck in her book *The Baby Trap*. The thesis of this book, that a woman's chief concern should be pleasing her man, that a penalty of having children was losing a youthful figure, and that staying at home makes women boring so that their husbands will turn for amusement to prettier, freer women, aroused a great deal of hostility from feminists and non-feminists alike. A young, childless Irishwoman who has strong views on the ways in which traditional roles exploit women, nevertheless says: 'I have felt the women's movement was against child rearing, especially after reading *The Baby Trap*. Although it made valid points I could also see many arguments against the author's views.'

Jane McLaughlin, no particular admirer of the organized women's movement, reiterated some of the feminists' arguments

against having children in an article in *The Guardian* during the
late Seventies:

'In my experience, the joy of motherhood is applied after the
birth like swaddling bands, a ritual pleasure played out by
everyone involved to dull the fear of the reality of parenthood.
. . . I could never see that my own existence or that of my
childhood friends in any way enhanced our parents' lives . . . it
seemed that their lives were curtailed because of us. I determined it would never happen to me. Later, you learn that the
decision not to have children because you don't want them is a
political decision, in terms of the dictionary definition "having to
do with organized form of society or government". Selfish,
selfish, selfish clangs the knell of friends and strangers down the
years . . . Apparently it is not selfish to have a child because you
want one, or you need to be needed, or you're looking for
support in your old age or a larger council house.'

Ellen Willis, attending the New York Radical Feminists' conference on motherhood, found herself sharing her private
conflicts with other women: 'As a group we put high value on
personal freedom, privacy, independence, mobility, self-deve-
lopment, and above all our work. We had put off having
children, or decided not to have them because we felt that
motherhood, under present conditions, was incompatible with
our priorities.' And yet it was a decision which left big, unanswer-
able questions. As Willis says: 'Many of us wondered if the
satisfactions of child-rearing might not outweigh the sacrifices',
and she found plenty of feminists who did not align themselves
with the militantly 'childfree' who were, she says, arrogant in an
insidious way: 'They seem to regard the worst aspects of
motherhood not as oppressive conditions that should be alle-
viated but as intrinsic disadvantages that should be avoided by
people with smarts.'

Undoubtedly the issue of children and mothering was
regarded as fundamental. The feminist press carried articles
about the issues, while the national media devoted expanses of
newsprint to sensational interviews with women who had
eschewed motherhood. A woman who went on to have three
children wrote in 1973: 'My belly is embarrassing because it
labels me a population exploder or an exploited baby machine. I
am troubled by this new lament. It seems to proclaim that

women are divided on the point that should most unite us. Right now a discussion of motherhood can shake sisterhood to its roots.'

But the discussions clearly influenced the assumptions and behaviour of a substantial number of women. In 1987 *Today* quoted a government study showing that one in five women were choosing not to have children because they were more interested in pursuing their careers. In the same year almost ten per cent of the women I interviewed said they did not plan to have children. Annette, twenty-seven, said: 'I've contemplated the idea of children over the last three or four years. Although I like and enjoy being around children I don't feel I want the responsibility of having my own. Feminism has undoubtedly been important in influencing those feelings — that is, the awareness that marriage and children are not the only way for women to live or feel whole.'

Brenda Polan, woman's page editor of *The Guardian*, acknowledges that the price of being as successful as she can be in her chosen profession, has probably been to not have children. She says: 'I have not sat down and thought it out, but I have certainly acknowledged by my actions that children would have lessened my chances of doing the things I want in a world which is still very male and traditional and makes few if any allowances for women caring for children.'

Hilary states: 'I never wanted kids as I would be expected to be a "mother" and I would rather play with kids than wipe their bums.'

The issue is still relevant. In 1980 The Women's Press published *Why Children?*, an exploration of the reasons women chose not to have children as well as to have them, while in 1987 Brigid McConville's *Mad to Be a Mother* appeared, a book which takes a feminist line on motherhood and also looks at reasons women have turned against it.

Less common and less explored is the phenomenon of women leaving the children they already have. Women who had felt trapped and oppressed by children but did not — perhaps could not — articulate it, learned through their involvement in the women's movement how to express anger at the injustice of their lot. Some women reacted by rejecting their children; others came out as lesbians and saw their battle against the oppression of those with a minority sexuality, as incompatible with the demands of mothering.

Lucia Valeska transferred custody of her three children to their father when she was living with a woman lover. She explains her position in an American anthology of writings: *Mothering: Essays in Feminist Theory* (Rowman and Allanheld, 1984):

'My children spend summers with my lover and me, and the school year with their father and another mother. The change was a necessity economically and emotionally. Perhaps we could have scraped by economically, although I had no vocational skills and was still working on a college degree. But emotionally the situation for me as a single mother was disastrous. My two-year stint in the women's movement had allowed a vast reservoir of rage to surface. The open resentment at being trapped began to far outstrip the pleasures of mothering, and the daily burden was too great for me or my kids to bear.'

Few British women speak out about leaving their children for the taboo is so strong, and those women who have done so face condemnation. Yvonne Roberts, a mother whose writing deals with feminist issues and who is sympathetic to the dilemmas women face, says: 'I have a woman friend who left her child and it horrifies and appals me, and yet I don't think it right to turn against such women — they need our support. Men walk out on their kids all the time and little is said about it. For some women the demands of motherhood in our society, clearly do make desperate action a kind of bid for survival.'

'I saw it then . . . and see it now as something incredibly ruthless . . . And something absolutely necessary' says Judy Sullivan in *Mama Doesn't Live Here Anymore* (Arthur Fields Books Inc.) in which she describes how, in the depths of despair at the sense of having lost her identity, she walked out on her husband and eleven-year-old daughter Kathleen, and later told her husband 'You'll have to pretend I died'.

One of the tenets of feminism has always been that women should support one another, and yet for a time militant feminists seemed not only unsupportive of mothers but positively antagonistic towards them. Ann from Wales writes how when she was twenty-six in the 1970s, lots of her friends disapproved when she decided to have a child: 'It seemed more acceptable in some

circles to have an abortion than to have a baby.' Another woman
has noted: 'If anything, the movement has all too often alienated
women with children by unthinkingly disparaging mothers and
motherhood.'

When Clare Moynihan, a sociologist, had her son and
daughter, the debate over children was at its height. She
remembers how dramatically her own life was brought to a halt
by their arrival, although, determined that she would keep 'the
intellectual bit of me alive', she succeeded in going to university
and doing a degree. She says: 'I feel feminism has taken away the
value of being a mother, but perhaps it had to be like that
because the other thing had been so inbuilt in to us. Perhaps we
had to scream to be heard. I never felt feminism should be about
saying *YOU MUST NOT BE A MOTHER* nor did many of the
liberal women I know think that, but for a while I felt ashamed of
just being a mother.'

To the thirty-three year old woman who describes herself as a
yuppie who was brought up in a working-class home, and is now
a mother; the main fault of the women's movement is that it has
done nothing to increase the importance of child care . . . 'I
chose when I had my baby to stay home and look after her but I
am now treated as though I have had my brain removed. What I
am doing is considered unimportant, especially by working
women. I think the women's movement should have concentrated on raising the status of child care rather than turning
against motherhood.'

Jude, thirty-two, the mother of two young children, saw
through her own experience the way that motherhood removes
energy from 'the cause' and says: 'In the early days that was the
feeling, not surprisingly, motherhood is so all absorbing that it
saps all energy which could go into political areas and makes
independence more difficult, so yes I do feel that then the
movement was against motherhood.'

Turning against motherhood may have seemed an appropriate reaction to some women, but other feminists who had,
deliberated over this in the early Seventies began to consider the
implications of denying themselves children. They realized that
rather than refusing to participate in what is, after all, the one
thing women have as uniquely their own, they should work
harder at drawing men into child care, living communally with

children and putting renewed effort into campaigning for the
Government to provide State child care.

Women who had not altered their theoretical position on the
oppressiveness of children in our society, nevertheless began to
contemplate the positive side of having children; they discussed
how childbearing and bringing up children could be empowering in a world where power was denied them in many areas. It is
a point that novelist Penelope Mortimer made, although she was
not referring to feminists who perceived themselves as in control
of choice, but of working-class women: 'Many women have
children, and go on having them, in order to assert themselves in
a world in which they otherwise feel totally insignificant.'

In a lengthy and thoughtful article in *Spare Rib* on the subject of
women and childbirth, Anna Briggs from North Shields stated
her feeling about the privilege women have in being able to bear
children: 'There's a lot of love, affection and caring that comes
from the actual physical contact with the child in the womb . . . I
think what men have done is to cordon off other areas of life to
make them their areas of power, because women have got this
reproductive power.'

Other women without any great rationalization simply decided
they wanted a child. This was the experience of Jane who wrote a
long and moving letter from Liverpool: 'I didn't start to want a
child until I was about thirty-one. Before that marriage and
motherhood were the two things I wanted to avoid. I saw
motherhood as the worst form of oppression — the combined
effect of my mother's influence and my fluctuating tangles with
feminism. Then, as many women do, I noticed the old biological
clock ticking away. The most surprising women started to have
babies. Then I really began to want to have a child.'

Despite this change of view, feminists did not forget the dark
side of having children — the fact that there are many mothers
who do not have adequate back-up, who are alone and in
poverty, who never have the opportunity to experience the sense
of fulfilment and joy brought by children — and continued to
campaign for more support. But for women in more privileged
circumstances, perhaps women who had managed to establish an
identity and a secure source of work for themselves, having
children often proved unexpectedly thrilling and brought a new,

deeply personal dimension to life. Novelist Lucy Ellman described it this way: 'It was someone to love unreservedly. My
daughter brought dignity and a sense of the world being a better
place to my life.'

Lucy Goodison, who wrote of how she agonized for some years
over whether to have a child or not, recorded her delight at her
child: 'I had no idea of the rewards. Children give so much love.
And honesty. And tenderness. My relationship with her is
sustaining like any close loving relationship. And the closeness
which is physical as well as emotional, is different in quality from
almost anything I have experienced with adults. I am not
denying hassles, demands, confrontations, boredom and the
times when you feel like murdering them. I am not trying to
drown the real oppression of childbearing in a flush of sentimen-
tal feeling . . .'

Another unexpected aspect of becoming a mother, for many
feminists, was the way it linked them up with other women.
Rabbi Julia Neuberger talked of how it led her to work with other
women and find satisfaction in that. Marie puts it this way: 'I
found myself enjoying a much deeper communion with women
than when we were simply discussing theoretical issues. It was a
kind of understanding of something truly amazing that had
happened to us. We did talk about nappies sometimes, but we
also talked about the importance of getting the world right for
children, our children, big philosophical subjects. Yes, I was
exhausted much of the time but I also felt enormously fulfilled
and that brought its own energy.'

Yet while the satisfaction of mothering was being experienced,
in the most traditional way, feminists did not, on the whole, want
to be at home full-time with their children. Nor did they see the
need for this at a time when John Bowlby was heavily under fire
and research was being published demonstrating that children
do well with good care and that fathers can be as valuable as
primary caretakers as can women.

Some fathers certainly wanted more involvement with their
children than was traditionally the case, and they became
conspicuous copy for the lifestyle sections of the newspapers and
for magazines. They came to be labelled the New Men. Books
were published about shared parenting and ways suggested to
draw men into child care. It was clear as the Seventies gave way

to the Eighties that more men were realistically involving themselves in child care and seeing the justice in role sharing.

Even so, the numbers overall were small. Jan Bumsted, an academic like her ex-husband, recalls the time, living in Cambridge, Massachussetts, when her generation began to have babies:

'The men around prided themselves on being in tune with new thinking and were keen on having children. There was a lot of talk about role sharing and women being able to carry on with their careers. But these highly educated men found, when their children were born, that it wasn't quite so stimulating and rewarding as they had imagined.

'I know when we had our first child my husband panicked. We had talked things through *ad nauseum* before but it wasn't as he had expected. I was getting tired and complaining because he really wasn't sharing much. He would sometimes offer to "help me" and that really was the attitude even though I was studying for a degree as he was. When we had the second child back in England I had a full-time job. I had planned to go back to work but I was beginning to feel I couldn't. My husband got very angry and said "but we need the money, you agreed". It was the absolute reverse of the other thing where husbands refused to let wives work, so what happened was that the feminist argument about women being entitled to work as well as have children actually got turned against them. There was no question of my husband, or the other men I saw behaving the same, turning to their wives and saying "poor you, you're tired" and recognizing that they were doing most of the child care — because that is certainly what was happening — or saying "let's work this out together". It was "Come on now, we discussed this, what do you mean you are tired? You have a career and you mustn't let it go." At the time it was happening to me I felt very guilty and any feelings I had that he was a shmuck had to be repressed because after all he was only repeating what I had said over the years.'

Not everyone's experience was this bleak; other women have been able to encourage men into sharing in the workload, partly by persuasion and partly by arguments of cool logic. Judging by the women who wrote to me, the efforts are bearing fruit — to varying degrees. Ann talks of how she and her husband bring up their child together: 'My man has done everything apart from breastfeed. We believe it enormously important to the kids growing up that they do get their nurturing from a man right from birth and that they see their mum spend significant amounts of time doing other things.'

There is little doubt that feminists who see themselves pitched against men as the oppressors in society, consider unity in caring for the new life they have created to be vitally important, and mothers of sons have exercised themselves a good deal over how boys can be brought up to challenge the undesirable aspects of traditional male behaviour.

5

WOMAN À LA MODE

THE POLITICS OF APPEARANCE

THERE is a sequence in Emma Tennant's novel *The Bad Sister* where Jane, the heroine, flees a party to carry out a ritualistic massacre of her carefully constructed feminine image. The long, highlighted hair is hacked to near stubble, the slinky, clingy dress replaced with trousers, and high heeled sandals give way to heavy boots. Her face is scrubbed clean. This incident is the climax to Jane's identity crisis, the war between her submissive, compliant self of many years and a burgeoning alter ego, fuelled by a militant rage which has come with her feminist consciousness. The new force is victorious and for Jane, the most immediate, powerful way of expressing her spiritual metamorphosis, her new sexual identity, is through clothes and style — by fashioning herself anew.

Jane's solution has a dual purpose: that of informing the world where she stands as a woman and a cathartic one of cleansing her spirit of conflict by demolishing the traditionally feminine persona she has built up, which suddenly represents a painful contrast to the way she is feeling. This sequence in the novel, written in the mid 1970s, dramatized an issue with which the women's movement was grappling at this time. Fashion and adornment were not among the first concerns to be put on the agenda of a movement which began with a strong Civil Rights perspective, but as women began to explore the subterranean world of their impulses and motivations, looking to understand the meaning of just about every area of life, the question of adornment came to be seen not as superficial, as mere cream for the crumpet, which was the way many feminists had so far dismissed it, but as an area of confusion, ambivalence and oppression. The intimate packaging with which women chose to present themselves was indeed political and loaded with significance.

It was for many feminists a difficult issue. On the surface the style of dress chosen, whether to make up or not, how much time is spent on perfecting the body, is an individual choice, an area where women have all the equality they want in terms of variety and possibility of adornment available to them, or the choice to reject all but the most functional elements, and so it did not so obviously fit into the framework of a feminist movement which many women felt was about tangible changes in legislation, the battle for equal opportunities and freedoms. Indeed, for plenty of women the idea of using precious time, intellect and emotion on something which was generally dismissed as frivolous or unimportant was a diversion from the main core of what needed to be done to better women's lives.

Lisa Tickner, who went on to write a series of articles on fashion from a feminist perspective, recalls: 'Many women shared my ambivalence about contemporary fashion, whilst rarely discussing it for fear of being thought trivial.'

Janet, who had been reading Germaine Greer and Kate Millett and was overwhelmed with the feeling that they 'make sense of lots of things which had confused me for ages', began to see the glossy, perfected fashion images in magazines as a personal insult: 'They seemed to be taunting me, saying you'll never be good enough. I took it very personally because I had spent years trying to look pretty and pert and sexy and saucy and all that stuff, and knowing I wasn't matching up. Of course when I thought further about it, I wasn't matching up to what I felt men would like — it never occurred to me that my women friends would like me or not because of how I looked. I felt very strongly about all this and decided I must bring it up at my women's group, which was difficult because we had been very concerned with things affecting working-class women — child care, decent conditions for part-time workers, adult education — and I felt uneasy talking about the pressures on women to adorn themselves.'

The meaning of adornment — its social function, its expression of conspicuous consumption, the way it displays an atmosphere of its time — has been much written about and there are many ways in which it can be viewed. But feminists focused on the way adornment had been used to contain women through centuries, arguing that it had led them to offer themselves up as vain victims in a double bind game: on the one hand, they were expected to see these trappings of adornment, the possibility of dressing up and improving on nature as their special privilege, at the same time it was those trappings which effectively handicapped most women from any participation in a man's world.

Tracing back through this century the willingness with which women have put on overburdening gowns and perilously tight-lacing corsets which did hideous things to their internal organs, weakened their health and sometimes wrecked their fertility, women themselves began to question what impulse led them to be so self-punishing. What quirk of the psyche had made women during the 1930s pay obeisance to designers such as Paul Poiret who declared with delight when he created a dress with narrow hem that he had shackled their ankles, and to Dior who after a war in which women had been demonstrably powerful, seduced them back into full-skirted dresses with cinched waists, and high, high heels. The answer they came up with was, once again, male power. James Laver, the late fashion historian, expressed it this way: 'Man in every age has created woman in the image of his own desire.' As the women's fashion industry — and the beginnings of haute couture — established itself at the turn of the century, it was men who (with a few interesting exceptions), were the designers, kings of fantasy whose creations were sewn into reality by seamstresses with no say in what they were making up. And these garments, which would presumably never be worn by their creators, had little concern for women's health and well-being, but a great deal to do with making them desirable and seductive. Conversely, it is worth observing that important women designers of this century: Madame Vionnet, Coco Chanel, Schiaparelli, Clare McCardell, Jean Muir, Norma Kamali and Katharine Hamnett come instantly to mind as creators who have brought to their designs an awareness of the need for women to have comfort and mobility (and in some cases humour) in their dress. But they were the exceptions, for fashion has been and still is dominated by men at the top designer level.

For much of this century to be packaged according to the fashionable male fantasy was a measure of a woman's success and contemporary feminists question whether things had changed that much. In the immediate post-war years, when women were working in larger numbers than ever before, what James Laver had named the 'Seduction Principle', still applied. Even if marriage was not the goal, proving you were a sexually desirable woman — with the aid of fashion and beauty products — was a profoundly important function of being female. Judith Thurman, an American journalist, described the experience of re-examining the clothes she put on: 'One of the greatest early shocks of feminism was to realize the way our clothes had packaged us, even the most radical of us, for male consumption. We were, even for ourselves, fantasy girls of one variety or another. We devised our costumes and competed, like so many circus acts, for attention.'

Julie Christie saw it from a different perspective. She described auditioning for a film early on in her career: 'I was asked to walk around by a producer and his comment was that my nylons were full of runs. That's how little I managed to make it in his eyes, but all those things remain as terribly humiliating — you might be angry and defiant but you see yourself as this terrible wreck. I suppose that was because I was trying to sell myself as desirable womanhood.'

American Karen Durbin, writing in *Ms.* magazine about women's feelings towards fashion, described at length a pair of dagger-heeled soft leather boots she had brought four years earlier and the wonderful, swashbuckling sensation they gave her — as well as crippling pain and a marked decline in her ability to walk. She wrote: 'Spike heels are combat boots in a sex war where women are the losers; an emblem of the old style vamp, who telegraphs a hostile eroticism . . . the futile gesture of the women whose only weapons are, as venerable fashion parlance has it, a "drop head" dress and a stiletto heel.'

The quest for desirable womanhood begins, of course, very young for women. Competitions such as Miss Pears, which select the prettiest girl and link that selection to the properties of their own soap, create early on a wish to conform to a standard which has been established in a world geared to male notions of beauty. This thinking underlies today's highly sophisticated, mega-budgeted world of beauty advertising. Images of perfect women display the expectations of how women should be physically, carrying the implication that the achievement of such perfection will make them more successful in attracting men.

These ideas surfaced in the Seventies and led women to see how their presentation throughout the ages had been geared to maintaining male domination. Bernard Rudofsky, an anthropological writer who claims no feminist perspective but a thorough knowledge of human behaviour, observes in his book *The Unfashionable Human Body*, the supplicating role given to women by fashion and beauty products: 'The burden is on the woman. She has to trap and ensnare the male by looking seductive. She has to keep him perpetually excited by changing her shape and colours by every means, fair and foul. In the traditional battle of the sexes, dress and its accessory arts are her offensive weapons.'

And even when a woman is not setting out deliberately to look sexy and thereby to ensnare a man, the style of dress she has been taught to wear marks her gender quite specifically. Women's clothes cause women to walk and move with less power and efficiency than men: they are frequently designed to emphasize the difference in body shape between men and women; they are often produced in colours and fabrics which signal femininity. Historically, feminine dress has been specifically designed to prevent women looking in any way like men and when determinedly defiant women, such as Radclyffe Hall, went out in male dress, society voiced its disaproval. In more recent years we have seen fashion take up items of male dress such as tailored jackets and ties, and sell them to women as part of a titillating game of gender confusion. However, the fun of this game has always been to put the clothes on to women who look unmistakably feminine. The Annie Hall look, the big, baggy butch clothes, the peg-leg jeans and Doc Marten boots — all these fashions were based on the idea of women playing with an awareness of masculinity but without ever letting go of their essential femininity. The contrast between the way these fashions were applauded and the feminist 'uniform' of clothes, also taken from a male repertoire of dress but worn to disguise not highlight the lovable woman underneath, was great.

The powerful influence of fashion and the advent of a body as contorted and contrived as those the Victorian women sought to attain, was a feature of the 1960s. The quest to be slim reached its apotheosis in that era. Models such as Jean Shrimpton and

Penelope Tree, tall and skinny by nature, were used to sell fashion and with it the idea that fashion could only look good on a body impossibly thin by most people's standards. It was a cult of the body elite which reached almost cartoon proportions with the 'launch' of Twiggy, a thirteen-year-old schoolgirl, by her consi-derably older Svengali-esque friend Justin de Villeneuve. Photo-graphic techniques were used to highlight her waif-like appear-ance and childish vulnerability, and looking back to those pictures it is hard not to see something redolent of child porn, although in this case the sexual sell was disguised as fashion sell.

Twiggy became the emblem of an impossible ideal during the late 1960s and early 1970s, the exemplification of what women could achieve if they would only work on their imperfect bodies. It was during the Seventies that the alienation women felt with bodies which did not match up to the ideal, became almost epidemic. At one end of the spectrum they boosted the slimming aids business into the multi-million pound league; at the other end they pushed themselves to the self-destructive illnesses anorexia nervosa and bulimia. Although these illnesses do not stem purely from a desire to have a fashionable body, they are illnesses rooted in finding the self unacceptable, and that sense was clearly stimulated by the ubiquitous message of desirable slimness.

The shape of the perfect body may have changed through the years, but whether it was curvaceous or lean, it has not been something most women could achieve, however much time they devoted to dieting, exercising or inviting the surgeon's knife.

As one women, who describes herself in mocking imitation of tabloid newspaper talk, as: 'a stunning forty-three year old mother of three with a picturesque home and impressively domesticated husband', says: 'I developed a large, rounded tummy after having the children, and my breasts were markedly more droopy than before the many years of breastfeeding I had put in. I was very proud of being a mother, of having produced kids who, I believe, are a good addition to the world, and I resent very much that I am not revered for this. Why isn't my body, which expresses its wonderful fecundity, which has been used as women's bodies are designed to be used, appreciated?'

Jeanette, who spent years trying to please a husband who wanted her to look beautiful, fasionable and to disguise anything about her body which did not fit this, talks with enormous relief of the life she has found since leaving him, and of living among women: 'I feel good. I like myself. I like my body too. I don't feel bad because it bleeds, has babies or breasts or does not turn some man on.'

Another woman, short in stature and inclined to 'put on weight when I am feeling content which is usually when I feel I have organized my life well', adds, 'All the images around tell me that I have no reason to reflect contentment with what I have achieved if it means my body does not fulfil the desired ideal. What I am actually told through advertisements and magazine editorials is that I'm weak, a failure and that I need to do better. It is quite a struggle to withstand all this and say hang on, if women are to feel strong and legitimate in being the people they want to be and not somebody else's construct, we need to stick two fingers up to the ideals being fed to us.'

It was a while before the issues attaching themselves to adornment became the subject of serious feminist writing, but Rita Freedman in her book *Beauty Bound* (Columbus, 1988), surveying the way the need for beauty has been marketed to women, assessed both the feeling women have that they must attract men, and also the flip side of why men so badly want a woman who conforms to cultural notions of perfect womanliness. She says: 'Women are aware that beauty counts heavily with men and they therefore work hard to achieve it . . . In a way men can reclaim beauty vicariously. The status one gains by association with an attractive mate or date has been called "the rub off effect". Preoccupation with female appearance stems in part from this. Attractiveness might be less important to women if it were not so unequally transferable.'

The irony is that adornment and display are arts which have been more extensively and imaginatively permitted in women's lives than in men's and, as attitudes to men displaying some signs of the feminine part of their make-up apparently loosened during the 1970s into early 1980s, a number of men chose to use fashion and make-up to join in the display game. But the difference is, of course, one of need and dependence. For women, display and the artistry of adornment have been underlaid with the message that not getting it right is a profound failure, because without an approved standard of attractiveness they are not worth having — inferiority is their heritage, adornment the means of overcoming it. Freedman, who has recorded the despairing feelings of women talking of their failure to match up to the perfected ideal, goes so far as to suggest that the construction of a physical appearance which wins approval is tantamount to a women offering up an apology for being female: 'The idealization of female appearance camouflages an underlying belief in female inferiority. Just as excessive narcissism has its roots in self loathing, the myth of female beauty grows from the myth of female deviance. Beauty helps to balance women as a misbegotten person. It disguises her inadequacies and justifies her presence.'

It did not take a lot to unleash the complex, hitherto buried feelings about fashion and beautification once it was acknowledged as an appropriate issue for the women's movement. Sara Scott, writing at length in *Spare Rib* in 1988 on the subject, said: 'Feminists questioned femininity because we recognized it was a set of ideas men had constructed to maintain their power over women. Clothes and make-up are one aspect of this. We know that femininity, including women's appearance, is historically and socially constructed, and within a particular society it can take many forms from a pastel pink twin-set to red fishnet stockings.'

Jo Spence, a feminist photographer who has worked for years presenting images of women designed both to explore their feelings about themselves and to show them as something other than objects of pleasure, recalls one of the early groups women set up to explore the issues around appearance and to discuss ways of breaking through the layers of conditioning: 'I was very large as a young woman and I never felt I could get my appearance right so I hid in voluminous clothes because at least I didn't look as though I was trying then and I couldn't be derided for failing. But it was wretched because I longed to be like the girls in the glossy magazines.

'One day in the group I was going to we made ourselves up into our fantasies and the idea was that we should be photographed like that. I made myself into a vamp, a real Golders' Green tart, someone who has really gone over the top and is flaunting herself. Then I looked in the mirror properly and hated it and wanted to cry. I couldn't do it, I would never be able to play that game even if I wanted to.'

All important to Mo was her regular women's meeting where they would tell each other how awful they looked: 'We would go just as we felt, and often that was scruffy, tired, end-of-the-dayish, a situation where normally you would pray not to be seen, not to meet anyone you knew. In the meetings we would say to each other things like "you look really awful" and "what a mess you are" but of course we went on liking, loving each other, nobody was rejected because of the way they looked, and for me that was terribly important. For about a year I spent an awful lot of time with these women because I felt safe and supported and I found that I wanted less and less to make up and dress in fancy but not particularly comfortable clothes, and more and more to live in blue jeans and sweat shirts. I began to go out everywhere like that and the world didn't fall about. Sure I got less wolf whistles and sometimes I did mind, sometimes I thought nobody loves me any more, but most of the time I felt truly liberated.'

Dress was not always a means to a desirable end. For some women it played the part of a *rite de passage*, the means whereby a woman attempted to establish her independence, and finding that, because of the messages associated with dress, she was plunged into a world of problematic femininity. Writing of the experience in *Spare Rib*, a young woman said: 'It is ironical that for me and my school friends the uncomfortable, constricting trappings of femininity meant independence and self-assertion in the face of parental authority. At home rows raged around false eyelashes, tight skirts and high heels. I soon found that the adult freedom supposed to be found within femininity was fraught with double binds — full of contradictions.

'It became clear that different forms of feminine clothing projected different messages and conveyed different sorts of power. Genteel femininity — high collars, small prints, pale pink — suggested social status and respectability. Sexy femininity — low-cut dresses, loud prints, shocking pink — suggested the power of sexual allure. If you opted for one you were in danger of being dowdy; if you went for the other you were accused of being tarty.'

Groups were also being held at the Women's Therapy Centre where women would spend two full days working on feelings about appearance and adornment. Exercises were held to help women look at their past, how they had been clothed through childhood and how they felt about their bodies, for example.

A lot of emphasis was put on the body because, a woman running the course explained: 'A lot of the reasons women choose clothes is because they don't like their bodies and they use clothes to try to be somebody different from the person who actually exists underneath. We get into trying to please other people because of alienation with our bodies. If you don't like your body you desperately need outside approval and because powerful people in the outside world are men, it is male approval we seek.

'During the course the exercises concentrated on "trying to get inside ourselves to see who we really felt we were, what we valued in ourselves'. From this, we could talk about the kind of clothes, and the kind of look which would express these feelings. Sometimes we did it with drawings. We also talked about how much clothes being worn were there to disguise disliked parts of the body, and why those parts were unacceptable. We also confronted the converse of dressing sexily and according to a stereotype, the situation where women would come in looking very drab and saying they were not interested in their appearance. It's like saying I'm not political — it's a political statement and very often it is hiding a profound fear of failure. The point of the group was to help women look at what they were doing with themselves, and to try to work towards doing what they wanted on their terms.'

The same sort of process was taking place over cosmetics which for some women, even more than dress, were an attempt to create perfection or to escape having the real person seen and rejected. In Mary's words: 'For years I put make-up on first thing in the morning and I touched it up all day so that the impression I was trying to achieve didn't fade away. The one thing I feared was being caught looking as nature made me. It became an absolute disguise. I found I disliked the way I looked without make-up. I appeared to have a puttyish face with little piggy eyes, and I felt quite certain that if anyone saw me they'd turn away in disgust. But somehow if they didn't find me attractive when I wore make-up it mattered less because somewhere, deep down, I knew that wasn't really me. It took me nine months of

forcing myself to go out everywhere without make-up to break
the pattern. I remember one day, I had had a bit of sun on my
skin and I was feeling very fit, and I looked in a mirror and really
liked what I saw.'

At a discussion on cosmetics, in West London, recorded in
Shrew, the first point raised was that quite a number of the
women were wearing make-up. This led to a debate which
revealed that many women considered make-up a way of building confidence — one woman spoke of using make-up most
when she was feeling unhappy and inadequate. Another
inveighed against a boyfriend who instructed her in how and
when to wear make-up. The meeting reached no conclusions but
the woman recording it took the line that: 'What becomes clear is
that the reasons for wearing or not wearing make-up are
extremely complex, deep rooted and go a long way beyond a
simple conditioned response to mass media manipulation.

'The implication for the Women's Liberation Movement is that
candid, self-searching discussion of the cosmetic issue is invaluable, while any kind of rigid stance recommending that all
"liberated" women throw away make-up, girdles, brassières and
"other devices" is extremely inappropriate — at least while we do
not yet understand fully why we do what we do in terms of
adorning our bodies.'

Yet since breaking the medium and the message of the
seduction principle seemed a crucial, practical and symbolic step,
many women could see no alternative to taking a rigid stance.
Feminists surveying the range of clothes available to them very
soon found how thoroughly the women's dress market has been
colonized by the fashion industry. In the hunt for clothes which
could not be interpreted as sexual packaging and which would
also allow them the mobility, comfort and seriousness afforded to
men by their dress, women had to search hard. The solution was
found in shops stocking work clothes such as donkey jackets,
dungarees, non-styled jeans, and basic men's shirts and tee-
shirts. Doc Marten boots was another item, and although by no
means all feminists adopted them, those who did inspired
cartoons up and down the country lampooning them as
'Women's Libbers', and deeming them man haters on the basis of
their appearance.

It was a fair measure of the case that clothes maketh woman, that while women's battles for equal pay and equal rights got at least an intelligent hearing and some sympathy, defying the code of adornment was clearly a profound offence, interpreted nationwide as a deliberate act of rejection of men.

The 'uniform' which emerged, added to by the feminist 'stubble' or the feminist 'fuzz', as the very short cropped hair, and the short perms worn, were named, gave women a sense of strength, unity and defiance. Joan Cassell, who explored consciousness-raising groups in the United States, brings up, in her book *A Group Called Women* (McKay), the relevance of dress to the group and the way 'Women's Liberation uniform' altered according to ideology: 'The most extreme manifestations were found among lesbian feminists. From the lesbians through radical to reform feminists, demeanour could be arranged on a continuum — the more radical the ideology, the more recognizable the demeanour. Lesbians generally wore jeans or denims or men's overalls, the baggy kind that hid the shape of the wearer. The pants might be topped by a man's tee-shirt or working shirt. It was apparent they were not wearing bras. Their hair was not so much styled as *there*, they wore no cosmetics; steel-rimmed glasses or sunglasses were frequent; footgear was comfortable with a predominance of heavy men's work boots or sneakers and jewellery was rare, with the exception of political buttons. Associated with this costume was a recognizable deportment and bearing — a freedom of stride or stance of language.'

Meanwhile, Susan Brownmiller, who followed her seminal book on rape with one on the nature of femininity, was making her own gesture: 'Along with others my conversion to pants at the start of the Seventies was slow but complete, accompanied by a sense of relief and relaxation. . . . it became a feminist statement to wear pants. Never again would most women wear skirts, I thought.'

To Wendy Chapkis, author of *Beauty Secrets* (published in 1986) the style of the dress feminists adopted was loudly and clearly the message. She says: 'Butch style whether worn by men or women, is a symbol of detachment. Dressing butch gives the wearer the protection of being the observer, not the object. A femme-y look by contrast, suggests self-display, whether in a quietly demure or sexually flashy fashion.'

My own conversion to a style which was not as extreme as the 'feminist uniform' but which was a very definite rejection of a kind of sharp-edged sexiness mixed with cutesy girlishness I had long effected, came, improbably, through being fashion editor on *The Guardian*. The job had always been a place of ambivalence for me. Trained as a general reporter, I, like almost every newspaper man I have met, regarded fashion as essentially unimportant, a woman's interest which confirmed men's entrenched view of female frivolity, and while colluding both personally and professionally in playing the game, I felt a marked unease, as, week after week, I wrote about the latest look or designer, the newest vagaries of the rag trade. I was writing for someone other than myself, and I didn't have too much respect for the person I was writing for.

It was an arrogant position to take and perhaps it showed. This was the early Seventies and plenty of women who had been rigorously looking at cause and effect in the female world, deluged me with, if not hate mail, then certainly highly critical mail. The essence of it was that in a paper like *The Guardian*, which took women's rights and the quest for equality seriously, I was an undermining force with my chirrupy pieces urging women to concern themselves with getting their look right. It hurt, I didn't see myself like that — I tried, after all, to pack in between the Paris collections the London shows which were usually extravaganzas of expensive and pretty impractical garb, articles about creative dressing from second-hand shops, the ideas of student designers, women designers creating with other women in mind. But these letters, which were relentless and insistent, caused me to stop and think, and this thinking led me to remember the many years since puberty I had spent packaging myself in a way planned entirely to attract male approval. Certainly the bum-hugging pedal pushers, low-cut tee-shirts, skimpy skirts and heels which had me teetering like a drunk on a windy night, and the undoubted sense of constraint and discomfort which went with them, were not put on to appeal to other women.

More often than not I looked like a caricature on a Brighton postcard, but I disliked my body, plump as a Bernard Mathews' turkey, and felt that the only way it could be appealing was by being displayed in a way which at least suggested I was a thoroughly sexual being. I was constantly exposed to be shot down. If men did not respond to me flatteringly I felt devastated, a failure. When they did, it was usually not in the way I hoped, which meant seeing beyond the leery packaging to the serious, dignified person inside. Most often came a raw sexual response which caused me a feeling of enormous vulnerability and shame, but I could not understand what I was doing or find another way. Thinking back, it brings to mind Simone de Beauvoir's way of expressing the dilemma for a woman struggling for the culturally accepted definition of femininity: 'The lie to which the adolescent girl is condemned is that she must pretend to be an object and a fascinating one, when she sees herself as an uncertain, dissociated being, well aware of her blemishes. Makeup, false hair, girdles and reinforced bras are all lies. The very face itself becomes a mask; spontaneous expressions are artfully induced, a wondering passivity is mimicked; nothing is more astonishing than to discover a young girl's physiognomy, well known in its ordinary aspect, when it assumes its feminine function. For a young woman there is a contradiction between her status as a real human being and her vocation as a female.'

As the letters to *The Guardian* unleashed more memories and my own involvement with feminism grew, I began to question more profoundly why and how the way women dress is oppressive and in what way, other than wearing boiler suits and bovver boots, it could be otherwise. I put the question to a group of women, all high-profile feminists — they included Ursula Owen at Virago, the writer Elizabeth Wilson, Julia Naish, a founder of *Feminist Review* — who broadly expressed the view that fashion was oppressive in two fundamental ways. One was that, whether at couture level or as an adaptation for the high street, it is almost always designed with the idea of presenting women in a stereotyped way, and, as discussed, marketed through glossy magazines and newspapers as well as through advertisements, to persuade women that success in life rests to a fair extent on being properly dressed (and made up). The other was that the kind of fashion which gets featured prominantly, which women are urged to be impressed by, is expensive. Most women do not have enough money to spend on that scale on their clothes and should not be made to feel inadequate because they cannot do so. Nor should a value system be promoted which encourages women, who may have low incomes and more important things to spend their money on, to think of fashionable dressing as a priority.

For all this, these women did not think that pages about clothes for women, in popular publications, were wrong *per se*, but that the idea of fashion with its built-in obsolesence and obsession with changing style every season, was not in the best interests of women. A clothes page, it was felt, should be about choices and ideas which would help women to find clothing which would be functional, reasonably priced and attractive in an enduring way. In tune with this was the member of a women's collective who said: 'I do feel very angry about women who are in a position to say something to other women about fashion and who say things which, I think, are going to make things much worse, who go on year in year out saying frills and femininity are back, get out the suspenders, men like stocking-tops. There are one or two women journalists who have been saying that every year for so long. They're really the counter-revolution.'

Carrying through these thoughts I asked the women interviewed to produce an acceptable fashion page, according to their beliefs on the kind of dress which could, usefully, be shown to women. The result included Scandinavian cardigans knitted by far-off relatives, a 1920s dress from a second-hand shop, blue jeans, a plain, well-made blouse, a fair isle sweater, a dirndl skirt and flat, comfortable shoes. The point of these outfits, the authors of the page explained, was that they had not cost much, could easily be imitated by women visiting charity shops, jumble sales, or basic clothing shops. The women wearing them felt comfortable, at ease with themselves and proud of who they appeared to be, yet the clothes had been chosen with care to enhance the wearers, to make them appear attractive to people around them. The point of it all was to explore a way in which feminists could enjoy clothes, on their terms, a way they could move on from that puritanism which caused Jill Tweedie to remark dolefully: 'I blame the women's movement for ten years in a boiler suit', and help women reclaim the positive aspects of adornment. Susan Brownmiller, criticized by the Left-wing *National Guardian* in New York for writing her book *Femininity*, expressed it thus: 'I was attacked because they said a feminist should not talk about clothes, but clothes are creative, wonderfully exhilarating and so can make-up be, but not when they are

compensating for lack of opportunities, lack of equality, not
when they are the tools with which we must fight for opportunities, status, men. If we can remove them from this arena and be
playful and creative in our dress, as feminists, that has to be a
good thing.'

Opting out of the adornment game was an important political
and emotional gesture for many women. It allowed them to feel
free of the competitiveness as well as the sense of being male
fodder; it allowed them too, to see that the unadorned woman is
appealing. Angela Phillips, who worked as a photographer
recording many of the early events of the women's movement,
remembers: 'The media was endlessly saying how awful and ugly
all these feminist women were with their scrubbed faces and
sexless clothes, but what I found, going to groups and events,
was the most beautiful women I had ever seen. They seemed so
alive, so confident, so full of energy and in a way the fact that
they weren't covered in panstick and lipstick and weren't wearing
clothes which attracted the eye, made it possible to see just how
lovely they were as people rather than women.'

Even so, a sense of displeasing puritanism was perceived
around the matter — women who felt a desire to wear something other than the neutral gear which had become *de rigeur*,
sensed sisterly disapproval. Jenny, a woman therapist, recalls: 'I
went through a phase of being very political and it seemed to me
that clothes, other than as protection from the elements and to
conform to required standards of modesty, were wrong. I got rid
of make-up, I wore brown trousers and brown sweaters and I
tried to look as inconspicuous as possible. A woman I was
working with had done the same and we both felt that we were
being oppressed by the clothes it seemed we had to wear, that we
were denying ourselves an area of creativity which has been
important to women for centuries.'

A young woman disturbed by the disapproval of women
around her, feeling what Jo Spence described when going to a
women's group wearing lipstick, that 'there were lots of disap-
proving Mums', said: 'There seem to be women who think that if
you wear flowered nighties or have long hair you are not a
proper feminist . . . feminists can be oppressive too,' while Anna,
who saw herself as having 'rebelled' when she went out and
bought a brilliantly patterned skirt and top, commented: 'I

believe feminism is about helping women to feel strong in doing what they want — not making them feel guilty if they don't conform to a party line. If I wanted to wear a skin-tight dress slashed to the waist and spike heels, I would expect my feminist friends to support me in the right to do so, not criticize me. I understand the point of the protest uniform and I do believe it's been important for women to explore what our ways of adorning ourselves have been about, but I enjoy clothes, I enjoy the different effects you can create dressing in different ways, I love the feel of certain fabrics, and I want to be allowed to play with my appearance.'

Susan Brownmiller, observing women like Anna among her friends, wrote: 'I think my friends returned to dresses because they felt that life was getting grey without some whimsical indulgence in the feminine aesthetic. They missed the frivolous gaiety of personal adornment, they missed the public display of vulnerability and sexual flirtation, and they missed the promised change in appearance that a new dress — and only a new dress — can hold.'

This feeling was shared by many feminists, who began to question whether denying adornment — an embedded aspect of women's culture — wasn't throwing out the baby with the bath water. They began to experiment with their appearance. Skirts appeared on the best of sisters, bright coloured garments like victory flags were to be seen at meetings and gatherings, close cropped hair was allowed to grow into shaggy manes and serious feminists began to write books and articles about the business of fashion and beauty. Wendy Chapkis brought together a variety of women with different views and experiences of dress and make-up and different attitudes to where these things stand in their lives, to create her book *Beauty Secrets*, quoted on page 104. And in her final chapter, which is optimistically entitled 'Towards a More Colorful Revolution', she voices a feeling which had by this time become a popular thought among feminists, that once they feel in control of their own sexuality, sure of who and what they want to be, clothes and make-up can be used to express and emphasize that self. She writes: 'Clearly the only way enhanced appearance can be a source of pleasure rather than anxiety, is if it is firmly rooted in a sense of our own value independent of it. Dressing up can only be fun when coupled with a confident knowledge that we are deserving of respect, affection, admiration and lust, even without the props and costumes.'

A fascinating contribution to the dialogue was made by Elizabeth Wilson, a feminist sociologist, who produced a lengthy exploration of the history and sociological meanings of fashion and beautification. While she acknowledges and discusses the feminist attitudes to these matters, in her book *Adorned in Dreams*, which was published half-way through the 1980s, she takes the view that 'to see fashion exclusively as an expression of women's subordination is to ignore the richness of its many cultural and political meanings'.

As late as 1988, when it seemed that the the passion over the politics of dress had subsided, Lorraine Gamman and Shelagh Young wrote an article for *Spare Rib* acknowledging the importance of a feminist style which refused to play the game of stereotypical notions of femininity: 'We're still portrayed as shrill, ugly and sexually frustrated if we try to take the working man's daily dose of tits and arse away from him. Many women justifiably resent the media for constructing a derisory image of the drag-dungareed dyke', but that: 'Feminists have participated in the image-making process and must accept some responsibility for forging an association between radical politics and looking a mess.'

They then went on to suggest that we should look at the puritanism which was still causing feminists to feel themselves politically compromised by choosing adornment: 'Current mythology is still that real feminists don't wear make-up, take pleasure in dressing or in being looked at by men. We're too pure and ideologically correct for these pleasures. White, middle-class and liberal guilt hinges around the notion that "as *a real feminist* I shouldn't be doing this". Somewhere along the line we've failed to acknowledge that the whole fashion industry revolves around women looking with pleasure (as well as envy) at other women, failed to acknowledge any radical potential in the production and consumption of multifaceted identities. Why can't we feel comfortable playing around with style or inhabiting a raunchy sexual image?'

The article drew a great many angry letters, condemning the Gamman and Young article as reactionary. But earlier than this,

Janet Radcliffe Richards, a lecturer in philosophy, produced a provocative book, *The Sceptical Feminist*, in which she took issue with a number of the dogmas taken as given by the women's movement. One of these was the rightness of turning away from wearing clothes intended to please men. She argued that for women to want to please men and attract them is not intrinsically wrong nor anti-feminist, but that the inequalities which mean that she needs to do so in order to have a livelihood are wrong and that these are the matters to be addressed. Given that a good many feminists actually want men as partners they need to make themselves appealing enough for the men they want to notice and desire them.

She writes: 'A woman should be able to make herself attractive to men, so putting herself in a position to have a wide range of them to choose from and increase the chances of finding one who comes up to her requirements, without being open to insulting remarks in the street and nasty comments about leading on men whose advances she will not accept. The problem is obviously a difficult one but what is absolutely clear is that it cannot be solved by women making themselves unattractive. To do that is to give up in despair.'

It was a thesis which plenty of women felt ignored the very real problems they faced: the belief that the fashionably dressed and decorated woman is desirable but also frivolous by definition of the efforts she has made to be attractive, the fact that men view women as being on offer to them or anybody else because they have turned themselves out becomingly, and that women who do not have the bodies or faces to be successful in the adornment game are passed by because the value system has not been effectively challenged.

In the words of a thirty-two year old woman who has spent considerable time debating these issues: 'You can argue all day about what level of adornment is acceptable without making the woman into a stereotype, what signals we give off under what circumstances and so on, but for many of us who certainly never intended to live in dungarees and donkey jackets for the rest of our lives, the point was and remains one of perception. Women who do not join in the party have to be condemned.

'If we will not make ourselves up according to a set of rules laid down by a patriarchal system which wants girls to look like girls and where business has a helluva lot of money invested in maintaining constructed standards of beauty, we are a very real threat. But what we want is to be allowed to be beautiful, attractive, appealing in a different way. I want the face and body nature gave me to be seen as beautiful in itself, not because I have spent a lot of time and money tarting it up. We may have an Equal Opportunities Act and Equal Rights legislation but we don't yet have the same freedom as men to be loved for ourselves.'

6

THE MEDIUM AND THE MESSAGE

FEMINISM IN THE THEATRE AND THE VISUAL ARTS

'IT was the beginning of the Seventies. I had begun reviewing theatre and I started writing plays as well. Suddenly there was a sense of urgency, there were things I wanted to say and a lot of them were about women. Feminism had become a central focus of my interest.' — Michelene Wandor.

'There was one remarkable weekend when I picked up a batch of plays from the Royal Court. There were three first plays by women in this batch and they were all good, very good. I couldn't believe it, it was Eureka time.' — Carole Hayman, actress, writer, director.

'I started to make work about my body which was small, precious, quite erotic. I started to make sculpture which could be worn as clothes, they were demonstrated live on the body and documented. My areas of concern became very specifically to do with women.' — Helen Chadwick, artist.

It was Vladimir Mayakowsky, the Soviet painter, who observed that: 'Art is not a mirror to reflect the world, but a hammer with which to shape it' and in those words he described a feeling which has been central to the way contemporary feminists involved in the visual arts and the performing arts have perceived things. Because art is a powerful provoker of thought and questions, a medium for challenging the *mores* of an era, artists

and the art forms are central in having an impact on the shape of
public thinking.

Throughout the 1950s into the 1960s the theatre echoed with
the words of the post-war Angry Young Men and their male agit-
prop successors. Men dominated the theatre, the important
drama: male actors took the key roles, male directors brought
their vision and values to the productions. The visual arts were
equally dominated by men who were beginning to break with
convention, to produce pop art and parody, anarchic work which
shocked the eye and sensibilities and questioned conventional
wisdom and values. The point which feminists raised was that
popular culture was almost entirely about seeing the world from
a male point of view and it was reinforcing the invisibility of
women who, accordingly, were believed to have done nothing
much worth recording.

The shaping of thought and ideas through art was being done,
then, by men, not women. Arnold Wesker wrote the rich, strong
character of Beattie Bryant in his *Roots* trilogy, but the point
made by theatre critic Ann McFerran was that Beattie stood out
because she was, indeed, a substantial woman but also because
other such parts were not being written. Otherwise, women
characters lived their lives through men, reacting to their actions.
Women's autonomous experiences and ideas did not come on to
the agenda. Nor did women express their view of the world as
writers or directors, except in very rare circumstances.

The Sixties into Seventies revolution in art was about ascen-
dant men moulding a new consciousness. There were a few
women (such as Elizabeth Frink, Barbara Hepworth — and
Georgia O'Keeffe in America) who were prominent in the visual
arts but they worked according to male defined standards, and
the burgeoning feminist awareness did not apparently inform
what they did.

Women working in many areas of the arts who had been
influenced by feminist thought and analysis, began to see how
thoroughly their lives were shaped by working in a world which
didn't acknowledge that they could be more than a sideshow,
applauded only for portraying a male created style of femaleness, whether on stage or on canvas. As elsewhere some of these
women looked to separatism in their field as an answer.

Gilly Fraser, an actress who turned to writing plays, spoke about the sense of being alone in a male world, in conversation with a group of women writers, in 1977: 'We're half the human race and our voice hasn't been heard. I spent a long time being that dumb dolly in the cops series and when I started to write all that resentment came out. You write what it feels like to be that dumb dolly and you write for the women who haven't been written for.'

Pam Gems, a playwright who wrote many plays about women and was seen within feminist circles to be an important voice for their cause, although she went on later to disclaim the tag 'feminist writer', also saw that the imbalance needed adjusting when she began working with the Women's Theatre Group: 'I certainly had the intention of writing parts for women. The paucity of them gave me a sense of outrage.'

As the Seventies got into its stride women began to look for effective ways of providing some balance to the artistic vision around them. As in many areas of life where under-representation of women meant they had been denied the same opportunities as men, women in the theatre saw the need for a specific effort to be made to provide them with more and better parts on stage, with the chance to have plays they wrote put on, and with opportunities to produce and direct. On this level the battle was seen as one of equal opportunities and overcoming a deeply rooted discrimination which was masked by a popular view that unconventionality and progressiveness in the theatre could be equated with emancipation for women.

Lou Wakefield, an actress who during the 1980s added writing and directing 'on my terms' to her repertoire, recalls her own struggle with this mythology: 'I had got into the West End as Janet in the *Rocky Horror Show* in 1975. I hated being dressed in underclothes on stage but I had no politics to tell me why. I had to put up with a lot of being touched and sexually harassed, sometimes to quite an obscene degree, and it made me furious, but you couldn't make a fuss. It was the swinging Seventies and we were all supposed to knocking hell out of each other and having a great time and this, we were supposed to think, was liberation.'

It was at drama school that Carole Hayman, who went on to act, write and direct, discarded the attitudes and values she had held through university where she expected and wanted to have male tutors: 'I was delighted at the notion that I was going to get away from the culture of women and into the company of grown-up people and men. I never realized how disenfranchised that made me or how incurious it made me about women and women's work . . . But when I went to drama school I found that they did plays that featured men and we got parts that were made for whores or the wife or whatever. In three solid years of work we didn't do a single play that actually featured women. I began to realize this wasn't quite it. I didn't know what was it, but I was pretty sure it should be otherwise.'

Julie Christie, who had made her name in John Schlesinger's film *Darling* in 1965 and was being offered plenty of roles, came to the realization that a part for a woman was not, *per se*, the point. In conversation with me at the end of the 1970s, she said: 'The reason I have turned down films in the last years is to do with a growing awareness, my consciousness of the political way women are used in films — the perpetuation of myths. So often the male is the functioning person and you operate through his function. For example, there is the scenario where you go through this marvellous conflict with a man which can be intelligent, political, and then you end up in love with him. There is a scarcity of films where the women's roles are making a statement about their oppression by men, although that is part of our lives.'

In saying this, Julie Christie touched on what many women saw as the vital second objective of feminism in the arts. Alongside the struggle for equal opportunities should be a commitment to representing a feminist perspective. Michelene Wandor explained it thus: 'I'm very conscious of trying to incorporate feminism in my writing. I'm committed to feminism as a political force that is actually going to change not only the position of women in society but that of society as well.'

Helene Keyssar, Professor of Drama at the University of California, observed the importance of this function on both sides of the Atlantic and in her book *Feminist Theatre* (Macmillan, 1984) she states: 'Like the early stage of the contemporary women's movement itself, the outburst of feminist plays and playwrights took consciousness raising as one of its primary goals. Parodies of stereotypes of women, role reversals, vivid imaginings of female sexuality and women's ambivalences about their bodies, were all non-reductive strategies intended to make women and men more aware of their gender-related behaviour and attitudes.'

But in order to achieve that objective, women had to find a way of controlling contents and the means of production. This, however, was impossible in the mainstream theatre. Women, happy to work according to the status quo, could progress but that was not what many feminists wanted. The solution was what it had long been for writers and performers who felt their wishes would not be fulfilled in the mainstream of theatre — to split off and put on their own shows as fringe productions. This began to happen almost as the women's movement was laying its roots.

In 1970 Midge Mackenzie staged *Me Tarzan, You Jane* at the Institute of Contemporary Arts, reviewed by Sally Wilkins in the *Daily Mail*: 'The women's revolution marches on and British Tarzans had better watch out — their Janes are getting fed up with being "sex objects". The aim of the show is to get Britain's Tarzans to think about how they are making slaves of their Janes. It will include films of women talking about the problems of being female, poetry readings and a strip routine.'

Midge Mackenzie said at the time: 'I gave the show its name because Tarzan and Jane are the ultimate stereotypes of a male-female relationship and the strip routine shows the way society puts women down. It shows the ultimate Jane — a creature programmed from childhood to win approval from men. To be a sex object.'

The following year a play by Jane Arden, *A New Communion for Freaks, Prophets and Witches*, was put on at the experimental Open Space theatre. Arden's intention, she said, was to convey, by dramatizing the interior life of a female patient: 'what it is like to be a woman in the mid 20th century.'

Following the first National Women's Liberation March in 1971, the Women's Street Theatre Group performed a play in Trafalgar Square on the theme of women's subordinated and sexually repressed place in the family. This group, unlike many others, survived and went on in 1972 to produce a show parodying the Equal Pay Act, showing what an inadequate piece of legislation it was.

Michelene Wandor, too, had committed her talents to the fringe and, describing this time later, in *Dreams and Deconstructions* (Amber Lane Press, 1980), a book on alternative theatre in Britain, she said: 'I wrote plays about the Miss World contest, and about ways in which women are trapped in the family; these were done on the art fringe and were directly related to my involvement in the Women's Liberation Movement.' The important point about the early, intensely personal, intensely political theatre was less the quality of writing or acting (although at times these *were* very good), than the fact that they were happening and demonstrating that women had things to say, were prepared to stick their necks out and say them, and do so in a medium which was so thoroughly male dominated.

Then in 1973 an eccentric, innovative American, Ed Berman, staged the first women's theatre festival at his Almost Free Theatre in Soho. It was intended as a series of events where women could come together to write, produce, direct and perform in plays by and about women. In 1973 the outcome of the venture was a season of 'women's theatre' and Michelene Wandor says: 'It was a season which had as its cohesive centre a frustration with the limited opportunities available for women, and served as a focal point for women to come together to argue about the best way to tackle the problem.'

The festival was a success in that the women involved proved their capabilities and realized ambitions which would have been well nigh impossible in the conventional theatre world, but a situation arose, as it did in many areas of feminism, whereby one group was primarily interested in demonstrating that women could compete with men in the theatre as part of a quest for equality, while others were primarily interested in purveying the feminist message.

Out of the Almost Free festival the Women's Theatre Group, generally agreed to have become one of the most interesting and successful, was formed with a mix of professional and amateur actresses. Ann McFerran remembers them with enthusiasm as a political agit-prop group: 'They would say their primary function was perpetrating the feminist message, feminist ideas, and they involved themselves in education, going round schools. They were very, very good in terms of what they set out to do politically, and theatrically they were very inventive, although

often not particularly interested in achieving stylistic excellence.'
Their first production was *My Mother Says I Never Should*, a show
with a sex education message which acknowledged that teenagers have sexual experiences. It toured schools and youth clubs
and upset some people, including the reviewer of the *Evening
Standard*. For all this they kept going and within a couple of years
they got an Arts Council grant.

It was the women's offshoot group from the Liverpool Everyman theatre company, which Lou Wakefield formed in 1978,
which generated the play *Trafford Tanzi*, subsequently made into
a television play and then a West End production. Lou explains:
'I had been on and on about the fact that there didn't seem to be
any decent plays for women and eventually the artistic director
said: "If you've got this big beef about there being no plays for
women, then you organize one, you commission one." It happened that the company were about to do a play which would use
most of the men, and leave most of the women spare. So as a sop
to us, we were allowed to organize a roadshow, a pub show. I
gathered all the women in the theatre together and included
cleaners, secretaries — everybody — and I said: "If we had a play
for women, what would it be about, what would the women be
like in it?" and everybody said things like "they'd be strong,
assertive, they'd win, they'd be the most important people" —
that kind of thing. So then we commissioned Claire Luckham to
write it and that was a success.'

The theme of *Trafford Tanzi* was women wrestlers. In it the
central character Mitzi Mueller is a 'goodie blonde', who is pretty
as well as being a wrestler. Towards the end of the play Mitzi and
her husband have a wrestling match over who should do the
housework, and Trafford Tanzi wins. She decides that subjugat-
ing another person is wrong and proposes that they share the
housework. However, when the play was taken to London, Claire
Luckham was asked to change the ending and allow Tanzi to get
revenge. It was a change which angered Lou: 'I thought it
reactionary. Feminism is pertinent to the whole human race, we
must not become oppressors.'

What she found interesting was that even in this democratic,
informal structure it was necessary to push the women performers into wanting bigger parts. Lou says: 'At the time they
really weren't ready for the kind of change I was trying to

galvanize. But some years later one of the actresses came to me and said that the experience had changed her life. I wished she had said it at the time. I felt very alone during the Liverpool years. It was a Socialist company but the men said I was divisive and diversionary because I was fragmenting the Left's struggle.'

Ann McFerran has reviewed feminist works over the past two decades and feels that her interest in the subject is important in allowing her a sympathy she does not think many male reviewers have. She explains: 'My view was that it was important to understand the point of what was being done. That did not mean saying the productions were good if I didn't think so — I was certainly critical on occasions — but I did feel passionately interested in the issues and the fact women were taking a stand, making themselves visible and letting themselves be seen and heard. And there were certain plays, such as Michelene Wandor's *Care and Control*, about the difficulties of custody for lesbian mothers, which I felt strongly needed to be reviewed by a woman. 'What was important was the ways these plays explored and celebrated women and feminism; they dealt with the many basic and complex issues arising from feminism, and in a theatrical sense they were a powerful means of consciousness raising. I felt, and still do, that as a *woman* reviewer I could take an active role. Initially men were confused by this or didn't want to know and in due course a handful became born-again feminists religiously applauding almost all that women did. I thought it interesting that when in the mid-Eighties Sharman Macdonald's play *When I Was A Girl I Used to Scream and Shout* was put on, there were just two women reviewers — myself and another. We were fairly critical, believing the time had come when it was possible to be so, while the men reviewers all praised it enormously as a feminist play.'

Around the mid 1970s other women's groups emerged which used sketches, parody, comedy and cabaret techniques rather than straight drama to convey their feminist messages. Glamour and spoofed-up sexiness were ingredients often used as a way of subverting the familiar way women appear in light entertainment. These groups indicated their anarchic intentions with such names as Beryl and the Perils, Cunning Stunts!, Hormone Imbalance, Monstrous Regiment. They were followed by the Raving Beauties and Fascinating Aida.

The early feminist theatre groups, boldly and determinedly establishing their own genre, were inspirational in creating an atmosphere in which these kind of shows were being put on. In America, Lisa Tuttle has noted, more than 100 feminist theatre groups were formed between 1969 and 1984, while Helene Keyssar calculated that between the early Sixties and the first years of the 1980s, some 300 plays by women had been published in Britain and the United States, more than half out of 'an acknowledged feminist consciousness'. The productions were not always particularly good, for polemic and proselytising, which were certainly dished up in some of them, at times meant that the plays were moribund and a long way from stylistically top class.

The members of the Monstrous Regiment company came together after being, as founder member Gilly Hanna puts it, 'purged' from John McGrath's The Belt and Braces Roadshow Company. That was thirteen years ago and although the company has no money and its members have to work individually to live, in between their own shows, they have survived and continue to put on productions. Gilly, sitting backstage at a Northern theatre where she was appearing in Dario Fo's quartet of female monologues *Female Parts*, recalled the 'somewhat haphazard' way she moved into creating a company with a commitment to women:

'I had "progressed", the daughter of nice, middle-class, Conservative voting parents from Trinity, where I led a pleasant sheltered existence, to the Liverpool Everyman theatre which was my first acting work. This was the end of the 1960s and there was a lot of Left-wing political thinking going on and it quite simply made me question everything. I was asked from there to join John McGrath's 7:84 company and then the follow-on company Belt and Braces. It was exciting in one way but terrifying in another because I had to try to catch up, very fast, on the political background to the work being done. But doing this made me look analytically at the structure in which I was working, how it functioned, and it became blindingly clear to me that all around was a battle of male egos with the chaps locking horns and carrying out stag-fighting sessions. The women, meanwhile, were of no significance until we were needed to vote or take sides on some issue. We were cannon fodder.

'The change, for me, came when, just as a production was due to go on tour, the Portuguese revolution happened and all the male members of Belt and Braces decided it was their revolutionary duty to go to Portugal. That meant they had to call on me and a group of the others who, earlier, they had purged for opposing them, and ask us to take the show on tour. We agreed. We started auditioning for the play and we got a stream of women coming for the one naff woman's part available in the play. They were extraordinary, they were talented and when they weren't working they were writing one-woman shows and other things. I just sat there saying "this is unbelievable!" And somebody said to me, "Look, you're always wittering on about women, why don't you get a bunch of them together?" So I contacted several of the women who had come in through the doors, and arranged a meeting. I remember it seemed a symbolic occasion because it was a dreadful night, torrential rain and a thunderstorm, yet every one of them got there. It wasn't completely straightforward, of course, but we did manage to establish a group and to some extent we operated as a collective, although later questions around this way of working came up, as they always do. Looking back, there were certainly moments when we were discussing something for hours, and it needed somebody to say "This is what we're doing! Come on chaps!" But that was the nature of women's organizations at that time. I think we very much wanted to do things differently from the very autocratic male way many of us had seen.

'Things really started when we applied to the Arts Council for money and a wonderful woman, Ruth Marks, said they would fund us if we could set up a tour and prove that it was viable. Three of us — myself, Mary McCusker and Chris Bowler, who are the three still with Monstrous — decided to make ourselves unemployed and doing that gave us, I think, an absolute commitment and determination to make it work.'

Monstrous Regiment got their name from a sixteenth-century pamphlet by John Knox called 'The First Blast of the Trumpet Against the Monstrous Regiment of Women', but they included men, although their base line was that there should never be more men than women on stage. The first production they put on was *Scum: Death, Destruction and Definition* about the women of the Paris Commune.

It was, Gilly remembers, an exhilarating, successful début: 'It caught a way of feeling. It happened because we read a book of documents — some educational publisher was publishing a series of various events around the French and just did these little volumes of contemporary documents. There was one in which women's clubs were listing their demands and we were going "It's a hundred years later and still we haven't got any of this stuff" — you know, education, creches, equal pay . . . The play was a success with audiences but the critics were not so keen. One, I recall, wrote: "When this fad for feminism has passed . . ." The other familiar critics' line is to damn with faint praise. These reviews begin with phrases like "unlike a lot of the strident stuff you get . . ." There's a mythology that's built up which has it that feminist theatre is about screeching harridans — in fact, I've never seen a strident play.'

The second play Monstrous Regiment produced was *Vinegar Tom* by Caryl Churchill, their next *Kiss and Kill* on the theme of violence between the sexes, which was not particularly well received.

They then tried something new, turning to cabaret, at times using quite unpleasant humour against men. The company stayed in business, going on to perform a play written for them by David Edgar, but by 1988 the original eleven people on the pay-roll had diminished to one and a half, full time, because of lack of funds, meaning that the three still involved spend more time doing work independently to earn their keep, than with Monstrous Regiment.

A tenet of Monstrous Regiment, as of most women's theatre groups, is that they should use women writers and, with the exception of David Edgar, this is what they have done. Gilly explains: 'It has been so hard for women to get work put on and there is such talent. I believe that backing women remains tremendously important.'

That has also been the view of Carole Hayman, who found herself becoming increasingly aware of the absence of women writers while working in Edinburgh in company with another actress who also felt frustrated at the lack of decent parts for women in men's plays: 'I suppose you could say we were crawling slowly towards the light. We realized something was wrong and that there must be some women doing work. We started to say things like "can't we have a women writer?" or "What about adapting such and such a book by a woman?" There was a kind of paradox in our situation because we were both completely involved in supporting the male in every possible way yet at the same time we felt the dawning of revolution with the conviction that there were more interesting things to say than in these plays by men.'

It was the experience of joining the largely male Joint Stock company which brought Carole to an angry, acute realization that women were quite simply of no interest in the male power house of the theatre world. She tells of the occasion when she asked 'Can't we do a play by a woman? We are supposed to be doing new work, encouraging new talent. We've never done a play by a woman', to which, she says, a now well-known male director, then a member of Joint Stock, replied: 'What women? There aren't any women playwrights because women haven't done anything in the world so they've got nothing to write about.'

Carole says: 'I suddenly realized what that meant in terms of men's estimation of us. And because at that meeting I had been unable to think of any women writing plays I decided I would go in search of women's work. This was about 1975 and my quest led me to Gilly Fraser who was writing plays which were all about women, and to the Soho Poly theatre where a woman with an interest in women's work was in charge. She put one of Gilly's plays on and I performed in it.

'By now I had the bit between my teeth and I had started acting in television and finding there were women writers there — impressive women.'

But for Carole it was discovering when reading for the Royal Court one weekend, the 'batch of great women's plays' — by Sue Townsend, Louise Page and Sarah Daniels — and finding those in charge of decision-making singularly uninterested, because, Carole believes, women were not seen as likely to produce the kind of theatrical fireworks which might come from a male writer, which created in Carole an absolute determination to get women's work produced. She directed Sue Townsend's *Bazaar and Rummage* at the Soho Poly and persuaded the Royal Court to let her do a reading of a Sarah Daniels' play *Ripen Our Darkness* upstairs. As other women were doing in different spheres,

Carole continued battling to be allowed to direct plays by women in various venues, and she was sharply aware of the need to apply stringent standards to the plays she was proposing: 'Women's plays were not liked, and plenty of men thought of the women writing them as frightening feminists with a capital F. But at the same time women were in the news, fashionable, and the boss-men were worried about not doing the right thing. I had a rule never to do a play I didn't think was very good. Choosing something simply because it is by a woman doesn't help anybody if it's not up to standard.

'In 1978 women's work flourished for a brief spell when everybody realized this was an "important thing". Women were coming out of the closet, as playwrights, all over the place. It was very sharp, vulgar, witty. But I think the tide has turned heavily against women and in 1988 the percentage of plays by women being put on is very low.'

But Ann McFerran disagrees: 'There are certainly not enough and if you are talking about true equality then it is still far away. But I know the Royal Court are proposing to put on several women's plays in 1989 and Greenwich will have a production of Wilkie Collins' *Woman in White* in the spring, for example. And I think with the increase in women artistic directors which has taken place recently, we will see more. But certainly it is a slow revolution.'

Caroline Gardiner's study of Arts Council revenue funding and employment among women in companies receiving Arts Council grants in England 1986, showed that just 11 per cent of works performed that year were original plays by women. The four women's names noted as being those whose work was most frequently performed were Agatha Christie, Caryl Churchill, Pam Gems and Sue Townsend.

Caryl Churchill has established herself as one of Britain's finest playwrights with a succession of plays — *Cloud Nine*, *Top Girls* and *Serious Money* — which were put on at mainstream theatres and reviewed with enthusiasm. Her early plays were, she has said, written from her own sense of pain and discontent with her life as a mother of three small children, isolated and finding it difficult to write. An awareness of woman's position in society has informed much of what she has written. But she has also tackled class oppression with a play (censored by the BBC) about the

Northern Ireland Diplock courts, and in 1987 *Serious Money* took
an excoriating, exquisitely witty look at the deification of the
world of money. She has succeeded in doing what a proportion
of the women's movement has always felt to be the ultimate goal
— established a reputation which makes gender irrelevant. And
yet speaking with Ann McFerran in 1977 she said: 'For years and
years I thought of myself as a writer before I thought of myself as
a woman, but recently I've found that I am a feminist writer. I've
found that as I go out more into the world and get into situations
which involve women, what I feel is quite strongly a feminist
position and that inevitably comes into what I write. However,
that is quite different from somebody who is a feminist using
writing to advance that position.'

Michelene Wandor, in company with Pam Gems, Olwyn
Wymark, Caryl Churchill, Fay Weldon and plenty of others,
wove her early writing around the demands of young children.
In her case the marriage had just split up and she was on her own
with two sons: 'The need to earn a living certainly pushed me
towards doing something with the thoughts and feelings which
were taking shape inside me. There was a sense of urgency,
things I very much wanted to say, and the writer in me surfaced
to say those things.' Some years on, she added to this thought: 'I
do write as a woman and I write of a particular kind of woman's
experience. I *am* more interested in women characters and
situations which tend to involve women. I can't separate the way
I try to look at things from the way I write, so I'd say I'm
conscious of trying to incorporate a feminist way of looking at
things into my work.'

Michelene Wandor had always identified herself as a Socialist
feminist, and class politics as well as sexual politics can be found
in the body of plays she has written. Helene Keyssar, writing of
her work, says: 'Wandor's dramas focus on major feminist issues
— women and work, caring for children, custody, divorce,
lesbianism. More than any single figure Wandor is responsible
for articulating and supporting the interaction of feminism,
theatre, socialism and gay liberation in Britain.' And yet,
although she had put together anthologies of women's plays,
seen a new generation of women writers such as Louise Page,

Sharman Macdonald, emerge, Michelene Wandor was not optimistic when reviewing the impact of feminist thought and
activities on the theatre:

'The pattern of what kind of play is put on, what is considered
to be serious subject matter, who really pronounces on it, who
reviews it and in what spirit, hasn't fundamentally altered. It may
sound a bit churlish saying that because even just having more
plays by women writers is a very important thing and it does
modify the landscape a bit. But it still feels very precarious.
When there is what looks like tokenism you actually don't know if
it's going to be there in ten years' time.'

By the 1980s a considerable number of women, working with
companies they had helped to bring into being, had got opportunities to direct. But it was far harder for them to move into
directing in the large theatres such as the RSC and the National,
although there were women artistic directors of small fringe
theatres.

The attitude which prevailed was, seemingly, that voiced by
Peter Hall in 1981 when he explained to a delegation of women
why there were no directors at the National Theatre: 'Name me a
single woman director that I could possibly respect.' It was a
remark which followed the début of Julia Pascal at the National
— the first woman to direct there — with her platform perfor-
mance of *Men Seldom Make Passes* in 1978, of which he wrote:
'goodness, women directors can direct just as birds can sing'.

A reporter, recording the next move of the women's delegation to the Royal Shakespeare Company, noted that: 'Their
answer was similar, if more evasively phrased: positive discrimination for women was sexist. Directors should be selected on
merit . . . '

At the beginning of the 1980s women made up less than 5 per
cent of the nation's directors brought in to work on individual
productions, and Gardiner's survey *What Share of the Cake?*,
published by the Women's Playhouse Trust in 1987, showed that
there were 34 women to 67 male artistic directors — the people
responsible for planning a theatre's style of production —
working for the 62 companies surveyed. The survey also pointed
out that 'women artistic directors are much more likely than men

to be artistic directors of touring companies, small-scale companies, theatres with small auditoria, and companies with low levels
of revenue funding.'

Women do get the opportunity to direct on a freelance basis
and it is here, Gardiner notes, that the greatest improvement in
women's opportunities can be seen. During the twelve months
preceding the research, 63 women and 77 men were employed
freelance. And although it can be argued that the reason for this
rise is that they may be considered more suitable if a 'woman's
play' is being put on, and that the 'risk' of taking a woman instead
of a man is minimized if she is only there for one production, the
fact is women are being given the chance to prove their
capabilities. A 1984 study by the Conference of Women Theatre
Directors and Administrators showed that 24 per cent of freelance directors were women and that figure is now 21 per cent
higher.

In 1975, one woman, Buzz Goodbody, did succeed in becoming a director at the Royal Shakespeare Company but she
subsequently committed suicide. She was the first woman director to work with this company and she operated in a renownedly
male environment. It has been suggested that the impact and
implacability of this contributed to her suicide. Certainly a range
of actresses over the years have commented on the difficulties
they have experienced working in a chauvinistic atmosphere. For
all that, in 1988 Di Trevis, Deborah Warner, Sarah Pia Anderson
and Garry Hynes were all directing productions for the RSC and
they told Ann McFerran that Adrian Noble and Richard Eyre
had instituted a situation where equal numbers of men and
women were involved in decision making.

In the same year the media seemed to have discovered with
delight, young, confident, determined women directors and they
were the stuff of serious articles and critiques making the point
that they were extremely able and talented. An article in *Elle*
commented breathlessly that in 1988 'suddenly it's fashionable to
employ them [women]' and profiled a number of women
directors: Deborah Warner, twenty-seven, widely considered one
of the very best directors around; Jenny Killick, twenty-seven,
artistic director of the Traverse Theatre Club in Edinburgh; Pip
Broughton, thirty, artistic director of Croydon Playhouse and
Paines Plough, a group putting on new work.

At the same time Ann McFerran was writing about Sue Dunderdale who had moved from a very successful few years as director at the Soho Poly to Greenwich, although before reaching these positions of autonomy she had been labelled 'difficult' because of her battles at her previous company with an all-male board; Jenny Topper at Hampstead; Nicky Pallot at the Bush Theatre; Di Robson at the Riverside; Annie Casteldine at Derby Playhouse and Jude Kelly running York Festival. Attempting to analyse the reason for the 'sudden spate of appointments', McFerran wrote: 'The reasons seem endless: the groundwork laid by the women's movement in the Seventies finally bore fruit. They might be confined to directing in small-scale theatres and in women's companies, but women directors in the early Eighties were gaining confidence with work experience; prestigious actresses, like Sheila Hancock and Juliet Stevenson who persistently demanded to be directed by women; research documents like *What Share of the Cake?*, demonstrating women's ludicrous lack of a statistical power base, commissioned by Jules Wright for the Women's Playhouse Trust.' It seemed that some of the hopes and strategies women had employed, could bear fruit.

Clare Venables was one of the first women to get the opportunity to direct, when, during the 1980s, she was appointed artistic director of the Crucible Theatre in Sheffield. Ironically her break did not come through a commitment to making it as a woman, on behalf of women, or to prove a woman's ability, but because she was well-educated, bright and brash — a girl in a man's world at a time when that seemed more of an amusing gimmick than a serious threat. It was only later that she began to understand how the theatre works for most women. She tells it thus: 'I remember when I graduated with a First from university and my mum said "you must be careful not to be too clever". Perhaps directing didn't seem too clever because I wasn't worried. I did a bit of directing at university and when I left I got an Arts Council bursary. I remember going for the bursary and seeing that Gwen Walford was also up for one and my reaction was "Oh damn it, there's another woman, that blows my chances". I felt sure they would never give a bursary to two women. After this I was made director at Lincoln Theatre Royal. I was always very much a woman in a man's world and I was quite happy with that. I realized at the time that so long as I did what they wanted, didn't make trouble or challenge their ideas I got on fine and fast.

McFerran noted: 'There was a big division between experimental groups and the committed feminist theatre and regional theatre where we were doing traditional plays quite a lot of the time and some new stuff, but not specifically anything to do with women. I was regarded as an Uncle Tom working in the establishment and when I went to meetings women from the "other side" would make their view plain. I remember it particularly at a women's directors' conference where I found it upsetting and I didn't know how to handle it.

'I find questions around the way women get on difficult. I feel that the best way is to be as good as you can and find a place to prove it rather than hammering on about the oppression women suffer. I honestly believe women have to do the job well and without letting the effort show. It is immensely hard and I had a breakdown after the birth of my son, doing it this way, but I believe it is how I have got where I have.

'Now I'm called a successful director and it's because I'm a woman. They wouldn't say that about a man simply doing his job well in a regional theatre. So there is still a distinction and in truth I don't think it's much easier now for women, across the board, than it ever was. The theatre has got more aggressive and competitive and when there's less cake to go around somehow women don't get the cake . . . '

Nor does Julia Pascal, who has directed for the Drill Hall in London, which has consistently put on plays by women, about women, produced and directed by women, feel too much cause for optimism. Writing in *The Guardian* in the summer of 1988, she said: 'The Old Boy system has hardly changed in State-funded British theatre. Over the past few years feminism has provoked moments of guilty reaction and the appointment of a few token women, but the power base has never really changed.'

Julia Pascal's view, given backing by shadow arts minister Mark Fisher's Labour Party conference The Missing Culture, in 1988, is that funding is the only way true change can be brought about. She would like to see organizations like the Arts Council and the Regional Arts Association refuse funding until theatres actively pursue equal opportunities. And Caroline Gardiner added her voice to this argument: 'For almost every level of appointment that might be expected to have a significant impact on theatre policy, where women hold such posts, they are disadvantaged financially, and therefore artistically, compared to men in the same posts.'

In the area of visual arts women have felt the same frustrations and handicaps as women in theatre. There is the same sense of an establishment which, quite simply, will not consider them on the same basis as men whether they are applying for jobs in institutions or offering their work for exhibition. And as with the theatre, women who see themselves as feminists, concerned with de-constructing a masculine value system and standard of aesthetics, have used their art to make their personal and political perspective public.

This was done controversially, emphatically and successfully with the exhibition of works of art by women depicting men, *Women's Images of Men*, which was put on at the Institute of Contemporary Arts (ICA) in 1980. There were pictures showing men as menacing and mean, domineering and despicable, cocksure and contemptible. Not all, by any means, but enough to give the sense that women felt sanctioned and supported in expressing feelings about male power which, individually, might have been far harder. Certainly for Argentinian artist Marisa Rueda, who works as resident artist for Hammersmith and Fulham, exhibiting was important because it attracted a good deal of reaction from the critics and the public and made her realize how, when women felt free to depict men according to their feelings, it was heavily condemned as sexist. It was, she said: 'the most important thing that happened to me professionally in England. I couldn't believe how cornered and uptight men felt and it surprised me. This exhibition opened my eyes to society's view of women artists. I began to see my work differently.'

Analysing the reactions to the exhibition, which drew a record 1,000 visitors a day, Sarah Kent (who helped to organize the event and edited the book of the same name, with Jacqueline Morreau) said: 'Collectively they [the pictures] presented a clear statement of dissent. A group of women artists was daring openly to challenge some of the basic assumptions of the culture. When a woman picks up the brush, chisel or camera and focuses her attention on the male, she invites an avalanche of patriarchal opprobrium.'

Waldemar Januszczak, writing in *The Guardian*, criticized the lack of calibre of the exhibition. This posed a crucial question: how far does the viewer's dislike of what is being done and who has done it, colour his or her ability to make a neutral aesthetic judgement? Women artists have grown used to interpreting the criticism as necessarily emanating from emotional reactions, as an attack on the subject-matter, rather than an appraisal of quality. It is one of the most difficult points of discussion which arises in the context of feminist or indeed any other specifically political work. The same questions arose over a later exhibition of work by 32 women artists, *Pandora's Box*, which travelled the country being exhibited at different venues. While a great many people attended, some critics again seemed to find women being outspoken about sexuality and oppression deeply offensive, although Pascale Petite, one of the organizers and exhibitors whose work explores the deep, psychic pains connected to being female, describes the reviews as mixed: 'Some welcomed it as a celebration, others damned it.'

In Hull the authorities insisted that a banner be put up saying that some of the work would offend parents and children. 'When has that been said about work by men and some of that is quite horrifying and grotesque,' Pascale says. 'Women commenting in an explicit and visually disturbing way is profoundly shocking, just as it always has been.'

Richard Cork, in a lengthy article about the state of the art for women, sought to be empathetic with the aim of *Women's Images of Men* and acknowledged both the point of the exhibition and that it was fair game: 'Neatly turning the tables on male art's traditional obsession with woman as an object of desire it demonstrated that men can, from now on, expect to be scrutinized in images which reveal them as aggressive and vulnerable, ridiculous and desirable, posturing and dependent.' But such rational consent was undermined with the round-up comment that women were 'obviously rejoicing in the chance to vent their stored-up spleen'.

Depicting men on their own terms may have captured the imagination of those who exhibited in the ICA show, and of the public who attended in extraordinarily large numbers, but most of the debate centres on how women artists painting about subjects which interest and seem important to them, can establish their presence.

The role of woman as mother has been the theme of a number of works, including Pascale Petite's vision of herself and her brother as foetuses growing inside their mother; Susan Hiller's document on her pregnancy; Judy Chicago's *Birth Project*, a five-year look at images of birth, which followed *The Dinner Party* in America; Mary Kelly's *Post Partum Document*, a six-part work tracing six years of her life and relationship with her son.

The reaction to these pieces of art — all dealing with a powerful and universal experience — was markedly less than could be expected if it had been dealing with an experience, such as war, perceived as universal and important by men. The subject-matter was seen as domestic — and hence trivial — and the feature which caused a riot of press reporting was the soiled nappy Mary Kelly used as just one ingredient of her entire project.

Describing what she had set out to do, Mary Kelly explained that she wanted to show that there is a moment of privilege in a woman's life, in our society, which is about the mother – child relationship, but adding: 'I'm not trying to say there's some essential feminine experience. I'm trying to look at the way femininity is produced in one specific moment or particular event.'

The issue of how far women's art should be a representation of the female experience, consciously depicting the way this differs from male experience and is hindered and handicapped by life in a patriarchal society, has been actively debated. That women have, historically, reflected their appointed role in society, whether consciously or not, is a point made by Griselda Pollock, who has written books on the experience of women working as artists. Commenting on the exhibition of *Women's Works* from the permanent collection at Liverpool's Walker Gallery, she said that the pictures were produced from 'within the socially constructed positions to which each culture assigns those it designates men and women'.

Dr Deborah Cherry sought to bring the same perspective to her exhibition *Painting Women*, which started at the Rochdale Gallery in Yorkshire and moved to the Camden Art Centre, London, in which she gathered a collection of paintings by

Victorian women depicting women and she explained the social circumstances in which they had painted, making a point about the obstacles women had to overcome in order to paint. The outraged reaction to this exhibition was remarkable when you consider that critics usually deal with small shows they do not like by either ignoring them or with a one-line thumbs down. Brian Sewell's review was a typical example, stating: 'rewritten as part of the history of feminism it becomes hysterical codswallop', and objecting to a conviction held by Dr Cherry (and others) that Victorian women did not have the same encouragement and opportunity to paint as men.

But if era and environment affect what a woman can do — and, in turn, are reflected in her work — that is not the same as a conscious decision to make work a pronouncedly feminist statement. Marilyn Crabtree, who writes on art, comments: 'Given that the predominant practices, values and knowledge systems of Western society are patriarchal it seems reasonable to assume that some of this might rub off on women artists . . . Feminist politics and theory have evolved and developed both in opposition to the mainstream and from women's direct experience and perceptions.'

The mainstream, oppressing women and protecting the interests of 'a mainly white male ruling/middle class', maintains the status quo, using its discourses and practices as a set of social tools, she argues, and to break through this, women must bring their own significance and views on to the agenda: 'By constantly insisting that our voices are articulated and heard, we can both change the shape of these tools and create and name our own, to construct a new social reality.'

That women have done this is noted and applauded by Pamela Gerrish Nunn when reviewing *Visibly Female: Feminism and Art Today* (Camden Press, 1988), a collection of writings and pictures from women artists: 'One of the most obvious achievements of the feminist art movement has been to disregard the accepted boundaries of the art world and to occupy other arenas with artwork and art criticism.' And yet it has been a difficult and isolating process in the view of Pascale Petite. Her powerful, deeply personal work concerned with exploring some part of her femaleness, most notably in *La Mère et Le Mer*, an almost life-size sculpture based on models of herself and her mother joined by a fish-net symbolizing the distance within closeness, the pain and powerlessness which bind and isolate the two women during the mother's five-year psychosis, was much criticized. She explains: 'I was at the Royal College of Art doing my final presentation. I had already had a lot of opposition from teachers because my work, from the beginning, was emotional and feminine. It seemed in some way to frighten them that I stepped into areas men don't usually touch.

'The argument put forward was that my work didn't measure up to the standards set. Of course these are based on male art. Yet there didn't seem a suitable argument I could bring up except to say that I was a woman, working on a subject which seemed very important to me and that it seemed to me the actual quality of my craft was not inferior to that of males working around me. But what can you say against the whole of the history of art?'

Helen Chadwick is an artist who has had her own exhibitions in small galleries. One of the most successful was at the White-chapel in 1988, based on cervical cells from a smear test of Helen's. It was, she explained, a way of trying to break the body down, to look at it microscopically.

Much of her work has been concerned with the body and, as other women artists have found in feminist circles, she discovered a taboo operating around the use of the female body for fear that it can become a subject of male voyeurism. Helen Chadwick, speaking with Sara Miles, said: 'The objection to using the body is that it has been so defined by male values in the past. But I feel we have to try to leave this behind and find new ways, new values. The body is the means by which we exist in the world. It is basic to human beings and it seems a very valuable starting point to define an orientation in the world, to negotiate reality with your body. It is your instrument.' She is, therefore, uneasy about the feminist label, saying: 'I cannot conceive of a thing called feminism. When I use the word I'm not quite sure what it is referring to. When I have seen or read certain things I've felt a relationship with the women and so I suppose for me feminism occurs in the exchange between people's ideas and perspectives, and it brings a kind of understanding of who and where we as women are. But what interests me most is the means of expression women are finding, the way they are articulating a position for themselves in the world, rather than living through the position already established.'

A woman artist who prefers not to be named and who is much concerned to be expressed in her own terminology because she believes the language we use can easily distort, has set herself the task of using a well-known, glamorous film-star, who represents stereotypical ideas of glamour, as an icon for much of her work. Through this figure she explores some of the difficulties she has experienced in her own life. She explains: 'My identity was intimately bound up with the requirement to give myself over actively to a sense of propriety and decorum and in my sexuality and appearance to be in good taste and decorative, at all times, in order to maintain a supportive and responsive attitude towards others.' The experience of creating an attractive image on society's terms as this woman sought to do, is a familiar problem.

It was a requirement which, she felt, meant putting the time and energy she needed for her work into fulfilling the stereo-typed feminine identity. This led to a painful crisis: 'Being the kind of artist I am involved putting the demands of my work first and accessing [making available] hither-to forbidden areas of pain, neediness, want, desire, excess, anxiety. Consequently I experienced an identity crisis for a time, a loss of identity, and my narcissism and vanity had to be undone. I felt I had to bring a work of art into the world which was in contradiction to the gendered subject that I had been raised to be.

'Feminist discussion groups, workshops, consciousness raising, gave me the support and strength and intellectual framework through which to understand my dilemma and therefore not to give in to the pressure to conform. And I find my work is talked about, criticized in feminist terms.'

As there have been and still are separatists in the fulcrum of the women's movement, although to a lesser extent than during the 1970s, so it has been in women's art circles. Some women have felt it vital to work only with women, to exhibit in exhibitions and galleries designed for women, to look to other women for comment and criticism, and the argument has been that only by doing this can the artists feel confident and supported enough to produce the art they wish to produce. Others have felt it essential to avoid being part of a ghetto, that they wish the definition 'woman' to be invisible when their art is viewed, they strive for recognition in the mainstream.

Susan Hiller, in an interview with Roszika Parker in 1974, explained her position: 'I want the art to speak. I don't want to label it — here is the work of a feminist artist. That notion has been very much degraded: to call people feminist artists is to box them off into an area which cannot insert itself, cannot contradict mainstream notions of art. Feminists are shunted off to a little side track called "Feminist Art".' Tess Jaray, speaking out four years later, said: 'Art has no gender. But women have to be given a chance to show their work. I look forward to the next generation, which will not find it in any way interesting that most of the work in an exhibition is by women.'

Ten years on, that generation still seems remote. Since 1910 there have been national exhibitions of just nine women's work, against 200 exhibitions for men. Less than half of the exhibitions supported by the Arts Council in the past five years, have featured women artists. When the winners of the 1988 Arts Council annual awards were announced no woman was among them, although women made up almost a quarter of the 670 applicants. Of seventy-one Royal Academicians just six are women. The Hayward Gallery has never held a retrospective of a woman artist, although in 1978 they selected an all-women panel to choose their exhibition of contemporary art. The panel chose sixteen women and seven men and as Lisa Tuttle has wryly observed: 'Some reviewers felt the work was of lower quality than it should have been because of this positive discrimination.'

But one of the most significant ways in which women face inequality both as workers and students is at the educational level. Within fine art education more than 57 per cent of the student population is female, yet only one woman is head of a painting department and staff female lecturers remain a rarity. Pascale Petite recalls her student days: 'There were no women teaching and that was a problem for me because my work is essentially feminine and I felt that a woman would have understood far better what I was doing. I now teach part time and the female students produce work which is qualitatively different from the male's — it's not a value judgement but it does mean that they get an understanding from me of where their work is coming from.'

Richard Luce, Minister for Arts, when questioned on this in the House of Commons, sidestepped the facts of inequality by saying: 'Any woman would take it as an insult if, in terms of artistry, she was picked on any other grounds than that of merit.' Many women felt insulted at the implication that among the burgeoning number of committed women artists so few were deemed meretricious.

But there are, manifestly, different attitudes at work. Maggi Hambling is an example of a woman being chosen in preference to a man. She was appointed as the first Artist in Residence at the National Gallery over several men contenders. Angela Flowers, with galleries in the West End and East London, has seven women artists on her books and regularly gives individual shows of the work of several of these including the popular Amanda Faulkner, Glenys Barton, Lucy Jones and sculptress Nicola Hicks, while Jo Brocklehurst has had more than one exhibition of her own in a West End gallery. In the autumn of 1988 Paula Weideger received considerable critical interest and at least one Sunday newspaper colour magazine featured her work, when it was shown at the Serpentine Gallery.

There is a growing body of literature examining why women have not been encouraged, nor had the same opportunities as men, to paint, notably Germaine Greer's *The Obstacle Race*, and also recording what they have done, as in Roszika Parker and Griselda Pollock's *Framing Feminism* (Pandora, 1987) and Pamela Gerrish Nunn's *Victorian Women Artists* (The Women's Press, 1987). Two other books worth mentioning are *Women Expressionists* by Shulamith Behr and Wendy Beckett's *Contemporary Women Artists* (both published by Phaidon, 1988).

The Women Artists' Slide Library campaigns on behalf of women artists, holds exhibitions and publishes a glossy journal which is particularly impressive in view of the small budget it must work with. They have an archive record of the work of 800 contemporary women artists and their *Women Artists' Slide Library Journal* publishes articles about the work of women, reviews of exhibitions and profiles. The organization was established in 1972 but the archive was not started until a few years later.

Pauline Barrie and Katie Peepwell explain that in the early days they were concerned with consciousness raising, discovering history and trying to adapt work strategies within organizations like the Artists' Union: 'Feminism took on an identity and these concerns became synonymous with feminist art. There have been important developments through this. Griselda Pollock's writing has put feminism on the agenda to the extent that art historians held a feminist art history conference in Brighton in 1986.

'And the most established women have come through the feminist movement. At the same time some women who have been involved in solid art practice for twenty-five years are still virtually unrecognized. The system does not support them and what you get is exceptional women being recognized as polar opposites, keeping hold of the notion of separate spheres — the feminine achiever versus the nice male genius.'

Where progress has been made is in community arts, which, W.A.S.L. say, is staffed almost exclusively by women. One reason may be that these positions are notoriously badly paid and, as has been remarked in the context of the theatre, women are found clustered in the low-paid positions. But that is not to denigrate the importance of the fact that they are there. Pauline Barrie and Katie Peepwell say: 'This has contributed to changing attitudes where the mainstream has been quite static. It is astonishing, isn't it, that a major gallery like the Hayward has not had one major retrospective of a woman dead or alive, national or international?'

The other piece of progress they point out is where women's work has been taken from basements, restored and put on display. Jane Sellars, Education Officer at the Walker Gallery, Liverpool, spent six years: 'bringing the women up from the basement.' She explains: 'While I was at the Walker I became very interested in how and what Victorian women had painted and I realized that in the nineteenth century there were thousands of women artists who were quite good and that in the collection the Walker keeps which is not on permanent display, there were some interesting women painters.' She found that, in a collection of 11,000 works, accumulated since the Walker opened in 1877, 2.7 per cent — 280 pictures — were by women. Caught up in the investigation of art history which had been going on through the early Seventies, she began to wonder why. She realized that when doing an art degree, she had learnt entirely about male artists. She subsequently read *The Obstacle*

Race and began to contemplate the role women had played in art history. Established in her job at the Walker, where she was allowed to mount exhibitions, she decided on one which would bring into public view the hidden women's paintings. The result was *Women's Works — Paintings and Drawings and Prints by Women Artists in the Permanent Collection at the Walker Gallery*, in 1988.

But if the show was designed to bring women forth it was not intended to make points, as Deborah Cherry had, about women's oppression by men and the question is begged whether this made a difference in the way the show was reviewed. Jane Sellars stressed that she did not find evidence of discrimination for or against women in the Walker's buying policy. Indeed, she says that: 'in fact the Walker in its first years was buying quite substantial, huge pictures by women. It was something of a pioneer.' She adds: 'Plenty has been said about women not having the same opportunity for an arts education as men. What I wanted to say was here are some who did well, their work is in this gallery, they did it for posterity and I'm getting it out to show you.'

Reviews for the show were, on the whole, appreciative. Steve Davies, writing in *The Times Higher Educational Supplement*, des- cribed it as: 'A forcefield of self-affirming energies . . . It is the assertive scale of these canvases, together with the level of technical competence they assume, that startles the viewer's imagination, recalling the needle's eye through which the Victor- ian woman painter must squeeze to get an education.' And Griselda Pollock specified that this exhibition demonstrated women's real ability: 'Major works which could not be and were not faulted by the establishment critics.'

Jane Sellars is now working on a book about 'the energies of women in Victorian painting', a pictorial book which will have a simple, non-polemical text, and yet, she says: 'This and all my work has been informed by the feminist ideas I've absorbed and find important. At the same time I have developed a deeper understanding of what it means to be a woman trying to develop my craft and creativity. I have a small son: I am on my own, and have to work to support him, yet my writing is important so I find myself writing until midnight because that is what has to be done.'

Marina Warner can see change and improvement in the way women are viewed because of the efforts of people like Jane Sellars and authors of books on women's art and the Women Artists' Slide Library. She has commented: 'In Britain increasing exposure for women's art has sharpened our perception that hitherto many major minor talents have been dreadfully neglected, due to gender, and that some are certainly major if not great artists.'

And as such work is validated, so it must create a greater interest in the work of contemporary women. But statistics and what we can see around us, do not give cause for much optimism. It is worth bearing in mind the words of the Labour Party's Missing Culture conference document: 'It can be argued that the disadvantaged position of women in our arts and media affects society far more significantly than in any other employing sector . . . because it is our arts and media which determine much of the agenda of public debate. If the images of and perspectives of women are under-represented there, society's prejudices are reinforced and this in turn slows down moves towards equality in other spheres.'

7

STAY OUT OF THE HAREM

WOMEN AND JOURNALISM . . .

'IT's easy to underestimate the value of _The Guardian_ women's page because it's become something of an institution, a joke even, but I know it's too important to be eroded or lost. It's the only mass circulation newspaper where women are allowed to stand up and be proud of their sexual politics' — Brenda Polan, editor of Guardian Women, 1988.

'_The Guardian_ women's page's "overt" commitment to feminism is too precious to be diluted' — letter from a reader, 1982.

The vexed question of whether women's pages are a good thing or not, whether they ghetto-ise women or validate them and their concerns by giving a serious allocation of space, has been going on since the term 'women's page' was used, apparently for the first time, of a column written by Jane Cunningham Croly in the American _New York Dispatch_, in 1859. In the past two decades feminists have brought the debate high on to the agenda. In looking at these pages they rarely found that a 'women's page' implied the reporting of serious women's issues, but was a page specially designated to women according to a male-devised idea of what women want. Traditionally these pages have been choc-a-bloc with advice on cooking, fashion, beauty advice and other subjects assiduously avoiding in the ghetto anything so demanding or stressful as political matters affecting the outside world. But there is one place where the mainstream press and feminism have traditionally and consistently found a platform, and that is on _The Guardian_ women's page.

It is true that other serious newspapers now carry important articles for women and about women which could as well be found on *The Guardian* women's page, but it is equally true that they will vary these with articles which may knock the tenets of feminism or be openly dismissive and disparaging of it. Nor would these papers wish to have a feminist flag attached to the pages they target at women. Twenty years on, feminism is still tantamount to a four-letter word to many male executives, even though they may concede that articles dealing with issues espoused by feminists, are topical or worth carrying.

One woman editor on the section of a serious Sunday newspaper aimed at women but painstakingly avoiding a feminist stance, explains her predicament: 'I would be very happy to do what *The Guardian* has done and stand up proudly saying feminism is important to women and we should acknowledge support for it, but to most of the male executives over me, *The Guardian* women's pages are anathema. Articles about serious women's issues, or things like poverty or wife abuse, which clearly are informed by feminism, tend to be treated like the dreadful relative you are obliged to have to stay from time to time. If I try to put in many such articles, or opinion pieces by women who have a feminist approach, so that the fun and frivolity gets cut back, I am quickly rapped over the knuckles.'

The reason why *The Guardian* women's page has succeeded in establishing itself as the one newspaper page where feminist writers feel they are welcome as both subjects and as writers, and where their thoughts and ideas will be treated with honesty and dignity, may have less to do with a sympathetic attitude from the men in power — the incumbent editor Peter Preston once told a former women's page editor that he had had enough of gynaecology on the women's page and wanted some easy-on-the-eye blondes, while another executive has openly stated his wish to kill this page off — than with history.

When the women's page on what was then the *Manchester Guardian* was first started in 1922 it carried articles by such women as Winifred Holtby and Vera Brittain. Mary Stott became the women's editor in 1957, pronouncing herself: 'a convinced feminist since my young days', and aimed to create a page which dealt with the serious issues she saw affecting women, with their inequalities and rights, and which reflected them as intelligent, thinking beings. While other newspapers were instructing women in crafts and cooking, the latest child-rearing methods and ways to keep a husband happy, Mary was establishing a campaigning page which won both her and *The Guardian* a formidable reputation. She established the women's page as something specific, exceptional and whether you loved it or loathed it, a hallmark of *The Guardian* and its avowed interest in justice and open-mindedness.

Not that *The Guardian* women's page has kept all of the feminists happy all of the time — far from it. Successive editors of what was tagged, from within, while I was there 'the head above the parapet slot', have received mailbags of letters bursting with anger, irritation, disgust, disappointment at articles which have seemed to certain women to be reactionary, hostile to the interests of feminists or simply not strongly enough worded.

Frances Cairncross, editor of the page for three years, put to paper her thoughts on the proprietorial nature of some readers: 'The advantage of devoting a daily page to women is that at least there is a regular flow of articles about women and for women into the paper — and they are chosen by a woman rather than by a male features editor.

'The drawback is more subtle. Unlike any other page in the paper, the women's page operates within a political commitment. This is not the result of editorial pressure from above, but of the combined weight of views of the people who work on the page, who write for it, and of its most vocal readers. The result is a *cordon sanitaire* around the page — there are views which it is considered appropriate for it to express, and views which it is not.' And certainly some readers objected to this. Julia Rahmer from North London wrote: 'It would be a great improvement if problems could be aired on the basis of facts and desirable ends, instead of entrenched feminist (and often prejudiced) views that may actually miss the point.'

Getting the formula of the page right has been a continuing dilemma for those in charge, but for most who have held the editorship over the past couple of decades it was important to give space to covering events, activities, philosophizing, and the impassioned first-person pieces.

It was Jill Tweedie who, in *The Guardian*, wrote the first feminist column for a mainstream newspaper and indeed there has not been another since which has seized the hearts and minds of so many women, nor galvanized such a committed audience or such a prodigious response. It was a column of enormous vitality, humour, fury, which was to last for seventeen years and which brought a wonderfully accessible analysis of the *raison d'être* of the women's movement. For many women not actively involved, it was a public voice echoing and validating their often unspoken feelings. Reflecting back on why she was able to touch so large a female nerve, Jill said: 'I came to feminism late, aged thirty-two, and I think it was all important that before I became a journalist I had been married, had children, divorced; many of the things the women's movement was concerned about had touched my life and seemed passionately important to me.'

Jill Tweedie's column boosted *The Guardian's* circulation and attracted many readers to the women's page, but that did not make it popular with those in charge. She says wryly: 'The men didn't like it, but because it was valuable to the paper, clearly it would have been absurd to axe it. There wasn't loud opposition but a kind of closing of ranks when I went in and remarks like "here she comes in her jack boots again".'

Nor have women's page editors had it so easy when carrying reports or analyses of women's feminist activities. Suzanne Lowry, a forceful and highly intelligent woman not easily brow-beaten, who edited for some years, would nevertheless emerge from conference on many occasions exhausted by the effort to convince the almost entirely male daily conference at which the content of the next day's paper was discussed, that she should be allowed to run a provocative feminist piece.

Brenda Polan tells how Liz Forgan, then in charge of the page, was offered an article on the case for separatism: 'She found it utterly fascinating, totally readable and did not agree with it. But she went to the conference and explained that she had this article putting the argument for a life lived totally apart from men. The editor did not agree with it. Liz had to go back with it several times, but she is a fighter and eventually she prevailed and the piece ran and the mail poured in . . .'

Brenda, articulate, witty and given to irreverence, is as committed to what the page stands for as any of her predecessors have been, but she also believes that the approach of the page has had to change and explains: 'The time for running polemic is over. The basic debate has taken place and, to a certain extent, with younger women, there's boredom. The whole thing about history, sociology, being amazed at the fact that a woman can get to a boardroom or be an engineer has had its time, you have to take it as read. I don't want to be running any more pieces about what it's like being a woman travelling alone and being given a table by the gentleman's lavatory. I like to think we have heard and been appalled by these things but that, also, we have moved on to be able to cope better, to feel more confident about who and what we are. It's been said, the basic feminist analysis is there and I think the point now is to go forward, bearing this analysis in mind. I am aware that there are debates and struggles going on on various fronts and that they have to be covered each time, but it must be done in a fresh, readable way. It's a question now of finding a way of creating a balance between men and women, so women get profiled and their work taken seriously just as happens to men elsewhere. And the quality of writing is as good, as informed, as serious as elsewhere in the paper and that is very important if women and their issues are to be valued properly.'

Yet before the women's movement was much more than a whisper from across the Big Pond, an Irish, convent-educated girl who reckoned that if you weren't pretty and hadn't been to Eton, you needed a lot of cheek and push to get on, persuaded June Levine, then commissioning editor on the *Irishwoman's Journal*, to let her write provocative, controversial stuff about women's feelings and urges. This was the beginning of a writing career which won Mary Kenny a reputation as a bold, committed feminist. June recalls: 'Here was the beginning of a new type of journalism for women. This would be the reportage of subjective reality rather than the external happenings of the day. Kenny, I thought, had a new concept of journalism.' A couple of years later she became Women's Editor on *The Irish Times* and it was this homecoming after some years spent abroad and in London which she looks back on as the catalyst for the fiercely feminist pages she edited. She says: 'I think it was a shock effectively going back to the 1950s and seeing all these anti-diluvian laws, the ways in which women were really held down and had no rights. It was obvious there was a need there and I got a tremendous response from all sorts of women. But if I'm honest I think I was also motivated by vanity and exhibitionism.'

Whatever the motivations, June Levine remembers the sense of excitement at the revolution having hit the formerly staid women's page: 'Almost immediately the women's page became so controversial and downright readable that it was often the biggest event of the day. Mary had two brilliant young Left-wing journalists, Anne Harris and Rosita Sweetman, on her staff. They both tackled sociological subjects in a way that needed doing and had never been done before in a women's page in Ireland.

'I was a freelance journalist by the time Mary came to the Irish press and it was great to work for her. The Women's Liberation Movement followed in the wake of Mary's established women's page and she used the page, as did other women's page editors, to further the cause. . . .'

It was ironic, then, that someone whose importance is so clearly put on the line, should have become in Mary's own words 'a renegade'. Today feminism is given virtually no quarter in the column she writes for *The Sunday Telegraph*, nor in articles she writes for other publications, while a traditional, reactionary, *Kinder-Kirche-Küche* approach to matters is the prevalent flavour. And plenty of feminists could and do see a particular disgrace in her having established herself comfortably and successfully and then deciding she wants no more of the struggle by women who have not been so fortunate. But what brought about a *volte face* which means that today she says: '*The Sunday Telegraph* readers don't know much about my feminist youth, and they see me now as the Catholic voice standing up for good Christian moral tradition'?

It was having children which, quite simply, altered Mary's vision of what she wanted in life. Feminism which had seemed the way towards fulfilment no longer appeared that way. It was a shift of perspective so absolute, she says, that she could not in any conscience have gone on writing as a feminist.

She explains: 'I was a lapsed Catholic and I went back to that when my first son was born in 1974. I wanted him baptised. I was overwhelmed. I wanted to worship and I was suddenly full of questions, nothing seemed very clear. It was having been so involved with the growth of feminism which is a way of discovering, it makes you ask who am I? what is life for?, which led me on to the new path of questioning. Because I was very fulfilled being a mother, I gave up my job on the *Evening Standard*, to have time at home, and then my second son was born and feminism didn't seem to be about me and my values. It seemed to be at odds with what I wanted and this applied particularly to my wish for religion, because the *filum bonum* of religion is, in the end, acceptance, accepting wisdom, accepting life as it is. Whereas feminism is about changing things, about saying I won't accept, I'll change. That is the fundamental contract and it no longer seems to me so clearly the way to make women's lives better.

'Of course I'm seen as a renegade and for eight years my former friends in the women's movement were very alienated from me — who can blame them? When you've publicly aligned with people, helping to lead the crusade so publicly and noisily, obviously they'll be furious when you change your mind.'

It is not difficult to imagine how galling many feminists find it to rely on the mainstream press to present, publicly, what they are doing and saying. For the press has got a great deal of mileage out of mocking, misinterpreting, misunderstanding what the women's movement has been about. They — mostly, but not entirely, the tabloids — have delighted in belittling 'Women's Lib. loses out' stories, they have invented a shorthand for any woman involved in any feminist activity regardless of how she looks or behaves, which is based on a core vocabulary: butch, hefty, strident, dungaree-clad, crop-headed, shrill. Feminists have been described as 'a formidable sisterhood', 'animal girls', 'bovver girls' and plenty more. But while nobody would claim that papers like *The Sun*, the *Star* and more recently the despicable *Sport*, have improved one iota over the years, it is cheering to find the broadsheet dailies all running news about women and pages which at least mix serious women's issues with the frothier material. The trend was noted in 1977 by Pat Barr in *Is This Your Life?* (Virago, 1977), a book about images of women in the media, which dealt with newspapers. She said: 'It is clear that, at all levels of the press, on-going and serious discussion about women's situation in society today increases yearly. More space is allotted to subjects that are considered to be of special interest to women readers.'

Yvonne Roberts, a freelance journalist and a features editor on the now defunct *London Daily News*, argued her case for placing features dealing with matters of interest to women — which would normally have been consigned to a particular page — throughout the paper, including the editorial and leader pages. She explains: 'My attitude is that issues which appear to be about women and for women are considered peripheral but in fact they are very central. Things like child benefit, caring for others in the community, the pleasure of children, whether women are safe on the streets, the culture women are producing, actually affect men as well and are, I think, of interest to them. But once men see something on a page they know is aimed at women I don't believe they see it applying to themselves in the way they may when it's amongst stuff about politics or things called hard news.

'I also wanted to have a specialist reporter on women's affairs, just as papers have specialists on industry or social services. At the time the GLC Women's Committee was in existence and there were a lot of women's activities which justified coverage but somehow didn't get on to news schedules. I didn't win that one and I'm not sure the climate is right now, but I do see these kind of initiatives as a way forward.

'Meanwhile, I know all the discussion about women's pages and that they are a ghetto and there is some truth in that, but my view is you don't give anything up until you have replaced it with something else. If we lost women's pages it would be all too easy for matters which concern women to filter away again. I am still convinced it was the right thing, but as Maxwell closed the paper we shall have to see if someone else will have another try.'

Women's writing and women's pages have thrown up their own dilemma for feminists. On the one hand the growth of material about and for women has meant more opportunities for them as writers and in many cases has given them a break they would not have got in other parts of papers, but on the other hand it has led to women being seen as specialists in women's writing and not suitable for other types of journalism.

Angela Phillips, who writes for several newspapers on women's health and child-care issues, is being honest, not modest, when she says: 'I think it is most unlikely I would have been successful as a journalist in a world which was not prepared to carry articles on subjects of importance to women. Quite simply it over-whelmed my life for many years and coloured my thinking and feelings thoroughly. It would not have been easy for me to switch from that to either traditional womansy subjects or male-conceived hard news.'

Another woman who writes for 'any paper that doesn't have a page three girl and doesn't distort my copy' feels that because the women's movement has been about serious, real, often topical matters, it has allowed journalists to write in a simple, authoritative style whereas, she says: 'In the past when the only work I could get was writing about women doing flower arranging, or acting in some silly one-bit show which had no story but made a "good" picture and my writing was as silly as I felt the subjects to be.'

Certainly during my quarter of a century in journalism I have seen the ghetto-syndrome at work and have seen how difficult it usually is for women to move beyond the 'feminine' confines of women's journalism in the way men move effortlessly from specialization to specialization, or to general news and feature jobs. But there has been a sign of some change here. Veronica Wadley on *The Daily Telegraph* is in charge of a range of features which includes the pages for women; Brigid Callaghan on *The Times* is in the same position, having been promoted from control over women's pages alone. Eve Pollard, one-time women's editor, now edits the *Sunday Mirror*. Suzanne Lowry, who when she was first looking for a job in London, was warned by the then *Times'* women's page editor, Susanne Puddefoot, 'stay out of the harem because once you are in you'll never get out', went on to edit the women's sections on *The Observer* and *Sunday Times*, after which she got a features editing job on the *New York Herald Tribune* and later became French correspondent for *The Daily Telegraph*. During the Eighties it suddenly became the thing to appoint women as editors of newspaper colour supplements, a job which had, traditionally, been almost without exception held by men. It could have been interpreted as a sudden realization of the value of women in high places or an ideological gesture — it was neither. As the colour supplements cut back their newsy, foreign, out-in-the-wilds-getting-the-difficult-story content, and the focus became home-based, with articles about lifestyle and home decor, cooking for parties and loads of fashion and bodystyle, women were put in the editorial chairs. The supplements were targeting hard at women, but women who ran the domestic domain on something more than a shoestring, and enjoyed spending on their environment; women who were making strides in their glitzy careers, with plenty of disposable income in their purses, and an appearance to keep up. Becoming the editor of one of these colour supplements didn't turn out to be quite the triumph for equality it might have seemed.

Felicity Green, known affectionately as the alma mater of journalism, was the first woman (and one of the very few ever) to reach the board of a national newspaper. She spent twenty years with the Mirror group of newspapers, five of them on the main board. Men were very supportive when she first joined, and during her years on the 'lower rungs', and they were not unpleasant as she climbed, she says, but she became aware of a certain frisson, a feeling that too much of this should not be allowed to happen. Having reached the top she worked hard at drawing in women.

There were, she says: 'Some excellent and worthwhile finds, but there were also some disappointments and it was important for me to be able to acknowledge these. You don't help women generally by allowing lower standards in someone just because she's a woman. That way it gets said that women cannot do the job as well as men. But I am disheartened at how little headway women have made since I got that position. I would have liked to think a lot of women would have been appointed to newspaper boards, there is certainly the ability around, and I would have thought we should have an editor of a national daily by now. Women's pages have been very important for women because they have allowed them to make decisions, have control, learn how to run things, and then when they do get another opportunity they can cope.'

Battling to make a mark within the established press, to get an executive position as a way of impacting more powerfully on editorial content, is a path some women have chosen — although plenty of women who do get promoted have no interest in espousing feminism or changing the agenda. But others have recognized that this is at best a long, hard way to achieve the sort of press they want and believe in, and at worst a hopeless quest. So some women have channelled their energy into producing publications which speak passionately and in polemical terms, publications through which women can speak directly to other women, knowing they share a common concern. Many of these publications have been run on the tiniest of budgets, written and produced on a voluntary basis and their circulation has been organized the best way possible without a formal structure.

Among the earliest were *Shrew*, *Red Rag*, which was aligned to the Communist Party, *Women's Report*, a feminist news service, *Wires*, the *Socialist Women's Voice*, and *Socialist Woman* which had a revolutionary Marxist line on feminism, and a bit later came *Outwrite*, and *Trouble and Strife*. These publications were intentionally persuasive and campaigning and few were interested in attempting dispassionate balanced journalism.

Dena Attar, writing in *Trouble and Strife*, explains why such publications were so important to women just finding their individual strength through activities in the women's movement: 'Countless women have experienced the impact of such direct writing and found it useful in our personal lives . . . the Women's Liberation Movement could hardly have existed without it. A lot of us can remember the effect of reading for the first time books and pamphlets which were full of anger but also gave us a sense of our own power.'

Angela Phillips and Anna Coote were founders of *Women's Report*, a well-produced black and white magazine which set out to report on all issues concerning women, to highlight important activities and events and give the kind of information not easily found elsewhere. There was foreign news, art reviews, writing on health and mind and on stereotyped women's images, and a wonderfully entertaining section called 'And a Free Consciousness-Raising Session To . . .' in which examples of sexism and bad practice were included. For example: 'Congratulations on her superb impersonation of Sally Oppenheim to Shirley Williams MP who never fails to preface a speech about women with the disclaimer that they are no worse off than any other oppressed group (by which she presumably means working-class men, blacks, the disabled, gypsies, rheumatic bank managers and the victims of blood sports), and with warnings that we should not take "the women's libs too seriously". Mr Leo Abse, one of the biggest private members around, for his book on Parliament suggesting that women politicians are motivated by penis envy, and describing the original members of the Abortion Law Reform Association as "intelligent, shrill viragos". The Pope has just announced that nuns and laywomen will in future be allowed to distribute Holy Communion — provided there is no male clergy around, or all the male clergy is ill, or there are so many communicants that the male clergy is desperate for help.'

Angela Phillips and Anna Coote founded *Women's Report*, Angela says, because the mainstream press were too often lampooning, misrepresenting and displaying mass prejudice about women's activities; and they did not present the news and information of interest to feminists.

In 1972 with £2,000, a great deal of optimistic conviction and bags of naiveté, Marsha Rowe and Rosie Boycott founded *Spare Rib*. Marsha can bring to mind, vividly, the day after a meeting at which it was decided they should start a magazine which would 'reach out to women and would test our own capabilities', going along to a distributor and committing themselves to producing the first issue in six months' time. 'It felt as though we were brave and insane but we recognized very well what a wonderful opportunity it was. From that moment on it was non-stop work. All sorts of well-known writers like Fay Weldon wrote for us, for no money, and women volunteered fascinating accounts of their own experiences. We started out with a fashion and cookery page but they were never quite sure what we wanted and in due course they got dropped. I don't think we had any idea of how long we might be able to keep going. The thing was to make the most of this wonderful opportunity, to produce the sort of magazine we as women wanted.'

In 1987 *Spare Rib* celebrated a decade and a half of growth with a circulation of 22,000. Although it has not compromised its committed feminist editorial policy by taking any but the most appropriate advertising, during the years the magazine has apparently bowed to the pressures of stand-appeal and gone for a glossy colour cover and a sharp new layout which, interestingly, gives the news and feature content a greater sense of urgency and bite than in the earlier days.

During the Eighties other feminist magazines were launched. *Feminist Review*, an academic magazine published three times a year, carried long, serious articles exploring different attitudes and perspectives on particular issues or bringing carefully researched information on a specific theme to the reader, and is widely held to have established itself as an important source of feminist thought and debate. In 1985 Barbara Rogers, who had been involved with the Women's Liberation Movement for many years and has written several books on women, launched *Every-woman*. Barbara described it as a magazine about women, *for* women but which does not have feminism stamped all over it. 'We do not want to be doctrinaire. We know there are women who have been put off the word feminist by the way it has been presented and we would like them to see the magazine as being for them too. That said, we do speak out on issues like pornography, women's rights, things like sexist advertising, and, yes, our language could be called feminist — I would call it pro-women.

'The point of *Everywoman* was to have a news and feature magazine which would cover the subjects found in the papers — and elsewhere — from a female perspective. If you read news reports they are almost all written by men, in male language, and they seem almost to say women need not apply themselves. Women are interested in everything but they don't want to be invisible in the news and they don't want to hear a constant clamour of men's voices informing them. Journalism for and about women is very important, particularly in a climate where so much is being done to push women's progress backwards. It *is* a way of making women feel strong, supported, part of a community which includes their own kind.'

On 8 May 1988 *The Mail on Sunday* carried a glossy, colour fronted supplement devoted to the Post Feminist Woman, an example of sleight-of-hand journalism which purported to be praising the wonderful products of two decades of feminism, women who no longer needed any of that nasty bra-burning, butch, strident nonsense but who had learnt how to make it for themselves feminine-style. It was full of glossy, glamorous pictures of women and drooling descriptions of short skirts, sleek stockinged legs, tousled hair, pillar-box red lips and high heels. But these were no dimbo bimbos, we were told — they apparently had brains like needles and executive jobs with minimum salaries of £30,000. What's more, they said reassuring things like 'I don't really feel I am fighting for feminism because I'm not really sure what the fight is about' . . . 'And if this is a man's world I haven't noticed.' And so on.

The only credit in all this must go to Sue Margolis who sounded a lone, salutory voice dissociating herself from the general message and saying: 'I'm still trying to be just a feminist, forget the Post.' And she added: 'I would like nothing more than to take whoever invented the phrase Post Feminist Woman and send him — I'd rather believe it was a man — eight and a half months pregnant, tired and frightened with another child tugging at his skirts, to an ante-natal clinic. . . . The PFW is nothing new. Women who crave success have always grasped the necessity to be frighteningly bright, hard-working or pretty — and preferably all three. There have always been the canny — some would say cowardly — who agree to live by the rules men lay down. They cop out. They dress provocatively, smell of Coco perfume and know that male employers like them to be bubbly. Post Feminist Woman needs to bubble. It stops her being branded a "libber" — and who wants a dyke in the boardroom?'

This attempt to point to some unchanged and unchanging truths was presumably put in to supply journalistic balance but it was conspicuous that the picture of Sue Margolis, a nice, straightforward looking woman with short hair and, apparently no make-up, was presented postage-stamp size in contrast to the blonde-haired, gleaming lipped model advertising the PFW tee-shirt alongside.

On the surface it was all a bit of good, harmless fun of the kind the tabloid newspapers particularly like — pretty pictures of women looking the way they think women ought to look, and, because it is fashionable for the fairer sex to have a brain, with that added ingredient. But this soothing reassurance that the status quo really does live on, that all those rampant viragos have been put in their place and girls still want to be girls is not harmless.

Scratch the surface and supplements like this are plain sinister. There are still millions of women in Britain living in poverty, women with few prospects struggling to make ends meet; women who could not afford a fashionable mini-skirt, and would not get near an executive suite. There are also women who don't want to have to achieve success by playing the male game, dressing according to a male construct and, denying the validity of feminism. Neither of these types of women was of course acknowledged in the *Mail on Sunday* supplement. Yet such subversive, reactionary articles, which set out to make women who fight male domination, who do not want to model themselves according to a retrogressive stereotype, seem passé and unpleasant, poses as journalism for women.

8

SOME ARE MORE EQUAL
THAN OTHERS

EQUALITY, LEGISLATION AND
WOMEN AT WORK

IT was Barbara Castle, then Secretary of State for Employment, who guided the Equal Pay Act through Parliament in 1970. She did it with alacrity, determined, she said, that it should be on the statute books before the forthcoming election. But that apparent dedication to justice for her own kind was somewhat undermined by her speech at the National Labour Women's Conference when she said: 'I don't think women have any right to equal pay unless they stir themselves up and exert their rights. I am providing a statutory framework, not spoon-feeding. It is all very well to say you want it now. Your patience has not got you very far over the past eighty-three years.'

They were harsh words and scarcely fair in view of the fact that the women's movement had been campaigning actively around this issue for some time. But more significantly, Mrs Castle was giving voice to an attitude which is historically enshrined, that women should not by right be entitled to the same remuneration as men. Otherwise why should women have to stir and exert themselves to achieve something which in any egalitarian scheme of things must be right.

But we don't start anywhere near that position, points out Elizabeth Watson, who has worked all her life in catering and has seen how men and women are paid differently as a matter of course even though the work they do may be similar. She says: 'The idea of unequal pay is conveniently wrapped in the cosy view of women as being meant to stay at home and make nests, and the idea is that they are rewarded with love and appreciation for doing so. Why, with all those perks, should they need equal pay when they do go out to work?'

Janet, who was involved in campaigning for equal pay, finds it depressing but unsurprising that the matter of equal pay did not immediately grab the public as right and proper: 'At the root of the opposition — or the indifference — to this issue is, I am sure, a fear which has haunted the women's movement from the beginning, that if women earn equally with men and have economic independence, they won't need men and the implications of that are clearly awful.'

Writer Nicholas von Hoffman acknowledged the underlying male fears too: 'A man's wife shouldn't work but if she does she shouldn't make as much money. Otherwise he would suffer a loss to his male pride. There is a layer of brutality in the way most of us think about women.'

But few of Von Hoffman's gender compatriots were so candid about the real reasons for antagonism to equal pay. The arguments which had always been put forward were straightforward economic ones and they were argued as though the fundamental injustice was of no concern. The TUC had first called for the same wages for the same work in 1888, although they have been much criticized for not doing so subsequently during the 1970s. In the words of Rabbi Julia Neuberger: 'We should have beaten up the trade unions for not supporting us in the early days of the equal pay struggle.' In 1950 the International Labour Organization floated the idea of equal pay for work of equal value. From then on it was hotly argued that this would be too costly, and many women chose pragmatism, and presumably a bid for self-preservation, rather than join in the struggle. In 1971 Kate Wharton in *The Daily Telegraph* voiced a fear many women felt, that the Equal Pay Act might well backfire. She wrote: 'To bring in equal pay in a world of rising unemployment is to pave the way for immediate discrimination against women. For the truth is we get the jobs we do because we are cheap.'

Patricia Ashdown-Sharp, writing in *The Daily Mail*, argued along similar lines: 'Beyond equal pay — what? By 1975, when equal pay should have been implemented under the legislation introduced, an 87-year old battle will have been won. But at what price? No one disputes the desirability of equal pay as a principle. Many injustices will be removed. But there are dangers. And the greatest one is that equal pay might actually reduce the number of jobs open to women . . . many women realize that in jobs where women and men are interchangable an employer will probably prefer to take on a man rather than a woman . . .'

Rabbi Julia Neuberger was not so compliant. She recalls: 'My feminism started with the idea of economic inequality. I was quite involved in the Labour Party from an early age and got interested in the equal pay issue in the mid Sixties. I was horrified when I realized how great the gap between men and women's earnings was. I felt and continue to feel that nothing can really be right until women have economic independence and until equal pay is accepted as a human right.'

When the Equal Pay Act first came in, some ten million women were in work, although then as now almost half — three million six hundred thousand — were in part-time employment. At that time their earnings were 66 per cent of men's. But between 1970 and 1975, the period allowed for implementation of the Act, employers dealt with situation in their own companies where there was clearly inequality, and women's earnings went up to 74 per cent of men's. By 1978 that figure had crept up to 75 per cent. But since then it has slipped back below the 1975 level.

The Equal Pay Act applied only to jobs where women were actually working alongside men, doing the same job but at a lower rate of pay, or work which had been assessed as the same under a work evaluation scheme. It was not going to deal with the problem of the large number of women in segregated jobs categorized as something other than the jobs done by men, where they felt they were doing work of the same value as men's but earning less. Although there was criticism that this was not built into the Act immediately, women were to wait fourteen years for this reform.

Confronting this criticism on BBC radio Barbara Castle explained why: 'It was intended to be a starting point: apart from anything else, I only got Cabinet agreement to this in 1969 and we were heading for a General Election and in case we lost that election I wanted to get an Equal Pay principle on the statute books. So we didn't have as in depth a preparation as I would have liked, but the women's officer of the TUC, with whom I had

had discussions, was delighted with it because it was a break-through.'

Many women felt the same. The Act might not be perfect but it was an important symbol of commitment to equal pay for women, and many women who had campaigned about the issue believed that once the Act had been established, it would then be possible to battle on for amendments and improvements.

Ruth comments: 'Suddenly it was there on the statute book, that to whatever great or small degree, women were entitled to equal pay. And when, as I had, you'd been involved in women's liberation battles, attempting desperately to get people to grasp the idea that women's rights were not about wild viragos wanting to bump off all men and run the world, but about being treated fairly, it seemed momentous. Oh yes, we celebrated.'

One of the most significant ways women's pay has successfully been kept lower than men's is through work segregation, a pattern which was established historically. Susan Yeandle (*Working Women's Lives: Patterns and Strategies*. Tavistock, 1985) points out: 'Before industrialization the tasks performed by all but the youngest children were clearly differentiated by sex and young girls were taught the domestic, agricultural and other skills considered appropriate for them.' They were not generally taught the skills and crafts which men learned and which were eligible for higher rates of pay. And when, during the mid-nineteenth century, women and children supplied all but a quarter of the labour in the textile industry, the men working alongside them still earned more. Added to this, as women were assumed to be in charge of the domestic tasks, an arrangement Yeandle describes as 'buttressed by an ideology of family life which has maintained women's subordinate position', they could not travel far to work, nor could they be available the same hours men could. Their bargaining power was not great, and many needed work, so employers were able to get them for a meagre wage. 'A wage which was not sufficient for them to support themselves and their children, hence their dependence on men', Yeandle points out.

It is a situation which has many parallels with the lot of nearly half of Britain's women workers in 1988, who are employed part-time. Part-time work has little employment protection, few opportunities for progress or improvement and is usually badly paid — sometimes very badly. Many women choose it because it is the only work available or which will fit in with their domestic lives. While this *may* be satisfactory where domestic lives conform to the euphemistic picture of the husband, wife and 2.4 children making up a well-functioning nuclear unit, it is not satisfactory for those women who are unhappy in their marriages and would like to be economically free, who suffer domestic violence, but who cannot afford to go. Nor can it be fair to the women in the one-in-three marriages which do end in divorce (many of whom are never given maintenance money) so that there are women heading more than 800,000 single-parent families. Both the First and Second World Wars drew women into work which was often more exciting and challenging than anything they had done before, and with it came a sense of being equals as they worked alongside and enjoyed comradeship with men.   Jacky Burgess, one of the women whose memories appear in Eric Taylor's book *Women Who Went to War* (Robert Hale, 1988), recalled the excitement of being in the ATS, aged twenty-five, in 1942. She worked for intercept wireless, travelling across the globe, and decoding messages — a challenging contrast to the job she held before as a bank clerk. When the war was over she applied to Cable and Wireless, hoping for a job as a ship's wireless operator. She was told all the jobs had gone to men and talking of this, said: 'I do feel that we women were doing such invaluable work at the time which has never really been recognized. I remember when I was demobbed it felt like an empty stretch ahead. No one seems to have any memory of us and the work we did.'

But remembering women as courageous, capable and with a stamina to match men's, was not what was needed once peace had come and there were homes to be re-built, men to be looked after, children to be born. Women were expected to revert to putting domestic life first. For all this there was a rapid development in women's employment in the post-war years. At first the bulk of jobs were filled by single women but throughout the 1950s and 1960s the number of married women increased steadily. The jobs available to them, however, were only in traditionally female areas such as the service industries, manufacturing and offices, and, as the welfare state was developed, in teaching, social services and health — but not in the significant managerial and professional level jobs.

Nor was there any sense that women should be treated fairly in the workplace as Coote and Campbell (*Sweet Freedom*, 1982) noted: 'Nothing hindered the steady progress by which women were eased out of skilled jobs throughout the twentieth century.' In the first sixty years of this century, women's share of skilled and better paid work dropped by almost half while correspondingly their share of unskilled work increased by more than 20 per cent. Nor has equality legislation changed this. Susan Atkins, a lecturer in law at Southampton University, has pointed out: 'Research shows that occupational segregation of women at the lowest levels of pay and responsibility is greater than in 1975.'

The Sex Discrimination Act, much heralded as the mechanism by which women could deal a legal body blow to anyone who discriminated against them because they were female, became law in 1975. It made discrimination unlawful in employment, training, education, the provision of goods, facilities and services and in the disposal and management of property.

Carolyn Faulder, who went on to be much involved in campaigning for the Act, recalls going to interview Joyce Butler, MP, who was putting forward a sex discrimination bill, for *Nova* magazine: 'I remember saying I couldn't see why we needed a sex discrimination act when women had already got the vote. She said, very gently, "Yes, women have had the vote for twenty years and where are they?" The bill was presented six times before it was taken up by Willie Hamilton and got through the Commons. It was Baroness Seers' comment in the Lords which made an impression on me — she said, "It's ridiculous to think that half the brains in the country are locked up in female heads and are not being used." She said it very emphatically and the bill got through.'

This Act opened up the civil courts to individuals, allowing them to present their own cases, and in due course women were to do this. Hand in hand with the Act, the Equal Opportunities Commission (subsequently described by writer Polly Toynbee as 'a poor, misshapen, misbegotten beast, with its teeth removed at birth'), was established. Carolyn Faulder acknowledged that it was far from perfect but felt that the fact of its existence was important: that it was up to women to try to put pressure on for it to become stronger and better. When, in 1988, Joanna Foster was appointed as head of the Commission, Carolyn Faulder spoke of her as being the first strong, optimistic appointment to this position — earlier leaders had not been interested in radical action, she explained.

The Equal Opportunities Commission had as its brief to facilitate the Sex Discrimination Act and re-educate the public into a consciousness of the wrongs of discrimination. What it lacked was the powers to deal with what Atkins describes as: 'the real problems of women's second-class status which is apparent worldwide. The problem is transformed from one about lack of power into one of barriers to single sex monopoly.' And in February 1977 Patricia Ashdown-Sharp had written a lengthy critique of the Commission for *The Sunday Times* in which she recalled that when the Sex Discrimination Act came into existence thirteen months earlier it had been heralded as 'one of the most radical pieces of social legislation of modern times.' She spoke of how the EOC had a 'propaganda role in changing the whole climate of opinion on equal rights. Its annual budget from public funds was set in its first year at no less than £1.2 million.' But at the time of writing, Patricia Ashdown-Sharp was expressing the doubts which would be far more widely echoed later on, that the EOC was dominated by blocs of TUC and CBI voting and, she commented: 'far from balancing each other out, the CBI and TUC tend to display a common interest in not allowing progress towards women's rights to upset the status quo'. Nor had the Commission by this time shown any alacrity in bringing investigations or in intervening in employment practices which appeared discriminatory.

However, the EOC did — and does — have the power to undertake formal investigations where discrimination is suspected. It may give grants to expose unfair and unlawful discrimination and it may help individuals in bringing cases to the Industrial Tribunal. The fact that the legislation was not followed by queues of women taking complaints to the tribunal probably had more to do with lack of understanding of how and on precisely what grounds this could be done, than that discrimination had vanished.

Ann Smedley, Women's Rights Officer with the National Council for Civil Liberties, when analysing the legislation in 1984, pointed to some of the reasons she believes women did not use the new powers more effectively. She says: 'There is a serious lack of knowledge about the rights provided or the scope of the laws. Few women know their rights and many see them as irrelevant to their own circumstances. The Sex Discrimination and Equal Pay Acts are extremely complex pieces of legislation — this is recognized by law and legal experts alike.'

But women have brought cases to the Industrial Tribunal and won. Mrs Vera Chadwick, a deputy headteacher for nineteen years, had applied for seventeen headships over a period of four years. She studied for an MA and BEd to improve her chances of promotion but failed even to get interviews for a number of jobs although, she said, her qualifications and experience were better than those of several of the men interviewed. The tribunal ruled that she had been victimized because she was a woman and she was awarded compensation.

It was the first case of discrimination which had been brought by a headteacher and the EOC regarded it as an important victory in a profession where there have been many complaints from teachers. Research by the Association of University Teachers based on an analysis of university records showed a striking pattern of career disadvantage for academic women. Statistics from 1985 demonstrated that although women equalled nearly 40 per cent of post-graduate students, only one in five of the academic staff recruited that year were women and many of them were on short-term contracts.

Joni Lovenduski, herself an academic, recorded these figures and pointed out that discrimination was even more accute at the higher levels — 97 per cent of all university professors are men. By the end of their academic careers just 15 per cent of men are lecturers compared to 48 per cent of women. And Lovenduski commented: 'Academe is male dominated. Senior academic and administrative posts are almost entirely occupied by men. The atmosphere varies a bit according to the subject balance of universities, with more women to be found in the humanities, social science and arts departments than in the male strongholds of engineering, science and mathematics. Moreover, universities have been notably reluctant to see the value of introducing sex equality policies of any kind. Frequently it seems senior posts are filled by search committees of old boys on the look-out for old boys. "Chap theory" ensures that the qualifications demanded

for important positions turn out when scrutinized to be qualifications which only men are likely to have.'

Other institutions were demonstrated to be equally guilty. In
1986 Dianne Robbins published a 100-page survey for the Equal
Opportunities Commission in which she reported endemic direct
and indirect discrimination against women in the policies of
British Rail and its unions. She pointed a finger at 'the average
British Rail manager' who regarded railway work as intrinsically
male and women as naturally unreliable, maternity leave as a
'skive' and complaints by women staff as 'whingeing' or 'banner
waving'. Out of a workforce of 17,000 just 6.5 per cent were
women and most of these were clerical and cleaners. The same
finger was pointed at the NUR which has a 6 per cent female
membership yet no policies specifically aimed at women.

There have been countless women who know they have
experienced sexual discrimination either in their attempts to get
a job or promotion, but who have not reported it because they do
not believe it worth it or they know any victory would be a
Pyrrhic one if they were to continue working in the same place.

Alanya, a journalist, went for an interview for a junior
reporter's job to replace a male friend with whom she had been
at college. She had worked exactly the same length of time on
another publication and it was he who had suggested that she
could do the job as well as he did. She recalls: 'The editor was
charming and interviewed me at length. I was confident I did
well in the interview and went away feeling good. I heard
nothing, so eventually I made contact and the editor told me he
had been very impressed by me but thought he needed a male
for the job.'

Lisa commented: 'At the beginning of the Seventies I was just
starting work and I was interested in finance so I applied for a job
dealing with the public, in a bank. At the interview the personnel
man scarcely bothered to ask me anything, and said very quickly
that he thought men were really better at dealing with the public
because they inspire more confidence. I remember being
enraged and feeling then the absolute injustice of it. I wasn't a
person, I was a gender.'

Ruth Moulting, a highly qualified computer programmer, with
skills which are unusual in either sex, began to recognize the
degree of sexism and discrimination in her work after joining a

Women's Academic Achievement Group at the University College of London, where she was working. She explains: 'This group examines what it means to be a woman in the working world and it led me to see how thoroughly sexist the computer world is. It is ironic because it's not seen as at all sexist as women are employed working with computers, but if you look, most are on word processing and then they may progress a bit to be operators or to be writing something like accounting packages. The women are always at the bottom. The other point is that all the language is male, all the manuals and projects are worked out in man hours, man weeks. Nobody really believes women can be technical. All the classic things which happen to women in worlds not instantly seen as feminine, have happened to me — people ringing up saying they have a technical question and wanting to speak to a man. Slowly I began to see this and as I did, it made everything harder. And it is maddening because computers are a golden opportunity for women as they can be worked on at home.'

In her present job Ruth is paid as well as the men of equal skills and she recognizes that, here, having gained exceptional qualifications, she can command the going rate. 'I am a rare species in terms of the experience I have got and they recognize that they have to pay for it — whether I am a woman or not!' But neither that nor the fact that she has reached a more senior job than any other woman in the company, alters her perception of the block on future promotion: 'I think I will have a very hard time to get any higher. I know the senior management just doesn't view me as senior management material. There is a space and I am fairly confident that if I were a man and adopted the right attitudes — they don't like my professed feminism — I would be all right. There is conspicuous discrimination in a number of ways — for example, in a meeting I might express a view and it would be completely ignored. Two minutes later a man expresses the same point of view and everybody says "good point". I think that's crazy, it can't be just that I'm a woman, but I've heard it from enough others to believe it is true . . .

'The other problem I have is the managing director who knows he's sexist, is proud of it, and he and I just loathe each other because I find his attitudes quite unacceptable. I like to think I'd feel the same if I was a man. I recollect him saying once, but not publicly, that no woman would get a very senior post in the company. When you are up against that sort of thing what can you do? He won't listen to reason, he won't judge me by my work as worth the same sort of promotion as a man. Now my plan is to try to go freelance and set up my own company with a group of women and to work outside of a male environment.'

Lucy Darwell-Smith, too, experienced conspicuous discrimination, and she has set up her own business where she employs only women. She has tried employing a man — 'A disaster,' she says with a dismissive laugh — but finds women harder-working, more reliable, less status conscious and a lot more loyal than the men she has worked among.

She is a success by any standards, having started her own public relations company at the age of twenty-six after reaching the position of associate director in the company she last worked for at the age of twenty-three. It was the help and support of a male colleague within this company which enabled her to become the only woman to be promoted beyond secretarial level, and the endemic chauvinism which forced her to leave. She explains: 'I was very pleased when I got the job as secretary within this PR company and I worked hard knowing I wanted to get on but wondering how it would be possible as they quite simply didn't promote secretaries. Then my immediate boss, a delightful man who had seen his wife through several degrees at university, decided he wanted to do one himself. He confided in me that in six months he would leave, and meanwhile, he said, he would train me up so thoroughly to do his job that they would have no option but to promote me. And that is exactly what he did. It was extraordinarily hard work but very exciting and when he left I had skills and knowledge that they would have spent time and money training a new employee to get, so they promoted me to assistant account executive.

'It angered some of the men and they combined trying to undermine me with showing they didn't take me seriously, but although I found it upsetting and infuriating I gritted my teeth and just went on working hard. But I did realize the extent of the antipathy when a client asked for me to do a job in Amsterdam instead of my immediate boss and I overheard him saying: "I hope the f..... bitch falls out of the sky." Luckily that man moved and again I was promoted because of the knowledge I had acquired. I was then made an associate director which didn't please the rest of the board at all because I would go into a meeting where they would all be sitting around, real YES men, and it was always me, aged twenty-three, who was challenging things. I got up their forty-year noses very thoroughly. But I then came to see that if I was to build up my department properly I needed to be a full director. All the other departments were headed by directors, the clients expected it, and besides I was making the most money of all of them for the company.'

Recognizing that it would not happen spontaneously, she gave her boss an ultimatum saying she must be made a director within six months or she would go. She says: 'I knew they wouldn't do it and one night I was talking to the marketing director of one of the big accounts I worked on, saying I would have to go, and to my amazement he said that if I went he would come too, bringing the business. That seemed like an omen and in my very naive way I thought that would be enough. So then I told the managing director and nobody spoke to me for the rest of the time I was there, because they thought I had let the company down.'

Starting her own company was 'terrifying', but within a year of starting with one account in a tiny space in Clapham she had moved to Beauchamp Place with several accounts and then on to a larger office in Smithfield with a fistful of prestigious clients and an accumulation of knowledge which led her to employ women who, she says: 'Are good at consumer PR, and seemed willing to work very hard to make the company work. In return I have tried, always, not to pull rank, to make everyone realize they are valued, and the atmosphere I aim for is more family than dynasty. I think I can confidently say that they do not feel as I did in my last company.'

In the case of both Lucy Darwell-Smith, who had an all-girls' education where it was assumed that she would be qualified to pick a career and do well in that choice, and Ruth Moulting, who went through university and targeted an area of work where she could see there would be demand and she could do well, education and the fact that women have seen that they can choose their careers have been all important.

Tessa Blackstone believes that one of the most important steps forward for women has come through the opening up of educational possibilities for them at all levels. Talking of her own life she says: 'I was always studious and I was encouraged, which was very lucky because at that time not all women were encouraged by any means. Once I had done my degree I knew I was capable and I knew I wanted to go on and work, using my brain, developing my knowledge and education had given me the conviction I could do this.' So it is that as Master of Birkbeck College, attached to London University, she puts particular effort into encouraging women on courses, and working on conditions and schedules which will allow the mature women students to combine children and study, just as it was made easy for her when studying as a mother at Bedford College. 'If there is a single thing which empowers women of all kinds it is education,' she says.

It is an attitude which can now be heard being voiced by people running the wide range of courses, educational workshops, re-starter programmes, polytechnic courses which draw in a spectrum range of women from those who have just left school and want to go on, to those who have failed at school and want to have another try, to women who have had their families and want to go to work but have no training and no confidence. Rosemary Auchmuty, who teaches Women's Studies to a group of women on a fresh-start course in London, says: 'In my classes I have women aged from twenty to seventy and among these are women who have, very definitely, recognized what twenty years of the women's movement has meant. They have drawn strength from it and they want to build on that. As a teacher and an educationalist, I see an enormous power in education which, of course, is why the Government wants to take control of us.'

The support system for women who want to educate themselves, who want careers, is now widespread, and careers guidance for girls as well as boys is well established. That is not to be sanguine about the many instances where girls clearly are not expected to achieve as boys are, or where career guidance will operate on a lower level, but the broad sweep of things for women is very different from what Carolyn Faulder remembers: 'In my first job at *Nova* I was asked to set up a careers advisory service — they were very forward thinking in wanting to do it, and as I began I realized there *were* no careers for women. I found no training, no courses apart from one part-time social work course in the whole country and some part-time teacher training courses.'

Although the Sex Discrimination Act has made it illegal for employers to question women on their marital intentions or whether they plan to have children, many still do it. Estelle Phillips, a lecturer in psychology, who questioned young women about their careers showed that at the initial interview for jobs most were asked about boyfriends and about possible engagements — in other words, the chance that they might become mothers was clearly a key factor. And Phillips, quoted in *New Woman* magazine in an article accompanying a survey on the facilities and allowances companies made available to women combining families and work, notes that although the women who did get taken on were optimistic about their chances of career promotion, that optimism faded quickly. She said: 'These organizations are leaders in the country and proud of their progress, yet it appears from talking to women in their employ that traditional attitudes are still rampant. In general, managers expect women to do well for the first few years and then be overtaken by men, because they believe childbearing will interrupt women's careers.'

Some of the triumphs for women going to one of the thirty industrial tribunals around the country, result from cases in which women have been discriminated against because they are expecting or have children. When Mrs Patricia Brown was offered a full-time job as a computer operator, she told her employers she was planning to have a family. However, when she became pregnant and spoke with the chairman about returning to work after the birth, he replied that he did not think it would work and Mrs Brown was sent a note: 'Due to your current state of health we have no alternative other to than to terminate your employment'. The ruling by the tribunal in Patricia Brown's favour was clearly a vital one for women.

When Mrs Shirley Ali Khan applied for a job as a grower in a nursery, she received a letter from her employer explaining that she ought to be at home looking after her children. 'Would he have written a letter like that to a *father*?' she asked, and the tribunal shared her view that it was discrimination. As they did in the case of Mrs Elizabeth Robbins, mother of four children, who had been teaching for sixteen years and was turned down for a primary teacher's job at Hamilton College in Scotland, according to the letter she received, 'because our policy is not to appoint lady teachers with very young children'.

The victories were small in number but they were important in the impact they made. Reports in the papers and on television succeeded in creating awareness of discrimination in a way the passing legislation on its own could not have done. And while covert discrimination continued to be experienced by women in many different ways at work, it could no longer be as blatant as the example commented on by *The Daily Mirror* in its leader column on 2 February 1971: 'For sheer, ingrained, insufferable masculine prejudice, with a dollop of self-righteousness thrown in, it would be hard to beat this statement from British European Airways [who had refused to give a qualified female pilot an interview]. "We may be old-fashioned but perhaps we prefer to have women in the home and not as airline pilots".' *The Daily Mirror*, wearing its feminist colours, spoke out: 'Women ought to have the chance to plan their own life, follow their own bent — according to ability and ambition. Fly an airliner. Drive a bus. Go to the moon. Be an engineer. Run a business. "There is," says the same BEA spokesman, "a dividing line between what men and women do." And who draws that line? In the BEA philosophy — which isn't limited to BEA — it stills seems that men do.'

Whatever the symbolic importance of the Equal Pay Act, it was not reaching the patent injustices many women were experiencing where women were doing work as hard, demanding, and lengthy as men's for less pay, but where because the job descriptions were different they could not go to court.

In the 1950s the International Labour Organization had floated the idea of equal pay for work of equal value and, according to Jean Snedegar, who made a BBC programme on the subject: 'It has been criticized by successive governments and industry as being impossible to define and to administer and for being too costly. Even after Britain joined the Common Market the Government argued that the equal value principle did not have a direct effect on member states and fought to give it the most restrictive interpretation.' In the event strong-arm tactics were used and the European Court of Justice ordered Britain to introduce it. That Mrs Thatcher, herself a woman who would probably be less than pleased if the men in her cabinet were paid more than she, was not enthusiastic about this commitment to women's rights, is manifest, but in the event, 'persuaded' by the European Court, the Government brought in an amendment to the Equal Pay Act, in 1984, which allowed pay claims to be made for work of equal value.

Julie Hayward was the first woman to test the new legislation, a case which spanned several years and proved her determination to see justice done, while her employers Cammel Laird demonstrated an equal commitment to countering her claim.

Julie's claim was that, as an assistant cook, her work was of equal value to that of a number of the men — a painter, a thermal engineer and a joiner. She explained that she had undergone a similar training period and during apprenticeship all were paid the same. But after training, the men were all put on a higher pay band than she was and by the time she brought the action the craftsmen were all earning £117 a week while she earned £92.

At the first hearing of the case in April 1984, an independent expert found that Julie's work was of equal value and she and the Equal Opportunities Commission, which regarded it as an important test case, were delighted. A year later the pay increase had not come and she had to return to court. At this hearing her employers produced new arguments saying they should not have to pay the same basic wage because Julie Hayward had better sickness benefits, paid meal breaks and more holidays than the men and that this compensated for the lower wage. This time the tribunal turned against Julie and ruled that she should not get parity of pay. But even when she appealed against the decision to the Employment Appeal Tribunal it went on to agree that Cammel Laird should not have to increase her wage.

Emotions around the case ran high. Women supporting Julie Hayward felt that employers should not be allowed to pay women unequally by giving them extra perks which they might not even wish to have and which, anyway, would be very unlikely to add up to the pay differential.

Ruth says: 'I felt passionately that it was yet another example of a hefty patriarchal organization feeling it was fighting for its life. There is a real horror of paying women justly. I know the implications are that companies will get a lot of claims if one is won, and it will cost them more, but it is hardly right that companies like Cammel Laird can protect themselves from having to pay out more of their profits in wages by being unjust to women.'

Then in a final attempt in June 1988 when the case went to the House of Lords, they ruled in Julie Hayward's favour saying that the Equal Pay Act stated that basic pay rates should be looked at, not perks. There was much celebration at the victory which was seen as highly significant in giving women a bit more muscle for the future in fighting jobs like those in the catering industry, where segregation means that women are valued less than men.

The case brought by Mrs Irene Pickstone, a warehouse packer, was regarded, too, as an important test case under the new amendment. Twice industrial tribunals had decided that Mrs Pickstone and four other packers could not bring claims for their pay to be made equal to that of male packers in the warehouse, because there was a man doing the work they were doing at the same rate. But it was widely felt that the man working with the women on the same money was a 'token' male put there to obstruct equal pay claims. Clearly the Appeal Court saw the danger in allowing such a situation to operate against potential justice for many women and it ruled that Mrs Pickstone could bring a claim for equal pay to an industrial tribunal if she wished, and that the presence of a single man should not affect this. It was hailed by the Equal Opportunities Commission as an important victory and the woman representing them declared: 'The ruling demonstrates that the change to the equal pay laws forced on the Government by the EEC is working as it should', while Irene Pickstone described it as: 'a small but important step'.

Another case which attracted a lot of interest involved the caring professions, where men's job descriptions and pay-cheques may be very different from women's even though the years they spend training are not. Here three speech therapists, seeking parity with three male pharmacists who received £4,000 a year more than they did, began a lengthy court battle in 1986. Elizabeth Clark, Kelly Atherton and Dr Pam Enderby claimed that with degrees and lengthy training they should be paid the equivalent of their male colleagues whereas at the time of going to court, their salaries were, in some cases, almost half. The final verdict was due to be heard in 1989.

The attention these cases received may have given the impression that the new legislation was changing women's working lives. Not so. Research done by Alice Leonard, the Equal Opportunity Commission's legal adviser, to measure the effectiveness of the laws and published in 1987, backed up findings from the period 1976-1983 which showed that only 11 per cent of all sex discrimination and equal pay claims before tribunals were successful and less than 100 people have been able to win comparable pay under the 1984 amendment. The view of economic writer Frances Gibb three years later was that: 'The new pay law which came into force in 1984, has so far made no impact.' By far the largest number of claims have been withdrawn (in some cases because settlements were reached outside court) or dismissed.

Nor was Lady Elspeth Howe, who helped set up the EOC, able to express much optimism when she wrote a retrospective analysis of the Act's achievements: 'Equal pay remains only a tiny speck of light at the end of the tunnel. Management clearly remains a "male" profession with only one in forty women among the two and a half to three per cent of top earners. Women are still concentrated in service industries and predominantly lowest paid, often segregated jobs.'

There have been less sex discrimination cases than those brought over equal pay, not least because it is an extremely hard thing to prove. Countless women know themselves to be discriminated against by bosses but cannot see how to prove it.

Taking a look at the way the Acts were working by the end of the 1970s, Dr Oonagh McDonald, opposition spokesperson on the Treasury and Civil Service, felt some fundamental changes were needed and she suggested: 'Far tougher laws are essential to overcome discrimination. These should include two vital changes: the burden of proof should be shifted from the person complaining about discrimination to the alleged discriminator and employers should be required to discriminate in favour of women by recruitment training and promotion into jobs not previously held by women.' But even if the legislation had become more user-friendly, one of the most effective and institutionalized ways in which women are handicapped in their working lives has been consistently disregarded at State level. As mothers and as the people who are assumed to be responsible for primary child care, women are discriminated against in a number of ways. Their choice of work is limited unless they can afford full-time, private child care — and most cannot. Some women cannot find child care at all because there is so little available. A survey of women in part-time work demonstrated that most relied on other women doing them 'favours' for their child care. Forced into jobs with hours which suit the needs of the children, many women are pushed into part-time work. As Phillipa says: 'I could only find a child minder to do five hours a day while the children were young and so I had to take what was going. There was shift work in a local office as a clerk so I took that. It meant I earned the bit we needed and it meant the kids didn't suffer — I just wouldn't want them to get home and me not be there, that sort of thing — but the work was boring. I had to accept that I couldn't expect any kind of career satisfaction because the people with the interesting jobs were all needed full time.'

Employers discriminate against women with children because they assume they will be more likely to take time off for the needs of the children and are less committed to work because they have other concerns. Marianne, a GP in a general practice, notes drily: 'If I phone in and say I'll be a couple of hours late because one of the children is ill and I need to get him sorted out, I can almost hear my male partners thinking it's no use employing women. But if one of the men phones in saying he'll be late because he has a hangover there's a kind of understanding acceptance.'

Magazines and newspapers have made much over the past years of women winning dynamic and much coveted traditional (male) jobs. And Marilyn Davidson and Cary Cooper (*High Pressure*, Fontana, 1982) said: 'On an optimistic note with more women working than ever before, there is also an enormous growth in women entering many of the formerly male-domi-nated jobs, including the field of management.' At that time 18.8 per cent of managers and administrators were women. But, they noted, these were mostly in traditional female occupations.

None of this alters the fact that, while some women succeed in demonstrating their abilities, reliability and commitment, to a level where they so clearly merit promotion that they are actually given it, there are many employers who hold the view that a mother is always more of a risk than a man unless those women can demonstrate very thoroughly that their children will not be put first under any circumstances. That has certainly been the price ambitious career women have had to pay. A woman I interviewed some time ago, who ran a successful chain of dress shops and had begun by working for big stores in the 1950s, told me: 'The reason I have been successful is that I have never taken a day off work. Even when my son had to go into hospital I didn't take time off.' It struck me then, childless as I was, that this was not right. Now, as a mother of two children, I know it is not right, and I am profoundly angry that men, and indeed some women in powerful positions, encourage it. For it is an attitude which discriminates against women having the freedom to use their education, their skills, to seek career fulfilment in a way a man does, *and* have children. The mother who tries to combine a demanding job with bringing up children often suffers from constant stress, anxiety and guilt, and the feeling that she is sacrificing her children's welfare or her talents. It is a conflict men rarely experience over their offspring.

Mary, who has a middle-management job, speaks for many women: 'I feel as though my life is a constant, precarious, act of juggling. I get the children organized with the childminder. I have trained my mind, at this point, to switch into work-mode, ready for the office. There I work very hard because I know I must be finished to collect the kids in time to give them their baths and to do the bedtime routine which seems all important to me. It is a matter of balancing everything all the time — the job which I see not just as a pay-cheque but also as something for when the children are grown and gone, and the needs of my kids. I don't want to feel they've had to sacrifice all the cosy, intimate bits of childhood because of my job. But it means I am exhausted most of the time and it hasn't done my relationship any good.'

Women who are ambitious and who feel, as so many men do, that they want to contribute their skills to the outside world, come to the point where they feel they must make a choice between career and children. Cary Cooper and Marilyn David-son conducted extensive research into the working lives of women managers and found that many women rising in their careers felt that having children would lessen their chances of getting on. Many chose not to have children. Another piece of research showed that just 7 per cent of women managers had children compared with more than 80 per cent of men.

It is, of course, grossly unjust that women, because they are biologically designed to give birth to children, should be penalized. Angela Phillips, who has spent years campaigning for State provision for children, says: 'The much heralded equality with men that was promised in the Seventies has proved a chimera, a prize only for the childless. Women should have the right to bear children without sacrificing income, career prospects and other benefits of employment.'

A tenet of the campaign for women's equality since the very early years, has been that there should be State child care. Feminists have pointed to the fact that in all other European countries governments recognize the importance of child care provision and offer just about every women a place. In Britain, when women were needed for work during the Second World War, State nurseries were provided to enable this. The nurseries proved successful, with much being said about the benefits to children of the social environment, but as soon as the war ended, they were closed down and no government since has seen fit to provide anything comparable.

So it was something of a surprise when, in the autumn of 1988, the Tory Government, which had shown a resolute disinterest in providing any child care for women who must or wish to work, announced the need for it. Earlier in the year, Mrs Thatcher had spoken out on the subject: 'I do not want State nurseries and I do not want State children.' But in November the National Economic Council published statistics showing that when the supply of 'baby boom' school leavers (which had, thus far, supplied the labour market) levels out during the 1990s, employers will need women to fill some 80 per cent of new jobs. The way this need can be met would be by bringing women with dependent children into the workplace.

At the time of the NEDC report, Britain had the lowest proportion of young mothers in work of all the EC countries because successive governments have refused to fund State child care. But after the report the Government promptly announced that it would set up an inter-ministerial working party to look at how child care needs could be met. The thrust of their thinking, it was made clear, was that employers should provide the care and not the State. In other words, recognizing the moral and practical right of child care provision, was not going to cost them money. It was a solution which caused anxiety among child development specialists such as Peter Moss at the Thomas Coram Foundation, who felt that it would be difficult to monitor individual child care schemes run privately. He voiced the concern that: 'Child care should be designed for children and be about doing the best possible for them and that may not always be the case with private schemes which must balance the books.'

Other solutions to the problems of working mothers vary. There are still many people who believe that mothering is an important job, and that this should be the commitment of a woman for some years, once she has given birth. There is an immediate flaw to this argument, which feminists have spent years pointing out, which is that a lot of women work out of economic necessity. One in four families in Britain lives below the poverty line and the figure would surely be higher if more women gave up the jobs they have succeeded in organizing around domestic demands.

There must surely be women who would prefer being at home with their children to working in jobs which give them no pleasure or satisfaction, a point acknowledged by Lady Elspeth Howe: 'When children are young, many would prefer a break from employment outside the home . . .' But with the Tory Government of the past decade, cutting back benefits and freezing child benefit, an allowance which if slightly higher just might allow some women to stay at home, such a choice is not available.

The rise of outspoken feminists, making the point that women want economic independence as men do, has given rise to a retort from those who disapprove of working mothers and are inclined to blame the wrongs of the nation's children on their absence from home, that these women should stop indulging themselves by working for frivolous extras. It is a retort which angers Joanna Foster, the new head of the Equal Opportunities Commission: 'I should like to challenge the view that mothers dump their children nowadays so they can work for those extra luxuries . . . the foreign holidays, the microwaves and so on. Economic realities are such that the choice to be a working mother barely exists.'

Lesley, who does voluntary work with women and children with social needs, says: 'I think there is a fear that with State nurseries women will stop wanting to look after their children at all, that there would be a kind of giving up of responsibility for them. It is ironic when you realize that women who are struggling to earn enough to help feed their families and to cope with the debilitating, wretched problems of poverty, must also worry about who they can get to look after their kids so they can go out to work. The stress on these women is enormous and of course their kids suffer as a result.'

Perhaps these words will be heeded; perhaps the burden which falls on women coping with children while also working, will get help from the private sector, and that would at least be a palliative to the Government's determined refusal. But none of this would undo the fundamental injustice of a situation where so many men are willing to abstract themselves from a sense of responsibility for their children, the commitment which handicaps women but which holds all but the most desperate back from neglecting or harming their children. Involving men in looking after children has been an aim of feminism for years.

Joanna Foster, who represents the most outspoken voice the Equal Opportunities Commission has ever had, stated: 'It is not cost effective to be discriminating against what is now nearly half the workforce. Women are playing an increasingly significant part in the workforce and at a time when Britain is really screaming out for skills . . . economically the country cannot afford not to make the best use of women's skills.' Although the anticipated demand for more bodies to fill slots in the labour market may make impossible the practical acts of discrimination which quite simply mean an employer will choose a male over a female and will avoid fecund women at any price, it will not remove the discrimination women face because, as mothers, they cannot and will not work the same hours as men and make invisible their domestic commitments. For this to happen, something fundamental is needed which will alter the subliminal discrimination waged against women by employers who see them as inferior employees because of their child bearing. It needs men to demand paternity leave, time off for their children's dental appointments and sports days; it needs men from government to factory floor to start speaking out about the importance of child care provision, child benefits, and sane working hours which allow both parents to care for their children.

Nor will the need for women in the labour market do away with the prejudice which prevents them getting through what Carolyn Faulder, who works in management training, describes as the 'glass ceiling' where women get to management level and find they can rise no higher although they see men who have done so very clearly.

Until there is a radical readjustment of the way men view women and a profound commitment from them to make equal opportunities a reality, some will always be more equal than others.

9

VOICES

WOMEN TALKING

THE voices here come from women who chose to write to me, in response to letters I placed in magazines and newspapers, asking for women's feelings about what feminism had meant in their lives. My original idea was to take excerpts from the letters and interviews to slot into the various chapters, which I have done. But when I had done that I realized there was a lot of fascinating, intimate, illuminating material which did not fit comfortably into my text but which should not be lost. In these words there is pain and passion, delight, discovery, humour, and many other things; there is a sense of what feminism has meant in the context of different women's lives. The voices let us see some of the ways women have come to feminism, the way a new awareness may have made women stronger, angrier, more sure footed, they also show how the changes wrought in women can have a profound effect on relationships. There are voices which criticize feminism, the women's movement, voices which see the good and the bad.

The way the atmosphere and events of the past two decades have touched women's lives, varies enormously. Some women have gone out to seek the feminist experience, others have found it compelling when it has come to them; still others have had their lives affected unwittingly. Some measure of the impact feminism has made even on the lives of women who have no professed interest in it, is indicated in the ideas and expectations revealed here which are seen as 'normal' but would not have appeared so twenty years ago. Conversely, some of the older women reveal clearly feminist thoughts and ideas which have occurred outside the 'new' feminist culture and have, perhaps, been drawn from knowledge, if not experience, of turn-of-the century feminism.

The women's voices have been organized according to age
rather than theme as this seemed the most effective way of
presenting them. Mostly the letters are published exactly as they
were written. The identification of class and age is as the women
have described themselves. Any changes made or re-organiza-
tion has been done to cut the letters down to a size which would
work here and to condense the material which seems in some
way to indicate the interface between feminism and these
women's lives.

Margaret Lincoln, seventy-three.

'I became aware of feminism shortly after my birth in 1915. My
mother was a Suffragette and a feminist throughout her life and
she gave me feminist attitudes (with peculiar nineteenth-century
undertones which she was never quite able to get rid of but which
I hope I have done).

'I have read a good deal of feminist literature since about 1966
but have had difficulty with local modern feminist groups. Most
of my political and social activities were through the Labour
Party and the Co-operative movement. Old ladies of over sixty
who were quite pleased that their marriage had lasted forty years
and over were not very welcome in feminist circles in Leicester,
which is where we lived until 1986.

'I did manage to do a little to help in the Women's Aid Refuge
and got a resolution put forward to the Co-op party annual
conference on the subject of battered wives. Some of the
attitudes adopted by young women in the feminist movement of
the last twenty years have seemed absurd to me. These are
usually the attitudes taken up with enthusiasm by men in the
Labour movement who are trying to pretend to support feminism in order to get feminists to support them in some matter or
other.

'My husband and I agreed ours was to be a partnership of
equals before we began in 1937. If either showed signs of
breaking that agreement we reminded each other. There were
sometimes terrible rows. My feminism has become much more
positive and open. I used to worry, thinking I was wrong
sometimes, but the progress which has been made in the last
twenty years, although limited, has been very heartening, i.e. it is
no longer possible for a Catholic husband to prevent his wife

having an essential operation on any part of her reproductive system by refusing to sign the necessary form. A woman can, at least by law, take her husband to court for assault. Refuges have been established up and down the country to which women and their children can retire from violent men. Women have far more control over their fertility than they did, even twenty years ago. And it is no longer possible for a man to treat his wife as a punch bag, purchased for the price of a marriage licence.

'I had a brief brush with lesbianism during the war while my husband was away in India. My friend married after the war. We both had children and remained friends until her death some years ago. There was a great deal of lesbianism during the inter war years. Nobody made much fuss about it. As far as I know, it was never illegal. I suspect that the present fuss is due to the fact that the balance between the number of women and men has changed so that some men feel they have been robbed of something if a woman chooses to have sex with another woman rather than a man. It is undoubtedly true that domestic life with another woman is much easier than with a man. No fear of pregnancy and none of this "Where's me shirt? Why isn't me dinner ready?"

'My hopes now are for my eleven grandchildren. I hope they will grow up to treat each other as equals and that changes will be made in the law so that society also treats men and women as equal. I hope my five grandsons will be able to work shorter hours than their grandfathers as a result of improvements in industrial processes and my six granddaughters will feel free to work with equal pay and proper child care provision, while they are working.

'During my time on the board of the Leicester Co-op I tried to get equal pay and equal training for the female staff. Being involved with the Co-op has made me much more self-confident and much less inclined to work through women's organizations only. Some of the things that are happening in the name of feminism seem to me to be stupid and irrelevant. There is enough to do in the fight for equality without diverting our efforts towards feminine dominance and matriarchy which might turn out to be as bad as patriarchy. Power brings out the worst in anybody.'

Anonymous woman, sixty-six.

'I was brought up in Edmonton, North London and grew up in a three-bedroomed semi which housed my parents, my maternal grandfather and grandmother, my brother, who was four years older than myself, and me.'

'I remember very distinctly the first time it occurred to me that women were unfairly treated. It was a Sunday in 1938 and I was travelling on a train past suburban gardens. There were men in those gardens, apparently relaxing and enjoying themselves, and I knew that their wives were working in the kitchens. The thought came into my sixteen-year-old head that I should have been better off if I had been born male. It was a long time before it occurred to me that I could be better off as a woman if somehow women's lot was improved. For many years I was determined that if I couldn't come back as a man I wasn't coming back at all.

'The war came, my brother died in the Med. and in 1942 I married his friend, a sailor and electrician by trade. In 1943 I had a son and in 1945 a daughter.

'I remember arguing with my husband during the first year of our marriage because he voiced the opinion that girls should be taught cooking in school and not Latin. It so happened that, being categorized as bright, I had been taught Latin and not cooking. I had not enjoyed the Latin but I was not going to relinquish my entitlement to it. I suppose that argument showed something of the pattern of our future.

'In spite of my thinking, I was easy meat for the indoctrination of the women's magazines and other media and did my best to be a "good wife", which included being a good housewife. At this I failed miserably and so suffered years of frustration and a sense of inadequacy. I think I succeeded in being amenable and submissive and still am to an extent. I argue the theory but still play the role.

'My daughter went to college in 1964 and it was through her that I became aware of the feminist ideas that were being discussed. I became interested in a range of thought of which I had previously been unaware.

'They talked of sexism in advertising and in children's books, of inequality in education and employment — you name it. I listened and I think I met their ideas with a sense of recognition rather than the shock of revelation. I knew that what they were saying was right, had always been right, although it had not been clearly stated before.

'My husband heard all this and reacted badly. Friends who were heard expressing the feminist point of view with enthusiasm went on to his black list. Somehow he has always persuaded himself that his daughter is not one of them — I don't know how he manages that because she most certainly is.

'On the domestic scene I fulfil the role more or less, as it was presented to me forty-five years ago. The big difference is that I no longer suffer feelings of guilt and inadequacy about it. I know that I am justified in not wanting to clean the house and only do it if I decide I want to. My husband accepts the principle that he should do his share but of course it doesn't work out like that. I keep my thoughts on many subjects to myself. I don't discuss what I read and don't voice my opinions on subjects I know to be controversial. Not, that is, unless he starts it! He doesn't know what goes on in my head most of the time.'

Enid Grimshaw.

'I am not really a "feminist" but fervently believe in equality of opportunity for all. I have campaigned since 1979 for more leisure facilities for housewives and working women. I was bowling in a British Isles Pairs Competition. We had four more ends to play and were a few shots down but on a winning streak. At 5.45 p.m. precisely an official of the Women's Indoor Bowls Association curtailed the match as the "Men wanted to play a friendly game" and of course 6 p.m. is the magic hour scheduled for the disappearance of Lady Bowlers from the sporting scene. Our opponents were given the game and I protested in vain, and continue to do so.

'I first experienced equality of opportunity during the war years. That was the time when men acknowledged our ability to contribute equally for the benefit of society. After the war I found it hard to accept a secondary role and found the game of bowls a healthy challenge which provided me with a competitive sense of achievement. We all need to experience some success in life and, sadly, the only opportunity offered to the majority of housewives, in the competitive field, is presented by the Welsh Cake Cream Tea syndrome. Oh the thrill of discovering that one's own sponge cake is more delectable than that of one's colleagues. Compare this narrow field of challenge with that offered our menfolk. Their choice is infinite — company management, banking, freemasonry, round tables, sport — i.e., rugby, soccer, snooker, cricket, darts, etc.

'I suddenly felt the urge to crusade for more facilities for women in sport and was surprised to find the most opposition came from *women* because of tradition. Sweeping changes in the economy of modern society have resulted in a worsening situation for women generally. Most wives now help to pay the family mortgage in addition to all the housekeeping chores, and statistics prove that more of them are contributing towards public revenue than ever before; but do they get a fair share of the goodies on offer to their menfolk? The answer is No!

'In 1983 Local Authorities spent some £900 million on sport and recreational activities . . . whilst women playing for National Bowling Honours have to pay their own way. The Sports Council, we are told, is primarily concerned with three areas of development — first, SPORT FOR ALL. Second, ENCOURAGEMENT OF EXCELLENCE and, third, PROVISION OF FACILITIES. In connection with the first, they do little to prevent the rotten system of Apartheid which exists at present. Many men can earn a luxurious living in sport — few women can barely scratch an existence. Sanctimonious sports*men* at Gleneagles heartily condemned the system of "separate co-existence" yet the hypocrites practise it daily in their private clubs, using all the constitutional rules and regulations to keep women out. It is inconceivable that in this day and age, working women in Wales are denied the opportunity to play bowls for their county or their country because facilities to play League and National competitions are non-existent after (*men's*) working hours. Because of my campaign, I have suffered ridicule and victimization by my bowling colleagues and my own "county" activities have been brought to a halt.'

Valerie, fifty-eight.

'I am non-party political, non-sectarian, non spit'n'polish orientated. We were brought up in the make-do-and-mend generation and have lived well below the national average wage all our lives.

'The more I think about it the more strongly I feel that Strident Women's Lib. has done man–woman–person–kind a great disservice. Each "real" partner in a relationship must be dependent upon the other. What does "equality for women" mean? Women and men are equally valuable, but they are *not the same*, and no amount of legislation or lobbying will alter the fact. In a "real partnership" there will be give and take — good manners and consideration on both sides. I get the impression that SWL women have not managed happy normal friendship with either sex. (Is this cause and effect?)

'By the end of the war women had proved that they were as good as men and most women with anything about them were able to do anything they wanted. SWL, though, was impatient. It rushed in with a lot of half-baked theories and tried to change the natural order (man+woman+children = family) and thousands of years of conditioning by bullying rather than persuasion. This alienated men in general, and quite a proportion of women.

'I could go on about the silly things SWL has done but the most damaging is surely that it has debased the stay-at-home mother. "Women's Lib." was freedom to do two jobs, and now women feel they *must* go out to work. Some women are strong and clever enough to do both jobs properly. Some earn enough to pay someone else to bring up their children. Many, though, can't cope. The result? A frightening increase in broken marriages, tranquillizer addiction and unruly children.

'I know there is much talk of sharing the domestic chores, but it's not all that simple, in practice. Someone has to be in charge to see that the household doesn't run out of bog-paper and baked beans. The hassle of organizing precisely who does what when is more than the average woman can manage! I can't see why SWL wants to do that and a boring full-time job!

'Yes, the place for mothers *is* in the home. We have pussy-footed round the question of child-rearing for too long — afraid of appearing un-trendy and pretending that it is just another simple chore, but bringing up contented, responsible children in a secure and loving home is one of the most demanding — and difficult — jobs imaginable. Every mother — and child — deserves the support of a husband and father who is treated as a partner, not just an irritating biological necessity.

'Perhaps I'll start an alternative women's movement. "Bring back responsibility, tolerance, and the family!" It is still true that the hand that rocks the cradle is the hand that rules the world, and the sooner modern women realize this, the sooner they will be truly and happily "liberated"!

'My son is twenty-one and coping with his first flat. He says he now realizes what a lot there is to running a home, and he would never expect the mother of his children to do two jobs. My daughter believes in "equality" and has trained her live-in-rock musician to clear up the domestic shambles she creates!'

Anne Walker, fifty-five. British, 'born working-class; now middle-class.'

'I was an "unconscious feminist" before I was a "conscious feminist". My mother was a "typical housewife" (but not happy in her role — she committed suicide when she was sixty years old). I observed her and my numerous aunts and decided I did not want to be like them. My mother did not want me to have an education. When an older female cousin went to training college she commented that it "was like asking not to get married". I thereupon resolved not to get married. My father (a very intelligent, self-educated, well-read, broad-minded man) backed me in my determination to go to grammar school and university. In a perverse kind of way my choice of degree was a "feminist" choice. I read chemistry and at university in my year there were only two women.

'It is clear that marriage was never for me (as I recognized in my early adolescence). But in 1953 well-brought up young ladies (especially those with a non-conformist background) did not screw around. So at the age of twenty-one I married the first man with whom I had been seriously involved. We stayed together for twenty-two years.

'It is fair to say that we both tried to make it work. We had agreed before we were married that we would both have careers and that we would not have children. In the event he had a career and I had a job. I resented this and I resented the fact that sex, as I saw it, was a "duty". So the sexual relationship became poisoned and eventually ceased. However, I still felt that I had made my bed and I should jolly well lie on it. It is to the eternal credit of my ex-husband that he realized that enough was enough and suggested we should get divorced.

'I then went through a delayed adolescence, sampling all the goodies that I felt I'd missed out on because of my early marriage; I found I enjoyed sex when I was free of the constraints of marriage. Concerning sexuality, feminism has been a force for good. It has enabled me to come to terms with my sexuality because whatever stage I was at in my sexual odyssey I felt that, because of my feminism, I was making the decisions. Almost three years ago I became a Born Again Spinster! and I love it. I have now lived alone for twelve years. My privacy, my autonomy and my independence are immeasurably precious to me. At the same time close relationships with a few female friends have become very important. I still have male friendships but these friendships are not as close (in general) as the friendships with female friends.

'I teach assertiveness courses and one manifestation of assertiveness in my own behaviour is that I am quite ruthless concerning whom I am prepared to spend time with. Women who are not committed feminists and men who are not at the very least sympathetic towards feminism do not deserve my attention!'

Ruth Barnett, fifty-three.
'I am a psychotherapist and ex-school teacher. My skin is colourless to people of colour, but a nice orangey brown to me.

'I was born in Berlin and came to England on one of the last "children's trains" to get through in 1939 under the London Refugee Scheme. I lived with three foster families. I always resented the preferential treatment given to my brother and foster brother — I was fobbed off with dairy technology when I wanted agriculture, suffered every kind of humiliation as a female in industry and built up enormous resentment about the treatment of female teachers in the male dominated teaching profession.

'I first became aware that women were getting together and saying things back in the Sixties. However, having been extremely well conditioned into the stereotyped patriarchal order of things, I was very busy bringing up three children in the Sixties and suffering torments of guilt because I was not at all happy at home all day with them as I felt I ought to be. I first became

interested in the movement in the late Seventies when my son
was doing repeat A levels, one of which was sociology. I thought
I was helping him by getting him talking each morning on our
half-hour drive to the station. In fact he taught me all about the
sociology of gender stereotypes and inequality and provoked me
into thought and action. I then started to scan the women's
sectors of bookshops, read reviews etc. Undoubtedly what most
influenced me were Simone de Beauvoir's *The Second Sex* and
Dale Spender's *Man Made Language* and *Invisible Women*.

'I did not have to, and have not, joined any organized women's
groups. I lead a very busy life doing far too much already. But I
do my "little bit" wherever I am. This consists of never letting go
by anything I feel puts women/girls in second place to men/boys.
I got a name for myself at the last two schools I worked in for
being a "rabid feminist", which I certainly was not, but the label
was always used to attempt to silence me. I stopped any meeting
I attended by quietly insisting such terminology as "girls' subjects" and "boys' subjects" was unacceptable and asking a lot of
provocative questions that brought out sexist answers into the
open.

'The effect on my family has been interesting. Apart from my
son who first triggered me into doing some consciousness
raising, the rest of the family took some time to realize they had
to take me seriously. My husband was always very sensitive to any
visible unfairnesses. My daughter said to me scathingly a long
time ago "I'm not going to let my husband get away with what
you let him [her Dad] get away with!" As a family I think we all
now feel that both men and women have lost out by the old
patriarchal stereotypying and pressures. Far from my developing female consciousness damaging our family relationships I
feel we have grown together.'

Valerie Taublin Booth — Ms., fifty-one.
'I use the title Ms. as I noted great confusion if I reverted to
Miss — doubts were placed upon my children's parentage. I
ceased the title Mrs. when an acned youth in the guise of Under
Manager in a branch of Curry's requested details of my husband's income when I required hire purchase facilities for a
washing-machine.

'I have never quite understood what "Women's Liberation" was about. Apart from the rather unlovely Germaine Greer extolling us, years ago, to ignite our underwear *en masse*, Joan Ruddock indicating those of us not prepared to be Socialist Feminists would be better off dead, and Glenys Kinnock trailing in her husband's wake yet causing more swell than the man himself made, Women's Lib. made no impact upon my life whatsoever.

I am fifty-one years of age — caught in the cross-fire of a changing society, as a child my world consisted of women — men were at war. My father died when I was six, my mother worked in a munitions' factory, my neighbour drove buses as an option to becoming a "land girl", school life was dominated by women, the male teachers were at war, cinemas showed film of women on land, women plotting for RAF, women nursing the wounded. It didn't occur to me women were not liberated as they appeared to a small child to dominate most avenues of life.

'I lived in an area of extreme poverty, had a basic education, studied at art college and dumbfounded the locals by staying in full time study until nearly eighteen and not being a budding Picasso or Hartnell, I opted for a male occupation — that of technical illustrator — to find that the office ratio was two women to eighty-four men. Once installed, the female presence was observed for a few days, then standards slipped and we lone females were absorbed into a male world.

'Having had a pleasant life style from mid-Fifties to early Sixties it came as a shock to be told via the media I was about to be "liberated". I was extremely angry as I never considered myself in bondage, although I was slightly confused in childhood — when eggs were rationed I noticed my father always had two eggs, my mother and myself one. I asked why and got my mother's stock reply "because your father is a man", and so early in life I had noted the difference in parents but never understood why being a man was a reason for having two eggs.

'I feel any mandatory enforcement, any restructuring of society should come by gradual change. To me it is a futile gesture to wake one morning and be told one is liberated, as is the instruction we will not be racist. In general people do not like being told by acts of Parliament they are free, equal, white, female — they prefer to find these things out for themselves.

Perhaps a better approach would have been to explain "Ladies, you are free to cox for Cambridge — should you so wish; you are free to apply for hire purchase in your own right."

'I had the best of both worlds. I had a career as long as I wanted one and my first child at thirty, the second at thirty-five — I have enjoyed raising my children — alone, as my liberated self couldn't combine liberated independence and marriage. I had four attempts at being a "wife" — all failed miserably but all four husbands remarried.'

Marianne Simons, forty-seven.

'I, like a lot of women of my age, experienced the dramatic swing in social attitudes to the woman's role in society during the Sixties. I feel that no one has yet given a voice to people like myself. The "in betweens". By that I mean those women who were conditioned from birth to the inevitability of marriage and children as their life's focus, and then having to adjust (quite cruelly it seemed) to a rejection of these values.

'I was married with two small daughters during the mid-Sixties. My husband worked in the media, and his very slightly younger than us friends and colleagues became my friends too. Our children were under three, and our friends, fresh from red-brick universities, were very critical of women who stayed at home. I had just missed the feminist boat, it took off rapidly, but it didn't matter to me since I was quite happy to be at home.

'My husband was a rampaging feminist, in theory, but a conditioned chauvinist by nature, so we became a "cosy pair". We were parent surrogates to our friends in spite of the fact that we were but a couple of years older than them. My own difficulty became apparent when I realized that I was trying to play two roles concurrently. The mothering instinct made me protective towards other people's sense of security, and their egos were therefore sacrosanct. I found myself playing the dual role of Mother Earth and progressive, enlightened wife of the media feminist. It was exhausting, in retrospect.

'To illustrate: we had invited two married, professional friends to dinner one evening. I looked through my well-thumbed Robert Carrier paperback the day before, and made prep-arations for the dinner early next morning. As the time drew near for our guests' arrival I removed all traces of the children so as to appear un-domesticated. I then got to work on myself. I bathed, plaited my hair and put on my designer "hippy" dress so as to complete the transformation. I wanted my friends to think I was like them. Independent and free spirited.

'The guests arrived and became locked in conversation with my husband. I prepared the meal in the kitchen and looked after the creature comforts of our guests. I heard a voice shout out to me from the other room "Got any nuts, love?" It was one of our friends. I ran into the room apologizing for the lack of nuts. It was at that moment that I became aware that I felt like a servant whose standards of service were being criticized. I sensed stirrings of anger in me towards our friends. They made me feel inadequate.

'Later in the evening one of my daughters woke up. I ran up to see her and could hear the conversation from downstairs as I rocked my daughter to sleep again. They were discussing children, and were all agreed that when they decided to have children au pairs or nannies would be a must, since they did not want their children to identify with role models. I burned with frustrated anger by this time. I felt I had been insulted and unrecognized.

'I decided when the children had reached the ages of ten and twelve, to go against the grain and become my own person. Social pressures from the media, the feminist literature and working friends had influenced my decision. The main incentive, however, came through my husband's attitude towards me. He had become bored with the cosy nest-maker at home. I began to feel like a household appliance ånd knew I had to ring some changes.

'I picked up a dead career and tried to revive it. It was a dangerous move, although I didn't realize it at the time. My new life and my new friends gave me a confidence in myself which had lain dormant during my married years. I became angry with my husband's subconscious need for his lost mother surrogate and rejected this role out of all proportion. Through trying to revive my husband's interest in me, I had learned to accommodate my own needs, and in the process destroyed our marriage.

'It could be argued that a marriage like mine wasn't worth having anyway. But I was happy. I'm more enlightened now. Feminism has given me confidence in myself, but it hasn't made me happier. The penalty for my feminist stand has been severe. Un-prepared and ill equipped for going it alone has meant financial deprivation, loneliness and single-parent responsibilities. We "in-between" women have suffered the emotional consequences of the feminist movement, since we are burdened with guilt which, I'd argue, is a common syndrome in the conditioned "mother" stereotype.

'I believe the feminist movement has brought about the most dramatic social revolution since the end of the Empire in this country. We pioneers may not have shed blood, but the tears shed have been immeasurable.'

Maureen Roberts, forty-three, working-class.

'I am not exactly sure what the women's movement is other than seeing the women at Greenham Common and people like Germaine Greer, Edna O'Brien and Erin Pizzey speaking out. I have slowly become aware of these things since I was married twenty years ago. I haven't joined any groups or organizations because I don't know how or what to join.

'My attitudes began to change after I got married and, if anything, I have become rather bitter. My husband cooks occasionally, washes up and shops sometimes, but he always lets me know it's my job he is doing. When my children were small he would look after them for me, so I could go out but he never got involved with feeding or nappy changing.

'About seven years ago I got a job in a comprehensive school as a resources assistant. It was considered by many people to be a good job. I worked 8.45 to 4.30 p.m. and had all the school holidays. I would never have got this job on my qualifications as I haven't any (I went to a secondary modern school) but I knew the headmaster through our local drama group, of which I was secretary. The three and a half years I worked there were the most difficult of all my married life. We came very close to splitting up. My husband works in a power station and often works weekends and holidays. He would often cook and wash up on his days off and then explode with rage at the end of the week. Why I don't know. Either he resented doing jobs he thought were mine or because he felt threatened and thought I was getting above my station working with well-educated middle-class people. Anyway, I left the job. He admits now he could have made my path smoother, but I couldn't cope with the stress at work and at home.

'Now I just work fourteen hours a week in a shop. It's boring but easy, but I resent giving up the most interesting job I ever had to do something I don't like — housework. If I had been a different person I might have left, but I feel it's very important to keep the marriage together because of the children. And anyway it's not all bad.

'Although I haven't been involved personally, I think things are gradually improving for women, i.e. legal abortion, the contraceptive pill, mortages, equal pay in some jobs. But I think it is very frustrating that with a woman prime minister the fight for women's wages has ground to a halt. Trade unions, of course, always dominated by men, were just beginning to make some efforts for women, but when they have all their powers taken away and aren't getting what they want, they certainly aren't going to bother about us.

'I suppose I was involved in a small way when I was about twenty years old. I was a shop steward for USDAW. I don't think it did me any good though. I often crossed swords with the manager, so when I asked for promotion I was passed over. When I was twenty-five I was working in a printing works and I organized with another woman to join SOGAT. It met with total opposition from the boss and no support at all from the men. I left a couple of months later to have my first child, but I was told that the boss slowly went round all the women one by one and persuaded them to drop out until only one was left and he gave her all the rotten jobs until she finally left.

'I was an only child but my mother told me she used to have to help her mother whilst her two brothers got to play out and she thought it was unfair, so I have always asked my son and daughter to do the same. But as my husband doesn't think that boys should have to do domestic work, more often than not, they don't do anything. Looking on the bright side, my son calls me "Red Mo", can cook, clean his bedroom, use the washer and iron when it suits him and so can my daughter. But I am quite happy to iron while she does her homework. If she makes a career for herself I will be very happy.

'My son has picked up some of his father's ideas, but hopefully some of mine too. I hope when he marries that he will be more broadminded and share all the housework and parenting so that his wife can be an equal. As for my daughter, I hope I have just made her think about the choices in front of her.

'I read an article in a magazine by Erin Pizzey who says she is now putting a lot of effort into a relationship and good luck to her. I have been doing that for twenty years. We can no longer say that women are better or fairer or kinder whilst we have Mrs T. on the throne, but we can say they are as good as and certainly not inferior to men.'

Carlan Ni Loinsigh, forty, 'middle-class (I suppose)'.

'My awareness of feminism began in the late Sixties, mostly through TV, books, and possibly because as an Irish woman I had always had a growing feeling that things were not fair for women. The growth of feminism confirmed for me that I was not alone. However, my confirmed interest in feminism did not grow or develop until I reached my early thirties. By then with one marriage and quite a few relationships behind me I actually felt that the "normal" woman's role was unbearable and I had to find some way to lessen the conflict between the me who was at times desperate to marry, have a family and "settle down" as my family say, and the me who was growingly and increasingly aware that it just wouldn't work for me.

'Feminism helped me to lift the burden of Catholic guilt and learn to enjoy sex. To begin to see sex for what it was, not so closely aligned to men and marriage, but an aspect of my life and being. My attitudes to men changed considerably. While at first I was a regular man hater I began to see that my behaviour left a lot to be desired. I still viewed them as "marriage bait", still played the lady role around them and was a victim of my own situation-creating behaviour. Anger towards men and the constraints which a society in which they have control physically, linguistically, economically, has grown in me and stayed. However, I tend now not to react as explosively as I have in the past. Having developed confidence in myself as a person, I tend to either ignore the ignorant (men and women) or find verbal arguments to show them that there is another point of view.

'I have always found it difficult to align myself with any group. There seems to be too much "dogma". One must dress like a feminist, or speak a certain ideology, or adhere to a particular view. From my experience these views appear to be symptomatic of "middle-class" feminism. I feel strongly that feminism ignores at its peril the differences between women — cultural, religious, race and class and also differing view-points on sexuality.'

Jean.

'I became interested in feminism in the mid-Sixties and at the age of forty I went on a social work course. This was after having spent from 1951–1969 as a "housewife" and mother at home. My only real motivation for taking up a career (would you believe it!) was that, as a mother of three sons, there was a possibility that I would not be allowed to slip easily into the Grandmother role — this doubt entered my mind because (a) I may not be allowed to have a role by daughters-in-law (b) their physical distance may prevent a role, so a career was seen to be second choice at that time, with a promise to the family that "nothing would change at home". In the event, of course, *everything* changed and resistance to my carrying on became a reality.

'My husband tried everything he could to sabotage my studies and women neighbours poured out their sympathy to my husband and children about being "neglected" — this after my having spent eighteen years as a full-time slave!

'Of course, greater awareness followed about the lack of equality in my marriage, by this time the battle was on which severely damaged the relationship with my husband. Of all the older women on my course and in my workplace *all* of their marriages have ended through their push for independence. My husband still thinks I have ruined our relationship; even though it is now nearly twenty years since I have been contributing financially to the home, he still only marginally shares domestic chores. The most important symbolic statement I ever did was to stop cooking the Sunday lunch, everything else was easier after that.'

Ann Jay, thirty-eight, middle-class 'from a fairly poor background'.

'I find it difficult to define what feminism means to me. There are certain obvious aspects such as equal rights and opportunities and control over one's own body and fertility. However, the last

thing I would want to be is a man and to me feminism also means
the promotion of traditional female attributes and strengths.

'I first became interested in the women's movement in 1971,
when I read Kate Millett and Germaine Greer for the first time. I
was enormously angry for a long time! As a result I became
involved in Left-wing politics and women's campaigns. I was
especially active in Sheffield Women's Aid and the national
abortion campaign. I left Sheffield after eight years in a so-called
radical practice which, on paper, and in many ways, had
wonderful attitudes to women's rights and women's problems. I
had a terrific maternity leave arrangement, for instance, and the
practice accepted and promoted home delivery.

'Yet within the partnership I felt undervalued and incapable of
self-expression. Two of the male partners in particular I found
extremely oppressive and yet arguably they had the "best"
politics. They wanted to define the agendas and I felt I was
expected to be a token woman without there being any real
dialogue. Things deteriorated to such an extent that I was
manoeuvred out of the partnership and forced to look for
another job. Interestingly, many women (another doctor, a
counsellor and a health promotion worker amongst others) have
also left or been pushed out. I was accused of being too much a
mother — too little a doctor! Yet women patients find me more
approachable than either of the two women doctors left there.

'Now I am in practice with three men who are not political in
the same sense and who have pretty traditional views about
women. So far, though, they have been very careful to offer me
good terms — financially and in terms of negotiating when I
work and also to discuss and request my ideas. Superficially it is
much less progressive but I feel more respected and that I am
being taken far more seriously.

'I find this one of the most fascinating of enigmas. My first
husband beat me up on occasion and yet said all the right things
about women's issues. I feel that my feminism was one of the
strains on my first marriage, even though in theory my husband
shared the ideas. As time went by he resorted to using his fists to
ends rows — more and more. Although he didn't want to in
many ways, I think he had a psychological need to be on top and
ultimately the only terrain on which he could feel superior was
the physical one.

'Feminism has also put a strain on my second marriage in that it has always been a tension. But because we usually resolve the problems in creative ways, it has been an enriching force. I have been with my present partner, Paul, for fifteen years, married for eleven years and we have been parents together. We have, I believe, an on-going dialogue about how to be real partners and how to share the business of life in our relationship. I believe we fight less than we used to and things have changed with circumstances rather than time. We have never shared fifty-fifty but we have negotiated something that feels okay.

'My politics have been formulated in my work. I don't see myself as a "doctor" or a "lady doctor" but as a "woman doctor" and this is very important to me. Women doctors are in a curious position and have been called, aptly, honorary men. You get nurses, receptionists, etc. to wait on you, you are in a position of power over each of your patients and their body's orifices and they usually respect you at least for the few minutes they are in your consulting room. Some of this is quite comforting to the ego but I do try to guard against it. As a feminist I try to offer women what I want when I'm a patient. It's difficult to describe but some of the essential elements are: respect, which means never invading, always saying why an examination is necessary and what it involves; giving choice in a simple way by being there — they can choose to see me — also by offering explanations and various solutions to problems. Not saying "I'm prescribing this, but you could take so and so" . . . Valuing — many women who come to see me aren't valued, even by themselves. If they are depressed they often say they have no reason. I would explore this and say "let's look and see exactly what's wrong with your life", rather than slapping out the tranquillizers.

'I try to offer things women need, such as sympathetic examination to rape victims, information to women's groups and simple access to abortion, contraception. Put simply, it means using my skills to women's advantage. It isn't awfully earth-shattering but I believe it is valued by patients. They say things like "no one has really listened to me before" or "nobody explained that before".'

Nina Kellock, thirty-seven.

'I can't really say that the women's movement has had any effect on me at all, and can't recall when I became aware of it existing. I didn't read any of the literature, join any groups etc., probably because I was happy with my lot and still am. As the fact that I am female never prevented me from getting a job, I suppose I couldn't see the point of women making a fuss about equality. But I was a secretary, which is a job predominantly female.

'I was brought up at a time when men and women had certain roles in life, i.e., the man went out to work and the women stayed at home for the most part, but once I got into my twenties I realized that it didn't have to be that way, and why should a working woman not do a job that was usually a man's job — engineering, surveyor, architect, bus driver etc? And if a woman was to do that, why should she not be paid the same as a man? So for that reason of equality I agree with the women's movement. However, I do think in some cases the women's movement came across as "butch" and that these women created animosity for a lot of women.

'They were forceful and aggressive and whilst I am not a mouse, and consider myself aggressive when I want to make a point, I think somewhere there is a fine line over which the really aggressive women stepped and so alienated themselves. There's no need to be unpleasant, surely?

'Having been widowed at twenty-six, left with an eighteen-month-old baby and a five-year-old, I had to quickly learn not to be dependent on men. However, there was no shortage of men offering to do the "typical male" jobs around the house and garden and I let them! Now I'm remarried I'm dependent on a man for the roof over my head, since it goes with the job, for the food I eat, the clothes I wear, my spending money, but I don't see that is wrong since I do my share in my own way. Our accounts are kept well, we never go in the red at the bank; we eat well; my husband's shirts are always ironed; the house is kept clean and tidy. During my unhealthy period, which lasted several years, he helped around the house, since some jobs were simply too much for me, and even now he does the hoovering at weekends. So there has never been any arguments in our relationship because of feminism. We consider ourselves equals in every way.

'I have never been convinced that women were nice anyway — I find them bitchy and sly, but not all, naturally. I'm not saying *all* women are the same but you have to get to know them really well before you find out if they can be trusted not to repeat things, and that takes time. I have always preferred male company socially. I find men in groups more entertaining, funny, etc. and being one woman amongst a group of men makes you feel good. In a group of women I'm quiet, shy, never contribute to the conversation, feel inferior and bored. In a group of men, I'm witty, extrovert, talk as much as possible, feel great and am never bored. So I guess I wouldn't be a good candidate for the women's movement.'

Unidentified Woman.

'To me feminism means truly being treated as an equal with men both in terms of an equal partnership at home as well as at work. It doesn't mean losing my femininity in achieving this. I got involved in the late Sixties when I was in the sixth form at my all girls' grammar school, although I had always been a tomboy in my childhood and hated playing with dolls and learning how to cook . . . I read all I could, books, newspapers, but I was already involved with my future husband so I was not an activist, although very verbal on the subject.

'I have always believed in women's rights and the unfairness of society's expectations as well as men's. I felt I was fighting with my husband the whole time for recognition. In fact, I was. We were constantly bickering because I felt undervalued and taken for granted and the more I tried to put my point the more entrenched his views and attitudes became. I gave in and became a doormat, trying to be like the traditional wife he wanted . . . and he left me for another woman. So my belief in Women's Lib. did destroy my relationship with my husband. I sublimated my ambition through him after I gave up work, had a child because I was bored.

'I had thought and believed that my husband believed in and supported Women's Lib. before we got married, but it turned out he was only paying lip service to the idea and turned out to be very much his father's son, a raging MCP . . . Separation and divorce gave me the freedom I really yearned for.

'Since then I have been lucky enough to share a friendship with a man on truly equal terms, a gift not many women are privileged to share in. We are both very independent people and value our personal space. I am also loath to give up my hard-won independence and I suppose I still am not convinced that a woman really needs a man around all the time. My life is simpler without a full-time partner at present, and I like it that way.'

Hilary Leighter, thirty, middle-class.

'I am not old enough to remember a time before feminism existed. I went to an ordinary Brent comprehensive school where I was the only girl in my year to study maths and physics to A level. My boyfriend of the time suggested that I go to Cambridge to study engineering and computer science — there were fourteen girls to 280 boys in my year. If anyone said "how unusual to be studying engineering" I always said, "oh no, there's loads of us" and denied their sexism. However, when I started work and went on a technical computing course with a number of men slightly older than me, they resented me being there and started going on about all the pornographic films they were going to each evening and when I hit one for constantly telling me to make tea etc. they ignored me.

'As soon as I got home I got *Spare Rib* for the first time and went with my friend Helen to a consciousness-raising group. This was very structured and dominated by two social workers who were trying to be "more working-class than thou" so I stopped going. Around this time I started writing Ms. instead of Miss, seeing myself as an independent wage-earning person.

'From 1980 I worked in New York for a year contract programming. Here I joined NOW (started by Betty Friedan in the Sixties). I wish we were so organized here. It's divided into chapters (areas). To join, you do a structured consciousness-raising programme discussing issues from promiscuity to pornography. Then you become a full member and take part in political lobbying — for example, writing letters to Congress to stop them banning abortion, helping women candidates secure nominations to become governors, taking part in International Women's Day marches and festivals and general evenings where we would talk about how to get on as women in our careers etc.

'When I came back here the 300 Group had just started so I joined — I then joined the SDP as they were an egalitarian party and the first to plug positive discrimination and to have more women candidates. I stood for Enfield North and hope to stand every election until I get in! I do see that one of my first priorities is to get equal rights for women and I will fight for this as much as I can.'

Mandy, twenty-eight, middle-class.

'When the man I lived with threatened to kill me, I knew he was serious and that I had to get out. It was in the women's refuge I fled to, that I got my "feminist education".

'I'd been with Greg for several years. We were drawn together by a tremendous attraction and the fact that we had so much to talk about, but there was always a big inequality because he was working-class with virtually no education, a kind of gangster with a lot of charm. I'd trained as a teacher and I'm very articulate and to Greg I was a "catch", someone who could lead him to knowledge, education and all the things he felt inadequate about because he didn't have them. I found him enormously attractive because he was rough, streetwise with lots of bravado and a sense of adventure. I was a country girl and although I'd been to university and came into contact with some of the women's thinking in the Seventies, I really was an innocent. Also, I'd got married and had a child very young, and that hadn't worked, so I had a strong sense of failure, that I couldn't get life right.

'Greg adored my little boy and I think that was part of my attraction — he desperately needed a mother and someone to love him that way. It was something he had never had as a kid. We began living together quite quickly and at first it was wonderful. But then we began to argue about small, not very important things but he couldn't stand the fact that I was good at arguing and I wasn't willing to give in to what he said. At first he would shout and scream at me, then it turned into shoving and slaps to try to force me to agree with him. Then within months he was actually beating me up because he was jealous, because he didn't think I was respecting him properly — anything that came into his head. It was terrifying because I couldn't believe this man whom I loved and who seemed most of the time to love me, could behave this way. And always after an attack he would be full of remorse begging forgiveness, crying, pleading with me. It was all terribly confusing.

'Of course I was angry and a bit of me said this isn't good enough, he shouldn't do this to you. But then he would say things like "if you wouldn't argue I'd never have done that" or "you made me do it" and it felt as though that was true, that somehow it had to be my fault.

'I began to be very scared but I didn't want to tell anyone because in between the beatings things were good and he was very affectionate and caring and this was what I needed. I felt I had cocked up my life so far and the only solution I could see was to make it work with another man. I was a prime target for an abusive man. But by the time I realized how dangerous he was I didn't know how to get out. There was a kind of unholy bond between us and I was colluding in the violence.

'I got pregnant with twins and he couldn't accept it. I think he was terrified of the responsibility and he began to get very angry with me. Then one day he beat me up very thoroughly and kicked me in the stomach, and I knew I had to get out. I realized that he would kill the babies.

'I packed my bag and fled, with my small child, to the refuge in the city where I was living. At the refuge they were very good and supportive and they talked to me at great length explaining it wasn't my fault, that I didn't have to put up with the beatings, that my life could be better without Greg. It was very comforting in one way but the women at the refuge took a very hard line on men, believing that they were the cause of most things wrong in the world and that the only way for a woman to be able to be strong and happy was to live without men. I just didn't feel that, it wasn't what I wanted. What I really wanted was someone to help me stop Greg beating me so we could live together — I can see now that this was an impossible idea, because violent men don't usually stop and the only way is out. Even so, even now, I don't believe all men are bad nor do I want a life without them.

'I went back to Greg and he promised it would be all right, but of course it wasn't and the beatings began again. This time I got an injunction to stop him coming into the house, but he simply came and broke the door down and beat me up very thoroughly. And I still let him stay. After years of abuse I was weakened and hopeless, and I had lost my reasoning power. The trouble was, too, that I hadn't told anyone [except for the staff at the hostel] because I didn't want to admit what was going on. But by now I knew I had to get out and I told my sister what was happening. She just came and took me and the little boy off to a refuge in London so that Greg wouldn't be able to find me and I wouldn't easily be able to go back.

'It was the best thing anyone did. At this refuge there were a lot of groups and I found that by sharing my experiences and listening to other women's I began to see that it wasn't just me caught in a crazy situation, but that there is a real syndrome of male violence against women. I also started to read a lot of feminist writing about violence as well as other polemical and academic writings and it all began to make sense to me. I began to understand how society permits male violence, how men are allowed — encouraged — to be tough, aggressive and macho and when that overflows into violence against women, it is seen as somehow an allowable male behaviour. Giving the wife a slap to make her see sense, is part of our mythology, it's what men have to do to make stupid, hysterical women behave. When you start seeing that kind of thing, and the fact that the police just don't bother about domestic violence, that our cinemas are full of male violence as entertainment, you begin to see that perhaps it isn't your fault, but the fault of our culture, that men feel they can use violence on women.

'I began to feel much stronger and to feel good about being a woman. I made good friends in the refuge and I learnt to value myself. From there I got re-housed. I had the twins and it was like a deliverance having them on my own. I felt wonderfully in control, that they were a gift and that I had to be a strong, sure footed woman to give them the life they deserve. That was a couple of years ago and I'm living on my own now. I haven't seen Greg and don't want to. I wouldn't have chosen to be a battered woman or to go through those years of hell yet at least I can see they have had some purpose in the end.'

Jenny who describes herself as 'middle-class (agh!), white (agh!), centre leftie (agh!), twenty-six (Thank God — still time to change).'

'I unwittingly found myself in a Women and Food self-analysis course, when about sixteen, thinking it would be an academic discussion which was all I was used to at school. University was the Big Bang which was about reading, joining groups, praising ourselves for having "strong" female friends, deliberately going for all female socialising, etc. etc. Piles of *Spare Rib* copies everywhere. Natural shoes. A definite group of "feminist" females emerged, scornful of our male colleagues for being underlyingly sexist but dreaming of them all the same and occasionally sleeping with them. Actually I became a ranting feminist bore out to educate my brothers' friends and parents by leaving *Our Bodies Ourselves* open at the cunt photos on the kitchen table.

'As you would expect, leaving university was a bit of a turning point when all we feminist female friends found ourselves scattered in different sectors of work and different counties/ countries. I think I then felt a minor "pioneer" role — i.e. to disseminate the information and wondrous enlightenment I had enjoyed. Holding on to progressive opinions also gives you a kind of inner, private confidence or self-praise — e.g. I may be working with (and behaving exactly the same way as), a load of "straight" office workers or whatever but when it comes down to it, I'm far more "right on" — witness my one ear-ring! When you find yourself in your third office job or similar situation (i.e. when you're still not down at Greenham or with Lambeth unemployed Mums) you can no longer kid yourself. You're part of the vast majority of the population — virtually politically dead.

'The best thing I've retained and still like to keep informed on is an awareness of women's health — *Our Bodies Ourselves* stuff. I've also retained some of the Susie Orbach school of thought on getting fat which I suppose is very useful, although it seems commonsense now. Finally, that awakening to the whole violence, real and social and political, against women, has never gone away and never will.'

Un-named, twenty-one, working-class woman with a 'professional' job.

'My partner and I have just got engaged and we discuss feminism and he holds a different concept of feminism than I do — he doesn't see the point of women getting married if they don't want to "depend" on men, that they want to stay as an independent individual. He believes that men appear as the "enemy" to such women and so they turn to lesbianism. He sees nothing wrong in women wanting to look nice by putting make-up on but feels that feminism doesn't allow this (I agree with the former but not the latter point).

'He moved in with me when we got engaged and we are just beginning to find out how to cope with day-to-day living and running of the house. We have discussed his apparent unwillingness to help with housework. At the moment he has to commute about twenty-six miles to work every day whereas it's only a quarter of an hour's work for me, so for practical reasons I do the bulk of the work with regard to cooking during the week and try to make him at least help in the cooking at weekends. I do the washing and ironing. I haven't the patience to watch him make a mess of it or teach him how to do something he has no interest in learning.'

Lynn, nineteen, 'working-class I suppose. I work in a factory.'

'I became aware of the way women are treated in our society as I was going through my teenage years. I now feel more strongly about it than ever; though I know very little about the political side of it I became aware of what was going on around me.

'I began to notice glamorous women being used to advertise and sell things, the less clothing they had on the more a product seemed to stand out and appeal to men — on the TV, on posters, in magazines and newspapers, literally everywhere. It made me angry. Women are being stereotyped to such an extent they lose their identity, we are no longer individuals. I saw men going into nightclubs with the "birds" on their arms, just quiet and smiling, an accessory, pretty and cute, obeying their every word and never stepping out of line, scared they'd be dumped.

'I looked at all this as I was growing up and thought to myself, "this is so wrong. I don't want to be one of those girls", so I gradually changed my appearance and attitudes and turned to an alternative style of life and group of people. The opposite sex did not like it one little bit, they told me girls should be pretty and feminine and not have views and opinions, but no way, not me. I was not going to and still won't give in to them. I get a lot of abuse for my appearance, which I suppose I should mention is generally classed as "punk". In being different the outside world shows up so clearly, and all that is wrong immediately jumps out and women today come across as still being treated wrongly. Over the years, since the women's movement, things have changed drastically, women can do so much now, more or less any career or job is open to them, but have men changed their attitudes? Not nearly enough.

'It seems to me most men either sleep around or think it's perfectly OK for them to do so, but when a woman does it, it's wrong, they get called slags, whores and the like, but when it's a man he's a big hero, a stud. It's so sad and wrong but it's always been like that and I can't see it changing.

'Men, to me, are a threat emotionally and physically. My views on marriage have changed. When I was just a child it was every girl's dream to grow up, get married in white, have children, buy a nice house and for a while I believed this dream, but it's not like that. Now marriage is to me about as wished for as a death certificate. Maybe you'll think I'm just another mixed up girl growing up in today's society, but believe me, I'm not the only one and our numbers are growing.'

These are just some of the voices which I have heard during the year I have been talking with and listening to women. I selected these because they seem to me to illustrate some of the issues, feelings, attitudes, experiences which are voiced recurrently, and also because they were expressed in detail and anecdote. It seems to me that they help to illuminate the way feminism has impacted on the lives of women who have not necessarily set out to embrace feminism but who, have been touched by it.

AN EYE BLINK IN HISTORY

WHERE ARE WE NOW?

'EQUAL opportunities may not have advanced very far but the most significant thing is that women's attitudes have changed fundamentally. I see that in my daughter and my son.' — Eva Figes, author of *Patriarchal Attitudes*.

'The years of women's liberation have been hard, they have taught women like me things we could not ignore and there has been pain because of the discontents it has bred, the questions which seem all important to confront. But I wouldn't have been without the revolution.' — Alys Kihl, forty-four.

'There is no formula for being a liberated person, let alone a free woman.' — Sarah Wedderburn, thirty-five.

'Feminism is responsible for the rising divorce rate, abortion, child-molesting and also rape.' — Isabella Mackey in *Cosmopolitan*, February 1988.

'It is twenty years since the Women's Liberation Movement came into being, a small tentative embryo which grew quickly into a tough, noisy, fist-waving, infant, defiantly making itself offensive and objectionable when necessary, opening its mouth and bellowing aloud the demand for equality, rights and status. It was preparing for an adulthood which would be no less vociferous but maturity brought a more careful analytical approach which would join forces with the agit-prop and demonstrations, and it was within the adult movement that women worked towards building and creating a culture of their own.

The movement gathered to it a range of women who found a vital, common bond in the message of liberation from the invasive, pervasive impact of a patriarchal society, of individual male control, of a status quo which had institutionalized second-class status for half the species. Some of these women have become important public names, controversial characters. Others who were not necessarily activists, have drawn from feminism strength, guidance, a belief in themselves which has had an important impact on their lives. Other women have assiduously avoided the arguments and actions, seeing feminism as threatening and destructive, out to take from them the way of life they have chosen.

So what has it all been about? Where has it all got us? Are women better off as a result of their activities these past two decades? Or has it been a grand brouhaha over not very much, ultimately? As the twenty-year anniversary has arrived, it is a time of assessment, a time when academics and polemicists are endeavouring to pull together the strands, and provide some answers or at least constructive thoughts on the matter. I have endeavoured in these pages to give some sense of what the Women's Liberation Movement has been about, some of the issues which have been important, some of the discussions which have arisen around them. Most of all, I have tried to answer the question which intrigued me when I started out: how have the activities and consciousness-raising of the past twenty years affected a range of women, from those who have been passiona-tely, energetically involved and those who have listened, thought, brought changes into their own lives, to those who feel feminism has happened in spite of them.

The difficulty in trying to answer this question is that the women's movement is an organic affair, which has grown, spread, spawned off-shoots, bred within its embrace conflict between sisters, dissenting allegiances and attitudes. It has been a vigorous, feisty campaigning body, a progenitor of networks and support systems, and also a psychic force leading women to new thoughts, ideas, perspectives and preoccupations. It has remained firm of purpose and intent in its bid for certain rights and conditions without which, it argues, women cannot be liberated, which are central to their well-being, and around these issues campaigning goes on. But it has also fragmented so that the white heat at the centre has disseminated. Although women's events, conferences, discussions are still to be found, they draw far less women than in the early days. Michelene Wandor, one of the most active and committed early women's liberationists, explains a familiar viewpoint: 'It's nothing like it was twenty years ago. I don't go to women's meetings. I've stopped going to the kind of conferences I attended in the mid Seventies. It doesn't dominate my life as a political activity because there isn't a Woman's Liberation Movement now in the way there was then.'

Some people talk about this fragmentation with nostalgia. They remember the heady days of a passion fuelled by the belief that all could be changed, that the revolution would succeed in re-drawing society, that a monolithic movement was the essential way for the end to be achieved. Others view it as a positive, confident follow on, the function of the movement in the Seventies.

By forming groups with particular, specific foci, women have concentrated energy into individual areas, so that we have seen support groups set up for women whose lives are hideously distorted by the misuse of male power, homes for battered women, rape crisis centres, a battle against pornography and the offensive depiction of women. A political forum around women's health has evolved empowering women to seek out and ask for information and to oppose the domination of medicine by men. It has also campaigned for and succeeded in getting Well Women clinics which are staffed by women and are there specifically to deal with women's health issues. Self-help groups for afflictions such as thrush and PMT have also been started. Programmes of women's studies now exist at all levels from *ad hoc* classes to degree courses. Women's crafts and skills are taught by local authorities and women's groups. Increasingly women make their living by these skills.

The feminist publishing houses Virago and The Women's Press, which set up in the 1970s specifically to publish works by women and about women, have been immeasurably important. Not only have they brought into existence an enormous body of work demonstrating women's skills as writers, telling us about the lives of women as subjects of literature, but they have also proved that such works are commercially viable. Many mainstream publishing houses have drawn pragmatic inspiration

from this, so that today there are a large number of women's lists
to be found. Small, committed feminist publishing teams have
also published books with little concern for profit. The wealth of
women's literature, history, philosophy, polemic, autobiography
set into print cannot now be erased and is an enduring and
exhilarating record.

Small groups have set themselves up to study the mystical, the
theological, the historical, the mythological aspects of women
and their lives. These and many, many more things have
happened because women have applied the feminist consciousness they may well have developed in the mainstream of the
movement and its activities, to areas which seem to them an
important part of building a female culture.

In discussing the way women's liberation has moved beyond its
early basic demands, Anna Coote and Beatrix Campbell, authors
of *Sweet Freedom*, write: 'There emerged new kinds of feminist
politics, which would carry the women's movement, profoundly
changed since the 1970s, into the 1990s and beyond. The black
women's movement, the peace movement, Women Against Pit
Closures and the new municipal women's committees were all
part of that.'

Midge Mackenzie, one of the earliest activists with Women in
Media, who set up a women's film-making group and helped
devise and then went on to make the BBC series on the history of
suffrage 'Shoulder to Shoulder', expressed it this way: 'The
women's movement as a central focus is no longer particularly
compelling to me, which is not to say I have lost interest in its
aims — not so. But what interests me now is to use my craft to go
on unearthing the wonderful things women have done, to build
a picture of just how much they have been capable of, because
that, in a long-term sense, is a way of creating an understanding
of women's equality and individualism.'

What can be measured, of course, are the tangible results of
the women's movement activities. It is easy to forget that before
1970 employers, without hesitation, paid women markedly less
than men for identical work, and jobs advertised frequently
specified that men only would be considered. The Equal Pay Act
and Equal Opportunities Act are now on the statute book and for
all the criticisms of these pieces of legislation they are proof of
the power of women's campaigning and an acknowledgement

that the principle of equality is right. That the number of cases brought and won have been small, the mechanisms to help and support women who want to bring cases inadequate, the ways in which employers can circumnavigate the legislation too numerous, should not be ignored, but nor should the magnitude of having secured public acknowledgement of fundamental, important rights.

During the Eighties the Labour Party formed a Ministry for Women designed to look at all the proposals for policy and see how they would affect women. This, presumably, results from raising awareness of the importance of considering women's thoughts and feelings, although, cynically, it can also be read as the pragmatism of a party which knows it needs to attract women voters. The real test of the significance of this Ministry has to come when the party is in power.

The GLC, before it was decapitated, saw leader Ken Livingstone set up a women's committee which supported and funded women's organizations around London, and set up educational and recreational services, advice and support groups for women. It also attracted a great deal of publicity from the popular press revealing the profound antagonism of the male-controlled media at the idea of public money being spent for the benefit of women. On the other side, the GLC became a public showcase for some bitter internal battles between the women on the committee. These may have disproved the notion held by some women that their gender is *per se* less competitive, aggressive, dictatorial than men's but the battles in no way invalidated the importance of a women's committee having been set up on an important policy-making body like the GLC. It was an important inspiration, so that now municipal women's committees are to be found in many different local authorities.

Women have reached boardrooms and management offices (although still not in very large numbers); they have become executives — although not bosses — in the media, in business, in industry, and having got the jobs, they have proved themselves at least as able as men in doing them. Women have broken into male employment bastions such as engineering and have increased their numbers in areas like medicine, and proved extremely successful in running their own businesses.

That is the optimistic picture of what twenty years of feminism has meant: a picture of disparate parts which add up to something quite substantial. But while this is all encouraging, it is not the sea change which was sought in the committed passion of the 1970s. As Janet Watts wrote in a lengthy two-part series on women in 1988, for *The Observer*: 'Women do not have equality with men at work; at home; in the classroom; in marriage; on the streets; in the professions; in the dark. Women have less money, power, prestige, status and say than men.' What this optimistic picture does not show is how little the women's revolution operating outside the political power base, has been able to do for impoverished women, to deal with the particular deprivations and abuses some working-class women endure, to break down institutionalized racism. It is a picture which bears testimony to how little concern for women who, for all sorts of reasons, do not and cannot improve their lives, has come from those in power. As Fay Weldon said, when talking about the situation of women today: 'We need to define which women we are talking about.'

The point has been made, too, by a substantial number of women sympathetic to feminism but critical of its self-delusory tendency. Jenny, a successful radio broadcaster, put it this way: 'So feminists have made their mark, establishing a lot of women's facilities and cultural things, but in the end how much does all this affect women whose lives are hard, for whom being a woman means a huge burden of work, for whom it means little freedom? Where are the improvements in child care? In facilities for the elderly who are looked after by women? Where are the truly equal opportunities for women?'

The Child Poverty Action Group attempts to monitor the effects of Government policies on families and they say that over the past two decades there has been little improvement in the conditions of women. With one in four families living below the poverty line, child benefit frozen and grants for such things as cookers cut, it is women who feel the brunt of the policies of a Government which has not had their needs on the agenda. And in the face of this, feminism for all its campaigning has not been able to change their fate. Fran Bennett at CPAG explains: 'Feminism has raised expectations but at the same time State provision has been re-designed to reduce expectations. Life is very hard for women who do not have the possibility of getting on to the upward ladder and you see clearly how little the women's movement can do when those in power do not wish to do anything about it.'

Material deprivation is a deadening and depressing situation to live with, and research has shown how people who have no faith that their situation will improve, become alienated, depressed and/or angry. This is not exclusive to women — men suffer it too. But for women it often means, additionally, greater physical risk. If they live in a place where there is bad lighting, no security, they are at risk of sexual assault and rape. Women usually spend a greater portion of time in their home than men, so if the housing conditions are bad, if there are too many children in too little space, if there is a problem with disturbing neighbours, for example, it is women who suffer. If women must look after home and children unaided, it probably means there is little or no time for study or recreation; and a woman with no financial independence may well feel she must put up with behaviour from a man which would not be tolerated by more privileged women.

On the domestic front, women, across the board, are still working hardest. Surveys have shown that in almost 90 per cent of households, women do the washing and ironing, in 75 per cent they do the cleaning and in 70 per cent they make supper. A number of surveys on child care have underlined the fact that women look after children a great deal more than men do whether they work or not. Nor has anything raised the status of housework or got it acknowledged as having value in monetary terms.

In early 1989 the Women's Organizations Interest Group at the NCYO (National Council for Voluntary Organizations) and the Fawcett Society launched a document 'Eliminating Discrimination — A Long Way to Go', which pointed to the fundamental changes still required before women will have any real equality. Jane Grant, who runs the Women's Organizations Interest Group, which acts as an umbrella organization drawing together, consulting with and acting for a large number of women's organizations and presenting their needs to Parliament, from the most radical to such as the Women's Institute and the Mothers'

Union, described the document as 'a response to the Government's initial report on the UN Convention on the Elimination of All Forms of Discrimination.' The Convention emerged from the UN Decade for Women and was ratified by many countries including Britain, although this only happened after considerable lobbying by women's groups, and it was done with a number of reservations. 'A Long Way to Go' pointed out that women's representation on public bodies, in Parliament, in top positions in almost every public field, 'remains abysmally low'. Although women enjoy equality with men before the law the fact that just three per cent of high-court judges are women means that the law is interpreted almost entirely by men. Women carry out most of the caring roles in society but do not get financial support, so their own career prospects are damaged. And child care provision in the UK remains among the worst in Europe. The final irony, pointed out by Jane Grant, is that the Government's own Ministerial Group on Women's Issues is chaired by a man, John Patten, who is described as 'difficult to communicate with' and just two of the eleven members are women.

Yet judging the women's movement only on tangible happenings, is to disregard the importance of the psychic impact feminism has had on women of all classes, colours, types and it is here that some transformations have taken place.

The earlier chapter Voices reveals just a few of these and there must be so many more. Women who, without knowing what it would mean, opened their eyes to feminist writings from Simone de Beauvoir to Germaine Greer, Shulamith Firestone, Eva Figes, Sheila Rowbotham and so many others, and found the words echoing stirrings in themselves, and used this beginning to explore further. Women who picked up through daily life and its encounters, the ideas and arguments of the women's movement, who found themselves offended by the sneering at the activities of other women whose quest for equality came across as reasonable. They moved forward. Through the distress of bad relationships, the inspiration of friendship, women were led to consciousness raising, and to evolving a feminist bottom line in their approach to life. Women who insist they were never 'card-carrying sisters' recognize the changes wreaked in their personal lives. Women who to this day protest 'I'm not a feminist but . . .' have adopted attitudes and feelings which appear to be drawn directly from the propagation of Women's Liberation activities. In *The New Women's Movement* (edited by Drude Dahlerup, Sage Publications, 1986) Joyce Gelb made the point: 'It is clear that the British feminist movement has succeeded in changing life-styles and consciousnesses', although they did not see those changes in the structure of life.

A number of key activists from the early days of the women's movement are now talking of the fact that feminism has mobilised working-class women, black women, women such as the miners' wives, into looking at their lives and what they are entitled to expect in a different way and into taking action. It is the lesson of strength learned through organization and solidarity which could be the dynamic to action through the 1990s.

Radical barrister Helena Kennedy who grew up in Glasgow, in a society where traditional roles died hard, says: 'The great advance has been in women's perceptions of themselves. I go up to Scotland and see my family and the women there and I can see how the ideas which the women's movement has put across have gone through large areas of the community. It's not true that it's just middle-class women they have reached, and I see that through my work too. I go to see my folks and I can see that their expectations have changed.'

A forty-eight-year old woman states: 'I think this is a good time to be alive and I've always felt very much a child of my generation, not out there being famous and changing things in a big way, but part of the pattern of transformation that began in the Sixties and still continues. It's a slow growth for me — no overnight change. The prevailing ambiance enabled me to think about things in a way I wouldn't have done before. It enabled me to leave my husband and in doing so to hang on the belief that women are not inferior. Now I have a new male partner and though we don't discuss feminism we do share chores and things are fair, or we are happy with them.'

And Sue comments: 'The peak of rage and activity may have passed but I feel that many women's expectations have been raised by that period, and attempts, for example, by the Government, to force them back into the home, will be resisted ferociously. Also, women who have discovered their strengths as individuals and parts of groups will not willingly give that up now.'

Janet Dixon who has contributed a vivid and illuminating account of how she turned to separatism then moved on from it, in *Radical Records: Perspectives on Thirty Years of Lesbian and Gay History* (Routledge, 1988), says of the separatists: 'It is my belief that without us, feminism would never have been more than a caucus of the broad Left. Separatism was right there in the middle, influencing all women, and, despite themselves, even those who were most vociferous in their resistance to our ideas. What separatists did was to reduce the very complex set of circumstances which combine to oppress women, to a single uncluttered issue. That is the stark injustice of the total humilia-tion of women on all levels, by men. Separatism was the source of this theme, and the means by which it spilled into every area of feminist activity.'

Marsha Rowe who, with Rosie Boycott, founded *Spare Rib* states: 'Feminism has changed everything. It informs my work, how I am as a mother and as a wife. It informs the way I work as an editor with a publisher and what I write myself. What is interesting for me now is to see how far I can go with this consciousness, which is not about a lot of specific women's movement activities but about taking the attitudes which inform my being further into bigger debates, to address bigger issues. I am interested in applying it to things which stretch my imagina-tion and take me further, outside the area in which I know my thinking and my thoughts are safe and appropriate.'

Zoe Fairbairns whose novel *Stand We At Last* (Virago, 1983) spans several generations of women's lives, finishing in the present, speaks thus: 'I am glad that I have lived in this era rather than twenty years earlier. I feel it is very important that the women's movement happened — important to me personally as well as for women generally. It is important for me to identify with the women's movement because I think it is vital to nail that colour to the mast. It's also an act of defiance because a lot of women these days use the line "I don't know if I'm a feminist, because I don't know what a feminist is" and I want to stand up and say "well, I do and I am one and proud of it". In my writing I cover different subjects and the fact that this is so, is testimony to my belief that being a feminist writer doesn't mean you have to keep writing about the same thing. The feminist perspective is my perspective.'

For Sarah Wedderburn, thirty-five, feminism has meant a tentative reaching out to new ways of seeing and behaving: 'My upbringing was scaffolded by an absolute belief in the patriarchy. I was a girl and I learned obedience, subservience, giving and giving way. I was afforded the best academic education possible and I didn't know what to do with it. I was frightened off by the aggressiveness of university feminist politics — the alternative ways of being were too deeply embedded in my psyche. It took a very long haul into the workplace, a marriage, two children and illness to bring me to a beginning of personal liberation and I owe much to the women's movement that went on in the middle distance all those years.'

Jeanette, forty-four, considers her experience: 'Throughout the late Sixties, I thought feminism sounded absurd, unnecessary, unpleasant. But I did not know why. I didn't investigate. I married as I was programmed to do and it seemed most important to have got my man. I was, in terms of the heterosexual world of looks, very beautiful — just what a man wants. I had lovely hair, a beautiful face, a lovely body (i.e. big tits), a lovely shaped arse, great legs, lovely ankles — I was slim trim and dim!

'I spent thirteen years in this dreadful marriage with a husband who believed "women are like blacks, if they need a law to make them equal then they have got to be inferior", "no woman should ever have a job while a man is unemployed", and so on. I often thought I was insane I was so unhappy but I was beginning to hear the ideas and things going on and in the early days, although I was not really involved, I can see now that I was changing. I thought I could forge these ideas into my marriage but that was impossible, so I left with my child in 1984.

'I am out of all that and I am a lesbian. I have never been so OK. I don't want to put happy or settled, that may not even happen, but I'm OK. I feel I like myself.'

There are clear words from Michelene Wandor: 'Well I think it's been absolutely worth it. I can't imagine the last twenty years without feminism for me. I can imagine it in the world because I don't think much of the world has really been dented, although I think there have been occasional moments. I suppose we've all got quite complicated responses to what's happened within

feminism and whether it could have been different. I certainly
feel that there is a kind of community of women and now others
are getting on with what they're doing, having also been inspired
by feminism.'

It is interesting, in glimpsing through a list of quotations on
friends and friendship, by some of the most highly acclaimed
male writers and thinkers, how negative, mistrustful, cynical
most of the sayings are — friendship is not something men seem
to find easy. In this area women have always been more able to
form friendships and emotional allegiances amongst themselves,
more able to explore feelings, confide and trust, despite being in
a world where they have had to compete for men and marriage,
where their success in life was so often measured through the life
the husband provided, and where friendship was necessarily
tempered. Fay Weldon depicted, most entertainingly, the double
bind of affection, dependence and enjoyment between women
friends, but laced with jealousy, hostility, fear of being rejected,
in *Female Friends* (Heinemann, 1975). Women reflecting on the
nature of friendship through the 1950s and 1960s talk of the
competitiveness between them and also the superficiality which
was brought to bear once they married — it was considered
disloyal, inappropriate to discuss feelings with someone other
than a husband. Of course women still confided in women
friends but many doing so had a sense of acting illicitly. Terence
Davies in his film of a family in the 1940s — *Distant Voices, Still
Lives* — showed the way women, once married, were prevented
by fear of their husbands' anger from visiting and communicat-
ing with long-standing, close women friends.

Feminism has applauded, encouraged, even exalted female
friendship. So many of the writings urge women to draw
together to share and care, stressing that there is enormous
strength and virtue in the qualities women can bring to their
friendships and allegiances. Consciousness-raising groups flourished because of the deep trust, affection, love which grew up
between the women.

Women with children found themselves able to share the
troubling doubts and emotions which so often accompany parenting. They found such communality of feeling and found the
joy of sharing it. Over and over in my interviews women have
talked about the importance of the friendship they have found

with other women. Fay Weldon speaks for many: 'For so long there was the sense of failure if you were in a room with a group of women; if Saturday night was spent with a girl friend. Now the status of one's women friends is so much greater. It is true of me and I know it to be of others, we are nourished by our women friends.'

So it is for Clare Moynihan: 'I live on my own, my marriage finished some years ago, and women are the people with whom I have strong and important friendships and I am sure these friendships are different: more honest, deeper, more acknowledged as very meaningful, than they would have been before feminism brought an analysis to us. I would like to live with a man as a partner, and perhaps I shall again one day, but I would not want it at the price of losing my women friends. They are not less important than a man or relationship. I see the close, loving relationships I have with women as something which will be part of the fabric of my life until I die.'

While Alys Kihl says: 'I have enjoyed women friends so much in the past years. We have made so many discoveries, we have so many things to share, so much to laugh about as well as cry about. The friendship of women is absolutely important in my life now. But I have seen women putting all their faith and energy into friendships with women sharing their struggle, and then perhaps the other women have moved on to different things, changed their ideas on what should be done, and the camaradie goes. Then there is such hurt. I have seen women in this position feeling discarded and desperate, saying feminism has let them down.'

Barbara speaks of her experiences: 'For so long women hated themselves because they were forever living through a man's eyes, trying to please men, trying to live up to their expectations, trying to get a man and keep him to feel all right, and when you live like this you cannot like yourself as a woman nor can you truly like other women. When I was in this frame of mind I had women friends but they were peripheral, the people I saw when there was not a man around. I saw much less of them when I got married and although I enjoyed their company I was so busy trying to please my man, giving him all my time and energy, that women friends became distant. I would not let that happen again. I am without a partner and happier because I like myself,

I do not have to strive to please all the time, and because there is space in my life I see far more of my women friends and I enjoy that, I enjoy it so much.'

Friendship among women stretches, too, across generations. Shared beliefs, interest in the history being written as they go along, an understanding of how older women's experience can be meaningful for the young, how youthful perspectives can enhance the life of older women, has created bonds and friendships.

Sarah Wedderburn comments: 'I owe an awful lot to one woman who has doggedly believed in herself through thick and thin over a long life. Talking to her over the years has taught me adaptability and courage and the good sense to know when it's better to duck under for a while rather than go on flailing around on the surface.'

Critics of the women's movement, sneering and glaring from the outside, have been plentiful, and it was an understandable article of faith in the early days, that feminists did not criticize their sisters or what was being done in the name of women's liberation. Jill Tweedie, writing in 1982, recalled the reasoning: 'It was a founding principle of the women's movement that women should not criticize other women. It was a good and necessary principle for many years. Women were conditioned, fearful, unconfident, isolated from each other and dependent on men, so whatever sins we might commit against our sisters had to be understood in the light of our historical handicaps and overlooked in the hope of increasing awareness and support.'

Yet a gag cannot be kept on debate forever — and nor should it be. Once the movement gained its strength from the communality of feeling, the confidence that they were, indeed, a united front struggling for fundamental changes, women began to express their disagreements: women with different feelings about men, different ideas about politics, women who wanted very different end results, women who used a variety of ways in their quest for individual power, position, acceptance said their bit. Within individual groups and in the public world there were some flamboyant examples of sisterly splits.

My own experience was of working with 'Broadside', the first all-women's current affairs documentary series, commissioned by Channel Four as its gesture of commitment to equal opportunities. The conflicts between theory and practice began almost immediately. Democratic meetings at which everybody was allowed a say and a vote, proved meaningless in the face of manoeuvring by some women determinedly getting the positions of power in making programmes and promoting their careers. Factions formed to take control of the organization and for many of us it was salutary proof that women, when there are prizes to be had, power to be taken, will behave in precisely the ways which have been so criticized in men, and which deserve to be equally criticized in women.

Many women felt irritated and aggravated by the battles over whether manholes should be re-named, whether lesbians needed separate cemeteries, whether school children should be allowed particular books, not because *au fond* these matters were considered unimportant, but because they gave the media wonderful ammunition for parody and because they diverted attention from larger, more all-embracing battles.

Eva Figes reflects: 'I think a lot of silly things happened in the 1970s. I think a lot of big issues got lost in a welter of extremes and symbolic matters. And there was a simplistic formula of man as bad and all men had to fit in to this. I had a strong feeling that younger women who hadn't made it were jealous and wanted to knock what people like me who'd made it, had to say, claiming we had only done it by compromise, playing into the hands of the opposition.'

Julia Neuberger feels that she has benefited from the women's movement and she acknowledges that she might well not have been made a rabbi without the movement's public influence. For all that, she is fiercely critical of some things the movement has and has not done: 'Most significantly I feel angry with the women who opposed entry into Europe. Certain conditions in many European countries are better for women than they are here, and if women had looked to that, aligned themselves more broadly with women and fought on that front I think it would have been important.

'I have also been maddened over things like whether political lesbians should have children or the debate over language, because these things have blurred the real issues, which are that we have more single women with children in our society than ever before, who are getting precious little help, that the majority of elderly in our society are women, extremely frightened, frail, who cannot go out alone. The women's movement should have concentrated far harder on economics and caring.'

Criticisms are one thing, but a central, essential flaw in the evolution of women's liberation hangs for many on the way they have felt themselves inexorably drawn to try to become Superwoman, to prove that it is possible for a woman to match men in the workplace as well as intellectually while also fulfilling the role of mother and often that of the traditional wife or partner as well. Many feminists would argue this was never the idea and that those women who took on such multiple responsibilities, who have felt themselves obliged to be so responsible, have misinterpreted the point and are themselves culpable. But the fact that so many women who have followed the politics and philosophies of liberation have found themselves juggling work, domestic chores and children alongside attending to a partner's needs, is one of the ways in which the women's movement has not thought through the consequences of its campaigning. The emphasis for some time during the Seventies was that women could and should be able to do the same jobs as men but the price of proving this, for many women, was to try to work the kinds of hours men have traditionally worked and, if they had families, to run those as well, without letting the tension at the seams show. No amount of lists pasted on the back of the door and carefully planned schedules, as suggested by Shirley Conran, author of *Superwoman*, altered the fact that life was stressful, exhausting and ultimately not much fun for the women striving to do it all. One described it as being like 'Spending life in a revolving door.'

It was not the way Betty Friedan had meant things to go when she wrote *The Feminine Mystique*, and in 1980 she produced the follow-up book *The Second Stage* questioning the rightness of what was happening and talking of the loss to women of losing the time and energy to enjoy their children, and the homes they had created. Carolyn Faulder, who wrote an introduction for the book, described the hostility from feminists which greeted Betty Friedan when she visited Britain: 'She's been accused of sending women back into the nuclear family and destroying the movement she helped to found.'

In demonstrating that they can be men's equals at work and working long hours and combining this with housework, shopping, cooking — employing others to perform these chores if a partner cannot or will not do so — may mean substantial cost, but it does not generally cause women in a position to do this, conflict. Once children are involved in the equation it all becomes a lot more problematic. For many women, it is possible to employ help with looking after children and should the child care situation improve there will be that option too, but none of this deals with the pain many women suffer at having to sacrifice their children so thoroughly, in order to succeed at work. In taking on the male agenda women, who have been biologically designed to carry and give birth to children, who for centuries have developed the primary loving bond with their children, and with it a deep cultural sense of the rightness of caring for them, must do as men do and put the domestic area of life out of sight. The women's movement has only begun to confront this recently. At the start of the feminist years, proving women could make it alongside men at work, on the one hand, and demonstrating loudly and publicly that they would not take biological destiny as their lot lying down, were *the* important things. And so women left their children the hours required, often departing before the children went to school, returning after they were in bed, working weekends if necessary. The cost of succeeding this way, was seeing little or nothing of their children, having a fleeting glimpse of the growing process, short intense bursts of 'quality' time. For some, like myself, the pain of effectively losing the child or children one loves and wishes to share time with to a successful career has seemed intolerable, a brand of searingly painful maternal deprivation which is not to do with the needs of the child but to do with the needs of the mother. Yet, equally, the prospect of giving up any chance of a fulfilling career to be full-time at home with children, was also a very high price to pay. The way women have chosen, which has its own drawbacks, is to cut back the hours worked, the prospects of promotion, or personal development, in order to divide time more evenly between children and work or study. That has not been possible for a lot of women, nor has it been the choice of others who, understandably, argue that for women to do this just when reasonable numbers are demonstrating their abilities to be equals in the workplace would be disastrous in terms of the public perception of women.

It is, I believe, a serious failing of feminism that it has not added to the dogged campaigning over child care a campaign to have this situation changed. There have been attempts at job-sharing, and flexi-time, which have never really taken off, despite the few examples of women who work hard at this, seeing it as a balance between work and children. Part-time work may be an option, but in terms of career it is a severe handicap. Besides, the real point is not to organize special deals for women but for our society to start valuing children and the role mothers and fathers play in their development. Nowhere is the importance of parenting backed up with money to allow parents to work shorter hours, or equally importantly, to get working hours cut back for *anyone* who is a parent.

Men must speak out on the need for time with their families, the children they have been as much responsible for creating as the women, to point out that bringing up children is a job which is important individually and to society. They need to demand time off for their children's dental appointments, to stay at home when the nanny is sick, to attend school concerts and confer-ences, to have holidays and after-school time with the children. If these things were to happen women would not be penalized in their career prospects because they are the ones who must almost always drop everything to meet children's needs, who are likely to need to leave punctually, to take time off during school breaks and men would get to know and enjoy their children far more than many seem to do these days.

Men, as the bulk of employers, should think about these matters, but there is too much evidence of their lack of the wish to do so, to be optimistic that this will happen. Less easy to understand are the many women who, when they achieve powerful positions, rarely work to change the agenda. For it seems an important way in which women could and should support other women, a way which would allow them to continue to hold jobs, progress, yet also enjoy their children. Is it that women who have achieved successful careers by seeing very little of their children will not do this because it would entail confront-ing the deeply internalized pain they have experienced in leaving their own children? By changing the agenda for other women they are acknowledging that children as well as careers are important and perhaps having sacrificed their own it is too difficult to face this perspective.

Yvonne Roberts, mother of a five-year-old daughter and a successful journalist and television reporter, expresses it this way: 'The myth presented to women is that there is nirvana, but of course it's not true. I think this generation of women in their thirties and forties are going for broke in management terms, in wanting to prove their capabilities and I don't think they are pausing to consider what it will all mean. For years men have lost their children to work and look at the alienation it has led to, look at how little we like what that denial of the caring, nurturing aspects of life leads to in men. I think women need to change the terms or we have not achieved the right thing. They are getting power now and they are in a position to start changing the terms.'

Marsha Rowe, too, feels that twenty years on it is important that women who have proved their commitment to feminism should stand up and say that they value motherhood, and allow men to say the same thing. 'Until the end of the Seventies we didn't allow ourselves to value domesticity. It was seen as reactionary but I feel strongly that we must and should challenge that view. I have one child and I see how quickly her time as a child, with me and her father, goes. I realize that it is not gain for me if I have to miss the experience of knowing her and being with her. I, like many women, have had to tailor my work to fit in with this and I think if women do this and find ways, that too is an important step.'

While Lucy states: 'The difficulty is that in the beginning the battle was for child care, for the right for women to be able to work and that remains important. Some women have to work, others wish to, and child care as a right has not been achieved. But for women who have had child care it has not proved the total answer as, of course, it isn't, and this is confusing. Women are having to work out what that all means, without finding themselves being forced back to the home bringing up children, doing housework, and having no status.'

Conflict within the movement, dissent among women about how things should and should not be done, is an inevitable part of a group made up of very different parts, but a lot of feminists agree that a focus of anger and despair is the woman who has gained the ultimate power in becoming Prime Minister.

The irony is that Mrs Thatcher, welcomed even by such women as Jill Tweedie for her achievement as a woman, and the role-model she provides, has proved a female Judas in couture suits and pussy-cat bows, artfully making use of her femininity while being mistress of policies which have made life worse for many women. In her treatment of other women politicians she has proved less than supportive, so that very few women have been appointed ministers during her reign, and those that have are women with voices selected to echo and reinforce her own in essence. Indeed, Mrs Thatcher displays the characteristics feminists have seen and struggled against so long in men — a deep contempt for women. She gives the impression of aligning herself with male perspectives, behaviour, power structures. If she can be called a feminist by dint of what she has achieved it makes a mockery of a word which embraces in its meaning support for other women.

Jeanette comments: 'I do not know if women can always do things better than men because, like Margaret Thatcher, most women just start behaving like men because that means they are equals — which, of course makes women equal in an inferior way. Yet there are women like Gro Harlem Brundtland in Norway, who demonstrate that winning the top position need not be so corrupting.'

Helena Kennedy expresses conflicting feelings: 'I find myself caught in a horrible bind, feeling admiration for the determination, conviction, ability not to be cowed by men, which Mrs Thatcher demonstrates, and if only she would use those characteristics to the good of her people, men as well as women, I would admire her enormously. But as it is, I see her damaging the lives of people who have no power to fight back, so badly. I see what she is doing to women who are especially vulnerable, as unforgivable. And because I believe the thing women have to show is that we can do things in a better way, that there are compassionate, caring, life-enhancing ways of behaving in life, Mrs Thatcher appals me.'

The policies of Mrs Thatcher and the values she publicly espouses convey a dual message which has at least contributed to the backlash against the Women's Liberation Movement which is hallmark of the late 1980s. On the one hand, she applauds and supports those who succeed and achieve and, within this framework, successful women too are embraced. Yet she holds strong aviews on the importance of the family in its most traditional nuclear form and holds mothers primarily responsible for the welfare of children. Supporting this view, there is a strong and voiciferous group of men and women, moral re-armers, who talk of the importance of the family, the harm done by women going out to work and most particularly *wanting* to do so. Central to the thinking is that women's liberation teaches women to be hostile to the historical idea that women should defer to men, seek to please them, and accept their authority. The public, publicity-seeking face of this came from David Stayt when he formed the Campaign for the Feminine Woman in 1978, specifically to oppose the spread of feminism, which he has described as 'a dangerous cancer and perversion in human society that must be eradicated.' His daughter Isabella Mackey, married with children, spoke out in *Cosmopolitan* in 1988 condemning women who work, women who will not submit to and aim to please their husbands and who are not prepared to make mothering and home-making a full-time job. Rape is the fault of women for going out unaccompanied and the reason for accepting male dominance is: 'Somebody has to talk and somebody has to listen. Someone has to decide and someone has to give way. Men can't lose face — they find it difficult to admit mistakes even to themselves. If only women and men too would accept these different and complementary sex roles, male/female relations would be full of romance, chivalry, harmony and love.'

Nor is this to be dismissed as a lone voice, there are plenty of women who see feminism as dangerous, who, twenty years on, continue to believe that women fighting for equality are subversive. In response to Isabella Mackey, Mary Higgins wrote: 'I found the views refreshing, frank and honest. She should have cited Eve, the first woman, who rebelled against God and her husband, bringing the human race to its present unhappy state.'

It seems the sins of assertive women are responsible for all evil. In America, it is reported, nouveau-skinheads, marauding in alienated gangs committing violent acts, blame the women who are a product of feminist-think. An article in *The Independent* stated: 'Affirmative actioned out of jobs, patronized by yuppie female executives . . . it seems inevitable they spill over into violence.' Helena Kennedy makes the point that: 'Women are still held responsible for public morals, for controlling men,

making sure they behave. That is why feminism is so threatening, because it is about women saying "we will not be forever
virtuous and self-sacrificing, giving up our needs to make men
happy, to hide their misbehaviour from the world." But my
grandmother voiced a very common feeling when she said,
talking of the case of a woman I was defending: "If there were no
bad women there would be no bad men."'

The view of women as deserting their duty is the revisionist
face of the backlash. Although in one sense it is almost an
acknowledgement of two decades of existence, the attack on the
Women's Liberation Movement appears to have gained vitriol
during the latter part of the 1980s. But the backlash has another
incarnation, more sinister because it is offered up in the guise of
progress. This is the 'Post Feminist Woman', an idea neatly
marketed in the *Mail on Sunday* as the woman who has made it by
being successful and highly paid in her career, who has relationships on her terms, who looks good, loves men and sex and who
sees feminism as old hat, a bore, and above all, something she
does not need. Siding with women, helping or supporting them
is not on the menu. The idea was a good media gimmick and
predictably it got taken up and the term Post Feminism slipped,
as an expression, into common parlance while the Post Feminist
Woman was extrapolated upon by journalists and ad. men, and
Brenda Polan described wittily in *Cosmopolitan* at the end of 1988,
the constructed ideal: 'Post Feminist Woman clinches the deal
and cooks cordon bleu. She flies first class and builds her own
bookshelves. She pays the restaurant bill with her gold Amex
card and she knits up Kaffe Fassett sweaters for her lover. She is
hell in the office and heaven in bed. She doesn't exist.'

Certainly this glamorized, de-humanized, all-achieving, stress
and problem-free construct is a media invention, although the
values of the late Eighties, deifying wealth, glitz and the go-for-it
mentality, has created women whose aspirations would be just as
Brenda Polan describes. And the propagation of the idea that a
Post Feminist Woman is a good thing, certainly does exist and is
the most cleverly marketed idea yet for attempting to put a full
stop at the end of women's liberation. Built into it is the all
important idea of novelty. It is cleverer to introduce an enticing
new alternative than to slag off feminists yet again, a stance
which is old-fashioned and unsubtle. Those promoting the Post

Feminist Woman make the point that they are not threatened by committed feminism as it certainly still exists, but here is something much more sexy and modern — the woman who has taken what she wants from the doctrines and forged ahead, remaining impeccably feminine, entertaining and, above all, fond of men in the process. What it is all about, of course, is diminishing women who remain serious about feminism and the fact that changes which have benefited the daily fabric of female life have been few, that there remains an enormous male resistance to it being otherwise.

The PFW is a construct which is designed to satisfy the yearning of men for a woman who does not appear to be in opposition to them. If she will look good, act sexy, be on their side, then she can go out and be successful at work and drive a flash car. But the design is not about making women happy or looking at their needs. Yvonne Roberts, writing in *The Independent*, said: 'If PFW becomes the dominant image of success waved before women, then everyone will pay a price. But none more than those women who buy the myth and try to turn it into a reality. Too late, the single-minded PFW will wake up alone, plug into the mail order catalogue on her computer and realize that the one thing money can't buy is a slice of ordinary life.'

Besides, many feminists are fond of men too. A great many live with them; those who do not, have male friends and allies, but they do not deny the central tenet of feminism that as the keepers of power, men represent a force to be challenged. This thinking has, as is well documented, led to some feminists deciding that until men voluntarily give up that imbalance of power they do not want to liaise with them, live with them, nor are they prepared to like them individually. Predictably it is this aspect of feminists' relationship with men which has received the most attention, and the man-hating tag stuck hard. But if that was overall an inaccurate label, it is indeed true that in the early days of the movement, as women discovered, in the words of Carolyn Faulder: 'what an enormous dirty trick had been pulled on us', as they considered the inequality which strait-jacketed their lives because of male control, as they began to examine the sexual power men have over women because of their historical need of economic support, many women did become extremely angry. Many relationships split asunder under the strain; others barely survived.

But time has passed; men will not go away and most women do not want them to. My findings reveal a strong consensus among energetically liberationist women that the way forward has to be in partnership with men. This feeling and thinking rests partly on the very simple belief of Yvonne Roberts that 'You can't say 48 per cent of the species are no good. You look around and see men who could be called feminists, although I dislike that. There are men who genuinely want equality and there are women who want to live with men like this. To brand them the "enemy" eternally in the name of women's liberation is nonsense.'

Tessa Blackstone, master of Birkbeck College, has brought in a number of key women since her appointment but she also works with men who, she says, absolutely support women's equal opportunities. She adds: 'Together with men who share our aims we can achieve far more than separately and it makes for a better world. I see little future in a movement which has to dislike, hate even, anyone who is not female. To me liberation has always been about equality with men, about sharing things like domesticity, child care, our interests and our aspirations, and this can only be achieved through consensus.'

Carolyn Faulder, too, describes herself as pragmatic and believes that the time has come when women's liberation needs to move outwards beyond the boundaries of women's issues to tackle bigger questions such as the environment, and in this she sees working with men as all important: 'We all belong to the same world. Certainly men have oppressed women and still do. In the area of health where I do a lot of work, it continues and I am very critical, but the point is to educate men, to galvanize them to join forces when we agree with them. I believe from what I have seen and experienced that men can be changed, can understand the point of view women hold and it is a basic understanding of human nature to see that they are more likely to be changed by reason and interest in them than by hostility. Some men always have been and always will be very threatened, but it is a very pessimistic view that believes all men are like that.'

This is a view which has considerable support in 1988, but has been much abused in the past. As Ann Oakley describes, when Betty Friedan and Alice Rossi 'repudiated the doctrine of sexual politics which formed the radical core of the women's movement in the Sixties and Seventies' they attracted much criticism. She adds: 'Friedan's argument that the feminist mystique has replaced the feminine one is, for example, used by her to defend the view that what women now need to do is actively to work for the transcendence of gender differentation.'

In assessing the 'real changes that have been wrought in women's lives' Jill Tweedie went along with the need for the gender divide to be put aside. She said, in 1982: 'The most difficult and crucial changes are still ahead and can come about only if *both* sexes recognize how much our very survival may depend on the speed with which we can manage to bridge the still yawning gap between the masculine principle of impersonal power and confrontation and the feminist ideas that seek an end to such sterile and dangerous attitudes. Until recently women fought for our own rights but, in doing so, we learnt a great deal about the way the world was run to the disadvantage of the whole human race.'

That point is picked up by Helena Kennedy who acknowledges, as do a large number of women, that men will not easily be persuaded to give up the lion's share of power, and that for feminists the battle to get a more equal portion should continue with an understanding of the fact that men, too, suffer oppression and in some cases are more oppressed by class, poverty and unemployment than some women. She says: 'If we take on their concerns then it is not so hard for men to work with us and, at times, for us. It angers me to hear the all men are bad line, because I know a lot of men who have been supportive of women's aims and who are not holding on to all the power.'

Others voice the doubt that we saw in the Sixties women and men working side by side for the common cause and that unison did nothing to change the status of women. The fear voiced is that too much consensus may blur or undermine the battle which, by necessity, must continue.

The other argument being put forward which presents itself as a charter for the future, is that the whole nature of democracy needs to be re-assessed and an approach constructed whereby the State is not regarded as separate from civil society — it should become involved with the household, the family, marriage and personal life. Sarah Perrigo in *Interlink* (1988) wrote: 'It has been left to feminists to argue that our conception of politics needs to include the so-called "private sphere" of the home, the family and personal life, and to show how the State is enmeshed in the maintenance of relations of dominance and subordination in that sphere.' The point Sarah Perrigo makes here is that the modern State poses as gender neutral and in presenting itself thus asks us to accept that people are equal. But she says: 'In reality the State, through a mixture of interference/non interference, structures the inequalities of women's lives in civil society generally and in their domestic lives in particular.' The regulation of marriage, the situation of divorced women, property rights, abortion and birth control; the refusal very often to act against domestic violence, to allocate resources for the care of the young, the elderly, the sick, because they are seen to be the responsibility of the family — and that generally means women — are examples she cites of ways in which women's inequality is ensured by the State's gender neutral stance and the fact that it has taken pieces of legislation which allow it to claim an equal opportunities position.

Through involvement with campaigns which have evolved out of the women's movement, women have learned to see that they can have power in altering their destiny. The work done to get the Abortion Act brought in was one example; the work done around rape has led to certain modifications and changes in the treatment of raped women by police and courts; campaigns around welfare benefits have involved women in their own fate. Perrigo cites, too, the different agit-prop activities women have engaged in, the growth of feminist culture, as ways women have set out to improve things on their own behalf. All of this has been important and empowering she argues but the next step must be for women to involve themselves with State institutions because it is through the power of politics that women can work to transform their environment and get such things as adequate legal protection for women from abuse and the provision of resources such as a social wage necessary for gender equality. At the same time, she says: 'The State must be opened up to public scrutiny and debate.'

Part of the process of doing this can be a Ministry of Women's Rights and a set of constitutional provisions which 'guarantee citizens an extensive array of social rights'. A key thought is that such things as State collective provision in the form of health, education, housing, child care and so on should be devolved on to non-State organizations with participation in policy making by those using the services. Sarah Perrigo explains: 'Women's experiences personally offer a vast reservoir of experience and knowledge about how these services ought to be run if they are to be truly responsive to individual needs. This devolvement of power to institutions in civil society is also crucial if women's dependence on men in "private" families is not to be merely replaced by a dependence on the State.'

It is a stimulating vision of a way forward and the kind of thinking which bring a renewed urgency to feminism. Clearly an important move would be for more women who share these views, to work to get into politics and ultimately Parliament, as the changes will have to be effected there. Jenny Sands is an example of someone whose involvement with the women's movement did not begin until the 1980s when she went on a Women's Studies course, but who has subsequently become active in her local Labour Party and has become a councillor. She has brought a fierce commitment to women's rights to her political activities. Sarah Perrigo makes clear, 'women have been handicapped in entering politics by their domestic commitments as in so many other spheres of public life. But already an increasing number of women are getting involved with local government and this is an important first step.'

As the two decades of the new women's movement have been assessed, inevitably some critics have judged that little has changed, that the movement has really only impacted on a very few women, that the fire has gone and little more is likely to happen until a new generation chooses to begin the good fight again. It is true that there is no reason to be sanguine about what has been achieved, for many women's lives are little or no better than they were twenty years ago. But I do not believe it is right or useful to be too pessimistic. Listening to women over the past year, recording the thoughts of young and old, of different class and type, it seems that there has been an extraordinary impact, that the ideas of feminism have touched the lives of a great many women, that these are young women adopting a vigorous feminist line in their lives, but not necessarily in a formalized sense, not always in a way which means they fully espouse the doctrines of the past twenty years. The number of transformations have not been enormous, but look back twenty years and consider the minds and lives of women then and it is easier to see the significance of the movement. And bear in mind, twenty years is just an eye blink in history.

BIBLIOGRAPHY

Arden, Jane. *A New Communion for Freaks, Prophets and Witches,* 1971 (out of print).

Barr, Pat. *Is This Your Life.* London: Virago, 1977.

Beauvoir, Simone de. *Memoirs of a Dutiful Daughter.* Trans. from the French by J. Kirkup (from *Memoires d'une fille rangée.* Paris: Gallimard, 1958). London: Weidenfeld & Nicolson, 1959; Harmondsworth: Penguin, 1983.

Beauvoir, Simone de. *The Second Sex.* New York: Alfred A. Knopf, 1953.

Beckett, Wendy. *Contemporary Women Artists.* London: Phaidon, 1988.

Behr, Shulamith. *Women Expressionists.* London: Phaidon, 1988.

Blackwood, Caroline. *On the Perimeter.* London: Heinemann, 1984.

Brownmiller, Susan. *Against Our Will: Men, Women and Rape.* Secker & Warburg, 1975; Harmondsworth: Penguin, 1976.

Brownmiller, Susan. *Femininity.* New York: Simon & Schuster, 1984; London: Hamish Hamilton, 1984; Paladin, 1986.

Cant, Bob and Hemmings, Susan. *Radical Records. Personal Perspectives on Lesbian and Gay History 1957-87.* New York: Routledge Chapman & Hall, 1988.

Cassell, Joan. *A Group Called Women.* New York: McKay,1977 (out of print).

Chapkis, Wendy. *Beauty Secrets: Women and the Politics of Appearance.* London: The Women's Press, 1988.

Churchill, Caryl. *Cloud Nine.* London: Pluto Press/Joint Stock Theatre, 1979; 3rd ed., 1983.

Churchill, Caryl. *Serious Money.* London, Heinemann, 1987.

Churchill, Caryl. *Top Girls.* London: Methuen, 1982; revised ed., 1984.

Clark, Wendy (editor). *Sexuality: A Reader.* (Extracts from *The Feminist Review*) London: Virago, 1987.

Coote, Anna and Campbell, Beatrix. *Sweet Freedom: The Struggle For Women's Liberation.* London: Pan, 1982; 2nd ed. Oxford: Basil Blackwell, 1987.

Craig, Sandy (editor). *Dreams and Deconstruction — Alternative Theatre in Britain.* London: Amber Lane Press, 1981.

Dahlerup, Drude (editor). *The New Women's Movement: Feminism and Political Power in Europe and the USA.* London: Sage Publications, 1986.

Daniels, Sarah. *Ripen Our Darkness and Devil's Gate.* London: Methuen, 1988.

Davidson, Marilyn and Cooper, Cary. *High Pressure.* London: Fontana, 1982.

Delmar, Rosalind (intro by). *The Dialetic of Sex: The Case For Feminist Revolution.* New York: William Morrow, 1970; London: Cape, 1971; The Women's Press, 1980.

Deutsch, Helene. *Female Sexuality. The Psychology of Women.* New York: 1945.

Dowrick, Stephanie and Grundberg, Sibyl. *Why Children?* London: The Women's Press, 1980.

Ehrenreich, Barbara; Hess, Elizabeth and Jacobs, Gloria. *Remaking Love.* London: Fontana, 1987.

Fairbairns, Zoe. *Stand We At Last.* London: Virago, 1983; Pan Books, 1984; Firecrest, 1986.

Figes, Eva. *Patriarchal Attitudes: Women in Society.* London: Faber, 1970; Virago, 1978.

Firestone, Shulamith. *The Dialectic of Sex.* New York: Bantam, 1971.

Fo, Dario and Franca, Rame. *Female Parts.* Trans. by Gillian Hanna. (Four monologues). London: Methuen, 1981.

Freedman, Rita. *Beauty Bound: Why Women Strive for Physical Perfection.* London: Columbus, 1988.

Friday, Nancy (compiler). *My Secret Garden: Women's Sexual Fantasies* (foreword by Jill Tweedie). New York: Trident Press, 1973; London: Quartet Books (for Virago), 1979.

Friedan, Betty. *The Feminine Mystique.* New York: Norton, 1963; London: Gollanz, 1963; Harmondsworth: Penguin, 1982 (Pelican).

Gardiner, Caroline. *What Share of the Cake?* London: Women's Theatre Trust, 1987.

Greer, Germaine. *The Female Eunuch.* London: MacGibbon & Kee Ltd., 1970; Paladin, 1971.

Greer, Germaine. *The Obstacle Race: The Fortunes of Women Painters and Their Work.* London: Secker & Warburg, 1979; Pan Books, 1981.

Harford, Barbara and Hopkins, Sarah (editors). *Greenham Common — Women at the Wire.* London: The Women's Press, 1984; reprinted, 1985.

Hite, Shere. *The Hite Report — A Nationwide Study of Female Sexuality.* London: Macmillan, 1976; New York, 1981.

Hite, Shere. *The Hite Report — On Male Sexuality.* London: Macdonald, 1981; New York: Ballantine, 1982.

Hite, Shere. *The Hite Report — Women and Love: A Cultural Revolution in Progress.* New York: Alfred Knopf, 1967; Random House, 1967; London: Viking 1988; Penguin, 1989.

Keyssar, Helene. *A Feminist Theatre: An Introduction to Plays of Contemporary British and American Women.* Basingstoke: Macmillan, 1984.

Kinsey, Alfred (and others). *Sexual Behaviour in the Human Female. By the Staff of the Institute for Sex Research, Indiana University.* London: Saunders, 1953.

Lowry, Suzanne. *The Guilt Cage: Housewives and a Decade of Liberation.* London: Elm Tree Books, 1980.

McConville, Brigid. *Mad to Be a Mother. Is There Life After Birth For Women Today?* London: Century, 1987.

Manning, Rosemary. *A Corridor of Mirrors.* London: The Women's Press, 1987.

Masters, William and Johnson, Virginia E. *Human Sexual Response.* Boston, Mass: Little, Brown & Co. Inc, 1966; London: Bantam, 1980.

Millett, Kate. *Sexual Politics.* New York: Doubleday, 1970; London: Hart Davies, 1971; Virago, 1977.

Mitchell, Juliet, *Woman's Estate.* Harmondsworth: Penguin, 1971 (Pelican); reprinted, 1986.

Morgan, Marabel. *Total Joy.* London: Hodder & Stoughton, 1978. New York: Berkley, 1983.

Morgan, Marabel. *Total Woman*. London: Hodder & Stoughton, 1975; Spire Books, 1973; paperback, 1983.

Morgan, Robin (editor). *Sisterhood is Powerful: An Anthology of Writings From the Women's Liberation Movement*. New York: Vintage Books, 1970.

Nunn, Pamela Gerrish. *Victorian Women Artists*. London: The Women's Press, 1987.

Oakley, Ann. *From Here to Maternity: Becoming a Mother*. (First ed. entitled *Becoming a Mother*: London: Martin Robertson, 1979.) Second ed. Harmondsworth: Penguin, 1981, 1986.

Oakley, Ann, *The Sociology of Housework*. London: Martin Robertson, 1974; 2nd ed, Oxford: Blackwell, 1984.

Oakley, Ann. *Housewife*, London: Allen Lane, 1974. Harmondsworth: Penguin, 1976.

Osborne, John, *Look Back in Anger*. London: Evans Brothers, 1957.

Parker, Roszika and Pollock, Griselda (editors). *Framing Feminism: Art and the Women's Movement 1970-1985*.London: Pandora, 1987.

Peck, Ellen, *The Baby Trap*. New York: B.Geis Associates, 1976 (out of print).

Phillips, Angela and Rakusen, Jill (editors). *Our Bodies Ourselves: A Health Book By and For Women*. New York: Simon Schuster. 1976; London: Allen Lane, 1978; Harmondsworth: Penguin, 1978 ; revised ed., 1989.

Richards, Janet Radcliffe. *The Sceptical Feminist: A Philosophical Enquiry*. London: Routledge & Kegan Paul, 1980; Penguin, 1982.

Robinson, Hilary. *Visibly Female: Feminism and Art Today*. London: Camden Press, 1988.

Rowbotham, Sheila. *Dreams and Dilemmas: Collected Writings*. London: Virago, 1983.

Rudofsky, Bernard. *The Unfashionable Human Body*. London: Hart Davis, 1972.

Sanders, Deidre. *The Woman Book of Love and Sex* (Research assistant Anne Rigg.) London: Michael Joseph, 1985.

Segal, Lynne. *Is the Future Female?: Troubled Thoughts on Contemporary Feminism*. London: Virago, 1987.

Spender, Dale. *Man Made Language*. London: Routledge & Kegan Paul, 1985.

Sullivan, Judy. *Mama Doesn't Live Here Anymore*. Arthur Fields Books Inc./Pyramid Books, 1974.

Taylor, Eric. *Women Who Went to War*. London: Robert Hale, 1988.

Townsend, Sue. *Bazaar and Rummage*. London: Methuen, 1984.

Trebilcot, Joyce (editor). *Mothering – Essays in Feminist Theory*. Rowman and Allanheld, 1984.

Tuttle, Lisa, *Encyclopedia of Feminism*. Harlow: Longman, 1986; Arrow Books, 1987.

Weldon, Fay. *Female Friends*. London: Heinemann, 1975; Pan Books, 1977.

Wesker, Arnold. *Roots*. London: Samuel French, 1959.

Wesker, Arnold. *The Wesker Trilogy* (contains *Roots*). Harmondsworth: Penguin, 1959; repr. 1984.

Wilson, Elizabeth. *What is to Be Done About Violence Against Women?* Harmondsworth: Penguin, 1983.

Wilson, Elizabeth. *Adorned in Dreams: Fashion and Modernity*. London: Virago, 1985.

Yeandle, Susan. *Working Women's Lives: Patterns and Strategies*. London: Tavistock, 1985.

INDEX